BLACK PRIVILEGE

Opportunity Comes to Those Who Create It

CHARLAMAGNE THA GOD

TOUCHSTONE

New York   London   Toronto   Sydney   New Delhi

Touchstone
An Imprint of Simon & Schuster, Inc.
1230 Avenue of the Americas
New York, NY 10020

First Touchstone trade paperback edition April 2018

TOUCHSTONE and colophon are registered trademarks of Simon & Schuster, Inc.

For information about special discounts for bulk purchases,
please contact Simon & Schuster Special Sales at 1-866-506-1949
or business@simonandschuster.com

The Simon & Schuster Speakers Bureau can bring authors to your live event.
For more information or to book an event contact the Simon & Schuster Speakers Bureau
at 866-248-3049 or visit our website at www.simonspeakers.com.

Manufactured in the United States of America

1   3   5   7   9   10   8   6   4   2

The Library of Congress has cataloged the hardcover edition as follows:

Names: Tha God, Charlamagne, 1980–
Title: Black privilege : opportunity comes to those who create it /
by Charlamagne Tha God.
Description: New York : Touchstone, 2017.
Identifiers: LCCN 2016059721| ISBN 9781501145308 (hardcover) |
ISBN 9781501145315 (pbk.)
Subjects: LCSH: Tha God, Charlamagne, 1980– |
Tha God, Charlamagne, 1980– —Humor. |
Television personalities—United States—Biography. |
Radio personalities—United States—Biography.
Classification: LCC PN2287.T337 A3 2017 | DDC 791.4502/8092 [B]—dc23
LC record available at https://lccn.loc.gov/2016059721

ISBN 978-1-5011-4530-8
ISBN 978-1-5011-4531-5 (pbk)
ISBN 978-1-5011-4532-2 (ebook)

This book is dedicated to the state that made me great, South Carolina. The 843, the 803, and the 864. To every dreamer living on a dirt road somewhere, this book is for you. In my story, may you find the inspiration to create your own greatness.

This book is also dedicated to my mother, Julia; my father, Larry; and my late grandmother, Rosa Lee Ford. The foundation of who I am came from the three of you. I don't know if y'all even want to take credit for my madness, but guess what? You have no other choice!!

Last, but certainly not least, this book is dedicated to my rib, my wife, Mook Mook, and our two beautiful daughters, A and Z. Yes, the name of one of my daughters starts with A and the other starts with a Z; we will fill in the rest of the alphabet at a later date. Please, when you two are old enough to read this book, don't judge your father for the sins of his past. I used to be a young savage, but I'm grown now and I hope this book will remind you that life is about constant evolution.

Contents

Introduction

Let me tell you about the first time I started living my truth.

I was fifteen years old and living in Moncks Corner, South Carolina. If you're not familiar with Moncks Corner, it's a small town of less than eight thousand people about thirty miles north of Charleston.

For most of my teenage years, my family lived in a double-wide trailer on a dirt road on the edge of town. My mother was a high school English teacher and a Jehovah's Witness, a straitlaced woman who did everything by the book. My father was her polar opposite: a contractor who was an occasional drug and alcohol abuser and a full-time hustler.

One of my favorite activities back then was to talk on the phone. Not a cell phone either, but an old-fashioned landline. If you think sexting is better than talking, you don't know what you're missing. I can honestly say that 90 percent of the times I got pussy as a teenager was because of phone conversations, especially the late-night ones.

My trouble started one night when I was on the phone with my friend Imani*; I don't think I ever wanted to fuck Imani (not that I would have turned it down if the opportunity presented itself) but we would just talk on the phone for hours for no reason. That night the conversation turned to a guy we knew named Darnell, who was Imani's cousin Deja's baby daddy.

*Names have been changed to protect the guilty, the easily embarrassed, and those who want to come up by suing me.

"Man, Darnell thinks he's hard," I offered.

"Oh, you think he soft?" drawled Imani.

"Maybe he is, maybe he isn't," I continued. "All I know is my father always tells me the dudes who act hard in this town all end up one of three ways: broke sitting under a tree, in jail, or dead."

After that the convo probably turned to something more pressing, like who was the best member of the Wu-Tang Clan. Neither of us gave my little rant about Darnell any more thought.

A few days later, after smoking weed I decided to go visit my neighbor Charles, who lived at the top of our dirt road. Charles wasn't home but as I was walking out of his yard, Darnell and his cousin came driving by. They spotted me and quickly pulled over, skidding to a stop in a cloud of dust and pebbles.

"Yo, Larry, what's good?" Darnell yelled menacingly as he hopped out of the car. Lenard is my government name, but people in Moncks Corner call me Larry, after my father.

I had zero idea what Darnell was yelling about. Number one, I was high. Number two, I talked SHIT about *everyone* in those days. I must have had a quizzical look on my face, because Darnell quickly filled me in.

"You was talking that shit to Imani," he announced. "So we gotta fight!"

I'd said what I'd said, so there was no need to cop a plea.

"Yeah, what about it?" I answered back defiantly.

But Darnell was already done talking. He unleashed a wild roundhouse that would have knocked my head off but thankfully missed. I managed to land a quick jab in retaliation. It seemed like he barely felt it. Despite being basically the same size as me, in one quick move Darnell scooped me up, lifted me over his head, and viciously pile-drived me into a ditch. If someone had taped it, we could easily get twenty million views on Worldstar with that footage today.

I tried to get up, but Darnell was already beating me back down. Punch after punch after punch after punch. Then he moved on to a choke hold. Now, in my experience there are two kinds of choke holds: (1) the "I'm just letting you know things can get real so don't play with me again" type, and (2) the "This situation is *so* real that I'm going to choke you until you die" type. I'm pretty sure option number two was being administered to me in that moment.

Thankfully his cousin stepped in before Darnell could finish the job.

"Chill, man, that's enough," he said, pulling Darnell off me. "Let the dude go. . . ." Darnell relaxed his grip, and I could breathe again (though I'm sure there are some folks today—Bow Wow, Ciara, and Birdman to name but a few—who would pay good money to go back in time and tell Darnell, "Naw, choke him a little longer!").

Think I'm exaggerating when I say Darnell was trying to kill me? Well, several years later Darnell *did* kill my cousin's mother by putting her in one of his choke holds and snapping her neck; he's serving a life sentence for it today.

At the time, of course, I didn't know I'd been in the grasp of a killer. I was more concerned that I looked like I'd just gotten into a head-on collision with a Prius. I didn't want anyone to see me with my face bruised up, so once Darnell and his cousin drove off, instead of going home, I limped across the road and crawled into a vacant trailer we'd used to live in. Sitting on the floor with all the shades pulled dark, I started crying, ashamed that I'd been beaten so badly. Not to mention afraid of what my father would say when he saw me ("Get the fuck out of here," he told me after I tried telling him someone accidently slammed a door in my face. "You think I'm stupid?").

Once I got over the shock of what had happened, I started feeling better. After a while my tears even turned into laughter. How could I not laugh at myself? I looked like Martin after he tried to box Thomas "Hitman" Hearns. I literally had a knot on my head so big a doctor would eventually have to shave it off.

I was happy because I sensed that I'd entered a new stage in my relationship with the truth. Most people would have walked away from a beating like that thinking, "I really got to start watching what I say." I had the opposite reaction. If I'd just survived *that*, there was no way I was censoring myself *at all*. One of my favorite songs at the time was Notorious B.I.G.'s "Unbelievable," where he rapped, "If I said it, I meant it / bite my tongue for no one." Sitting there in the trailer, I could hear Biggie's lyrics over and over again in my head. In his words, I'd found my own voice too.

Bite my tongue for no one was the mantra I was going to live by. If I had something to say, I was going to say it. If someone wanted to know what I'd said about them, I'd tell them. To their face. What's the worst that could happen? I'd get beat up? I just survived a five-star ass kicking! If that was the worst that could happen, I was all right with it.*

Bite my tongue for no one.

Throughout my years as a radio guy—first on local stations in South Carolina, later as a cohost on Wendy Williams's show, then

---

*Do you know they let prisoners on Facebook now? I didn't. And the other day I got a friend request from Darnell. When I saw his face pop up on my screen, I immediately thought, "Nooooooo, he's out?" and almost had a heart attack. When someone beats you like that, you never get over it.

as the host of my own show in Philly and eventually as part of *The Breakfast Club*—the syndicated radio show I host on New York City's Power 105.1 with DJ Envy and Angela Yee—I've been asked (not to mention threatened) to watch what I say more times than I can remember. I've been hated on for my honesty, fired for my honesty, even punched in the side of my head for my honesty. But I've never for a second doubted that honesty is not only my best friend but also my secret weapon. Almost twenty years later, my tongue remains unbitten.

Perhaps the best example of the depth of my commitment to honesty is the first time I interviewed Kanye West on *The Breakfast Club*. To give you a little context, the interview happened while he was out on tour supporting his *Yeezus* album, which I thought wasn't up to his usual standards.

To make matters worse, Kanye had been delivering long rants about how the fashion industry wasn't giving him a fair shot. How he was a genius but no one in power in the industry understood his vision. How he felt like a slave to major corporations.

In my eyes, instead of trying to keep up with the Kardashians and worrying about whether an editor at *Vogue* liked his blouses, Kanye should have just focused on what made us love him in the first place: compelling, heartfelt music. I knew that as long as he was connected to the people via his music, all his other dreams and aspirations would eventually fall into place.

In order to get him back on track (at the end of the day, I am a Kanye fan and want him to succeed), I started calling him Kanye Kardashian to poke fun at his new image. I also named him Donkey of the Day several times, a daily feature on the show where I give someone the credit they deserve for being stupid.

Of course when word got out that Kanye was coming in for an

interview, the question on everyone's lips was, "Will Charlamagne really call him Kanye Kardashian to his face? Will he tell him *Yeezus* was wack?"

That's certainly what Natina Nimene, Kanye's rep from Def Jam Recordings, was worried about when she arrived at our studio the morning of his interview. "Charlamagne, whatever you do," she implored, "please don't call him Kanye Kardashian. You gotta understand why that's not cool."

Being the pain in the ass that I am, I crushed that dream right away. "Since you asked me not to say that, that's the *first* thing I'm going to say," I told her, though in truth I was always going to say it regardless. I added that little dig because I really hate when publicists and label reps ask me *not* to do my job. I'm here for the listeners, not the artists, and certainly not the labels. If there's something I feel listeners would want me to bring up, then that's what I'm going to do. Here's a little Radio 101: listener benefit trumps everything else.

True to my word, as soon as the interview began, I got right into it. "They said it would never happen, a repeat Donkey of the Day offender," I said as Kanye smiled uncomfortably. "Kanye Kardashian!"

I wasn't done. As soon as the talk turned to *Yeezus*, I was truthful with Kanye. "I didn't like that album at all, and I was a Kanye West fan," I told him. "But *Yeezus* was wack to me."

Was I being a bit of an a-hole by calling *Yeezus* trash? Or by introducing him as Kanye Kardashian? Of course. But Kanye's a certified a-hole himself and he respected my honesty. Despite the rocky start, we ended up having a great conversation. The interview created so much heat that I ended up getting profiled in *Rolling Stone* and the *New York Times*.

That's a lot of attention for an ex-felon from Moncks Corner with a night-school diploma. And while I appreciated that people found the Kanye conversation compelling, the fact is, mainstream America was just learning what people who had been listening to me for years already knew: every interview I do, or conversation I have, is rooted in honesty. Whether on the radio, on my podcast, or on TV, I'm always going to be honest.

Honest about myself.

Honest about my opinions.

Honest with whomever I'm talking to.

That commitment to honesty was one of my main motivations to write this book. I've lived a great life thus far, and enjoyed every step of the process, the highs and the lows. I don't like to label those experiences good or bad, because they're all part of one life-long process. I've learned something from each and every one of them. I've been a bully (and been bullied). I've been a drug dealer. A so-called thug. A so-called nerd. I've been to jail a few times. I've come within inches—on more than one occasion—of fulfilling my father's prediction for Darnell and all the other knuckle-heads in our town: broke under a tree, dead in the ground, or rotting in jail.

But despite all that, to quote the great Pastor Young (aka the rapper Jeezy), "Here I stand a grown-ass man." Yes, that little boy on the dirt roads of Moncks Corner, South Carolina, is a grown-ass man now and has managed to realize all the dreams I had for myself.

My goal for this book is to pass along the valuable principles I've absorbed through living what I feel has been an eventful life. Some of the principles I've developed on my own. Others have been passed down to me by the wise elders I've been fortunate to meet (despite having a big-ass mouth, I pride myself on having big-ass ears too: I'm a great listener). Regardless of their origin,

INTRODUCTION

I'm hopeful no matter what your background or situation, you'll find value in all of these:

- Success isn't determined by the size of the town you're from, or what sort of home you grew up in. When I first started doing radio in NYC, people tried to make me ashamed of coming from a place where you pull over when you see road-kill. (Pro tip: If it's cold, you leave it there. If it's warm, it's dinner.) But even if Moncks Corner was a small town, it had a magic in the air. Magic that I was able to harness and moti-vate myself with. There's something special wherever you come from too: find it and use it to help it propel you toward your pursuit of greatness.

- In order to change your life for the better, first you must change your lifestyle. Which can't happen unless you change the people around you. My family didn't have much, but I still got off to a good start in life: wearing glasses and a fanny pack, reading Judy Blume books, and hanging out with nerdy white kids. Then I made the mistake of ditching all that for my "cool" cousins who were thugging.* I had one foot under that tree my father always told me about, one foot in jail, and let's call it my dick (aka my third leg) in the grave. Thankfully I woke up and realized I had to cut all the losers loose, even the blood relatives, if I was ever going to reach my potential. I hope this section will help you see that no one is a victim of circumstance in life. No matter how or

---

*A note on the term "cousin": I'm going to be using it in the Southern sense: a "cousin" refers not only to blood relatives, but a lot of other folks too. Truth is, I still don't fully understand who my true cousins are. It's very confusing when you don't know which of your cousins are actually related to you, not to mention very awk-ward after you've had sex with a couple of them. . . .

where you were raised, you can make the choice to live a different way.

- Often the most valuable advice you can give someone is "fuck your dreams." Sounds like pretty depressing advice, but it comes with a qualifier: fuck your dreams when they aren't actually *yours*. For young African-Americans, relatable images of success are often limited to sports and entertainment. Too many times the dreams you think are yours are actually someone else's; you're only chasing them because you've seen them working for others. I should know: I wanted to be a rapper because that's what I saw young black men who were successful do. Thankfully, someone who could see I didn't have the skill set to be an MC had the courage to tell me, "Fuck your dreams of being a rapper." It turned out to be the single best piece of career advice I ever received. This is why I often say, "If you don't have anything nice to say to anyone, say it anyway."

- As someone who has been fired countless times, I can promise you there are no "losses" in life, only lessons. From getting let go from Taco Bell (by my own sister no less) to getting canned from Wendy Williams's show to every single time I've been fired, a short time later I've always landed in a better position. As long as you don't compromise who you are, no matter how many pink slips you get, there's always going to be something better out there for you. Learn how to trust what I call "divine misdirection."

- When you're starting off in your chosen field, just focus on "putting the weed in the bag." If you don't know classic hip-hop cinema, I'll explain that quote in greater detail later. For now, just know it speaks to the importance of embracing the process, instead of what may seem to be the results. Too many people, especially millennials, lack the vision to recognize opportunity when there's not a paycheck attached to it.

- Always live your truth. When you live your truth, can't nobody try to use that truth against you. For instance, do I look like a Teenage Mutant Ninja Turtle? Of course I do. By embracing my egg-shaped dome, I've taken all the ammunition away from people who call me "the fifth Ninja Turtle," or "a burnt Ninja Turtle." By laughing at those comments instead of getting uptight, I've replaced a perceived weakness with power. You might not look like a Ninja Turtle (unless your name is Ne-Yo) yourself but chances are there's something you're uptight or embarrassed about that you could actually turn into a positive by just embracing the truth about yourself.

- Give people the credit they deserve for being stupid—starting with yourself. I walk through life assuming that I've got a lot to learn, and I happily soak up any knowledge that comes my way. Too many people take the opposite approach and decide they've got it all figured out by the time they're twenty-five. That's a mind-set that is *guaranteed* to block your blessings. You must stay open to new ideas. To new kinds of people to work with. To new mentors who can coach you. Otherwise, you are always going to be stuck in place.

- Finally, embrace the concept that you are privileged. I believe in the power and privilege of God. And God created me exactly how he wanted me to be and who he wanted me to be. I believe I'm just as privileged—if not more—as any white person out there. I *have* to believe that. Otherwise, I'd never have transcended the circumstances I was born into. No matter what your circumstance in life, you must adopt the same attitude. You must believe—strongly—that you've got Latino Privilege, Asian Privilege, Tall-Guy Privilege, Smart-Girl Privilege, whatever your particular situation may be. And then you've got to have complete faith in your privilege. This book is only for those who believe that they can create their own opportunity.

Because if you don't believe in your ability to create breaks for yourself, then this book can't do anything for you. In fact, just put it down now. Then find your receipt and return it before you accidently get some Polynesian sauce from your Number One at Chick-fil-A on one of the pages and can't get your money back.

I need to share these principles in a book because I know just how much power the written word holds (plus it didn't hurt that the publisher wrote me a nice-size check). Remember, I'm the son of an English teacher. From an early age, my mother kept a book in my face. Those books, combined with her love, are what nourished my imagination and inspired me to transcend my circumstances. Books are what provided me with a sense of escape when the tension between my parents made our home feel suffocating. Books helped give me the confidence to dream bigger than I was supposed to as a poor black boy growing up in the rural South. Books are where I got the name Charlamagne (even if I did misspell it). My life is a living testament to the transformative power of books.

Having said that, as you might have noticed, the language in this book is going to be raw. I'm raw on the radio, I'm raw on social media, I'm really raw on podcasts, and I'm not going to change up now just because I'm an author. That means jokes, most of them tasteless, will be made at people's expense. Including my own. It also means some of the topics I touch on might make you uncomfortable. Especially realities that many in America would prefer to sweep under the rug. Realities that are inevitable when cycles of poverty and neglect are repeated year after year, generation after generation. I'd say sorry in advance, but the truth is I don't give a fuck. If you're looking for a book that sugarcoats situations and runs from reality, then you're in the wrong place.

If you're wondering how uplifting principles could come out of a potty mouth like mine, it's simple: I'm a firm believer in the concept of "ratchetness and righteousness." By that I mean embracing the full spectrum of the human experience includes both ignorant and inspiring moments. Far from being mutually exclusive, they're the ying and yang of a fully lived life. So enjoy the ratchet moments and get inspired by the righteous ones. Remember shit is the best fertilizer; it's what helps the flowers grow.

Finally, I'm not going to spend a lot of time talking about all the famous rappers I've broken bread with, or bragging about every beautiful woman I've talked into my bed. Yes, I've been very fortunate to meet a lot of the artists who inspired me growing up. Yes, I've had sex with more beautiful women than anyone who looks like me has any reasonable right to. But I've got bigger fish to fry. I want to show you how opportunity truly does come to those who create it.

I want to tell you about the people I grew up with in Moncks Corner. How I learned the right way to live from my father's words, just as how I learned not to get down from many of his actions. I want to speak to you about the village that raised me and how so many of the mistakes I made could have been avoided if I'd listened to my elders. I want to tell you how the spiritual legacy of the African slaves can still be felt in South Carolina four hundred years later. You're going to hear about UFOs behind my grandmother's house, tales of my crazy cousins, the dudes I slung crack with, the teachers at my high school who we tortured, and the guys I got locked up with (including my pops). The colorful cast of characters that made this rural southern town feel like the center of the world to me. Because ultimately those people and experiences, much more so than any celebrities I've met in New York or Los Angeles, represent who I am. What I could have been. And what I've become.

I went from Moncks Corner to Madison Square Garden, all "on MTV telling 'em how I sold D." (There really is a Jay Z bar for every situation.) From reading liners on a fifty-thousand-watt station in South Carolina to hosting the biggest nationally syndicated hip-hop radio show (actually one of the biggest radio shows in the country *period*, which just happens to be rooted in hip-hop). From not even being registered to vote to actually interviewing presidential candidates and having them vie for my endorsement.

If you've ever wondered whether you can change your trajectory in life, I'm here to tell you that you can. While everyone's paths are different, have confidence that no matter your situation or your perceived stature in our society, your truth is more than enough to take you where you want to go.

BLACK PRIVILEGE

It's Not the Size of the Pond but the Hustle in the Fish

Geographical location doesn't determine what kind of success you will have, but your psychological position always will. How are you going to make waves in a bigger pond when you haven't even learned how to cause a ripple in the pond you're in? When you stop complaining about where you are physically and start focusing on where you are mentally, that's when you will start to transcend your circumstances.

The Origins of the Dirt Road Dirtbag

I was born in Charleston, South Carolina, one of the oldest cities in the nation. For a long time it was also one of the richest, thanks to being the center of trade for several industries, including deerskin, indigo, cotton, rice, and, most lucratively, African slaves.

Sullivan's Island, which lies in Charleston's harbor, on the Atlantic Ocean, is where hundreds of thousands of African men, women, and children were brought to this country in chains during the Middle Passage. If you're African-American, there's an almost 50 percent chance one of your ancestors landed at Sullivan's Island. Despite having so much historical significance, you

1

won't find any Statue of Liberty–size monument commemorating what scholars call "the Ellis Island of slavery." Nope, all you will find is a couple of plaques and a memorial bench Toni Morrison arranged to have built overlooking the ocean. Chances are, you've never heard about any of that. This is why, as Public Enemy once rapped, "History shouldn't be a mystery / Our stories real history / Not *his* story."

Specifically, Sullivan's Island is where most of the Bakongo, Mbundu, Wolof, Mende, and Malinke peoples of West Africa were brought to America. It's probably safe to say I'm descended from one of them. I went to a family reunion a few years back and heard some relatives say that the McKelveys (that's my father's last name) have Irish ancestors, but it's more likely we just had Irish *owners*. I did some research when I started working on this book and found that there had been a lot of slave owners in the area with my last name. If you look at some of the old records, you'll find actual sales receipts like this one from 1805: "McKelvey, David to Ebenezer Hopkins, Bill of Sale for a slave named Ben, a Barber by trade." Maybe Ben the Barber was one of my ancestors.

Probably the most famous former slave to live in Charleston was Denmark Vesey. Denmark was born on St. Thomas in the Caribbean in 1767 and ended up being sold to a ship captain, who brought him to Charleston. After some time in the city he won $2,500 in a lottery and was able to buy his freedom. He stayed in Charleston and cofounded the Emanuel African Methodist Episcopal Church in an effort to aid the slaves in the area.

After doing all he could for the slaves through his church, Denmark decided that working with local white leaders wasn't getting him anywhere. So in 1822 he started secretly organizing a slave revolt in Charleston and the surrounding area. The plan was that on an assigned date, all the slaves in the area would rise up, overwhelm their masters, and then march to the port in Charleston. From there they'd sail to freedom in Haiti, which had recently won its independence from France.

The plan might have worked, except that Denmark and his fellow leaders got dimed out by a local slave (now *that's* snitching) and everyone was arrested before the revolt could happen. After a short trial, Denmark and thirty other slaves were hanged.

I've always found Denmark incredibly inspirational because he didn't have to help the other slaves around Charleston. He'd not only literally won the lottery, but he was also a skilled carpenter and could read, which was a rarity back then. It had to be tempting to say, "Peace, Charleston," and carve out a nice life for himself up north. But he didn't go that route. He was committed to his community and ultimately gave his life trying to liberate it.

Unfortunately, if the Emanuel AME Church in Charleston sounds familiar to you, it's probably not because of Denmark Vesey. No, the church Denmark helped found over two hundred years ago to help slaves is also where the terrorist Dylann Roof killed nine innocent black folk back in 2015. So, clearly the more things change, the more they stay the same in Charleston. This is why we need to celebrate heroes like Denmark Vesey whenever we get the chance, instead of letting them become a footnote to history. I wouldn't even feel right putting my name on this book if it didn't tell his story.

Another thing you should know about Charleston is that it's a center of Geechee culture. Geechees, or Gullahs as they're also called, are the descendants of slaves who lived along the Atlantic coast in the Low Country regions of South Carolina and Georgia. Even though they've been in America for hundreds of years, Geechees still have a very close connection to African cultures and languages. I've met Geechees who speak a dialect that's closer to African languages than English. Clarence Thomas comes from a family like that and claims one of the reasons he never talks in the Supreme Court is because he grew up ashamed of his heavy Geechee accent. Other kids would make so much fun of him that he became more comfortable listening than talking. Or at least that's his story. Chris Rock, Michelle Obama, and Trick Daddy all have Geechee roots as well. Even if you've never heard of Geechee before this book, you've probably heard some Geechee phrases, like "gruber" (aka peanut) and "Kumbayah," which means "Come by here."

Growing up in Charleston, I wasn't aware of all that history yet. I do remember going on a field trip to the Charleston Museum, which is actually the oldest museum in the country, but only because I pushed open an emergency door on purpose and set off a fire alarm. Even as a little kid, I was always a bit of an instigator.

Our family, including my older sister, Teresa, and my younger brother Julian, lived in a trailer park in the North Charleston neighborhood. The trailers were packed tight together—if you stepped into your backyard, you were also stepping into someone's front yard. One reason I never minded the close proximity was there were two girls in the trailer behind us who would flash me whenever they saw me looking out my window.

Even though I lived there the first seven or eight years of my life, my memories of Charleston are pretty scattered. However, I can distinctly remember that my father had a stationary bike behind our trailer that our neighbors would come over and ride. They'd pedal on it for a couple of minutes (that's what passes for going to the gym in a trailer park), then they'd hang out and drink beer with my pops, just shootin' the shit. White neighbors, black neighbors—it didn't matter. The sort of solidarity Dylann Roof was trying to rip apart.

The Dirt Road Less Traveled

When I was about to enter the second grade we moved to Moncks Corner, which is where most of my people are from. My maternal grandmother lived on Route 17A in Moncks Corner, while my father's folks are from Kitfield, which was just down the road. Since we spent so much time in the area visiting family, my parents already owned a little piece of land off a dirt road on the edge of town. Eventually it just made sense to move our trailer over there rather than stay in Charleston.

Even though it is only about a half-hour drive from Charleston to Moncks Corner, culturally they are two very different places. Moncks Corner doesn't have any of the history, sophistication, or energy of a city like Charleston. Or *any* city for that matter.

Put it this way: think of a place like New York, Los Angeles, Chicago, or Atlanta, full of restaurants, stores, infrastructure, opportunity, and access.

Then picture the exact opposite of that. A place with no opportunity. No access. No infrastructure. No stores or restaurants.

The place you're picturing is Moncks Corner.

Okay, I'm exaggerating slightly about the stores and restaurants; Moncks Corner has plenty of barbershops (a lot of them black-owned), banks, and grocery shops. As well as a McDonald's, a Sonic, a Chick-fil-A (just got that in the past couple of years though), a Wendy's, and, of course, the holy grounds that are Walmart. The "downtown" also has a courthouse, a detention center, the depot for the train to Charleston, a YMCA, and Berkeley High School, which was my alma mater even though I got thrown out. Over by the Old Santee Canal Park is the Berkeley County Museum and Heritage Center, a little building that has memorabilia from some of the local plantations, as well as dinosaur bones that were found in the area. That might not sound so bad, but trust me, there really isn't much to do. After a day or two visiting Moncks Corner, you'd be ready to get back on the road.

Having said that, there were great aspects to growing up in Moncks Corner—the best being the relationship it helped me develop with the outdoors. Almost as soon as I moved in, I started playing in the woods with the other kids in my neighborhood. Any day we didn't have school, we'd be up at eight and out the door by nine, exploring every part of the country we could.

The woods that border Moncks Corner were filled with otters, beavers, coyotes, bobcats, raccoons, and deer. We'd also visit the swamps and rivers that were home to gators. We were never too scared of gators, but we were always on the lookout for the snakes that seemed to be hiding under every rock and fallen tree trunk; cottonmouths, copperheads, diamondback rattlesnakes, and timber rattlesnakes are all native to the area. One time we biked down our road and found our neighbor Mr. Wilson standing over a diamondback rattler he'd just killed that was literally ten feet long. He'd chopped off its head and was pouring gasoline over its body because as he explained, "You gotta kill the devil." You see, to country people a snake represents Lucifer in the flesh. So you don't play around with them.

Another time, my mother drove me and my friends over to Kitfield because my father wanted to show us something special. When we got there, we found him with a huge rattler he'd just killed. "This is why I tell y'all to stay out of those damned woods," he yelled, shaking its limp body at us. "Because this is what's waiting for y'all in there!"

My father didn't like us roaming the woods, but ultimately the only rule we had to follow was to be back home before dusk. That's the universal law of the hood, urban or rural: get your ass inside before the streetlights come on.

There weren't any neighborhoods where we were afraid to go. As we saw it, all of Moncks Corner was our turf. People tend to think of the South as heavily segregated, but race never felt like a big issue in Moncks Corner. When we moved to the trailer park there were five other black families living on our road: the Trotters, the Wheelers, the Presidents, the Gibbses, and the Wilsons. Over time a few white families moved in and a Mexican family as well.

When those white and Mexican families arrived it wasn't an issue: they were just there. My parents might have experienced racism in their day, but my friends and I didn't feel it as kids. There is a neighborhood called Pinopolis just north of Moncks Corner, and that's where I imagined all the rich white people lived. But I never did bother to go over there. Looking back on it, all the homes I'd imagine as mansions were probably regular as hell anyway.

I didn't go sightseeing in Pinopolis because I've never felt envious of what other people have. Most folks I knew lived in trailers, and that felt regular to me. An African-American family named Gibbs did have a brick home down the road with a formal den and a nice-size kitchen. Plus a big basketball court outside. As a kid, that was the most immaculate house I'd ever seen. When I did dream of something better than what we had, that's all I saw: a nice little two-story brick home with a basketball court.

The Supernormal

Snakes and gators weren't the only creatures that roamed Moncks Corner. Plenty of supernatural creatures abounded as well.

Or as I prefer to describe them, "supernormal." Because to me, there has never been anything out of the ordinary about encountering the spiritual realm.

My first encounter with the supernormal came when I was five or six years old, with one of my favorite toys, a little plastic tractor with a farmer sitting on top of it. Suddenly, that plastic farmer hopped off the tractor, walked over and started messing with me. Not in a threatening way, but almost more as if he was issuing me a warning. As if he were telling me, "Hey, you're not alone in this universe. I can get off this tractor if I want to."

Every few days, that farmer would mess with me. I even told my mother about it, but she just blew me off with, "Well, you don't say . . ." and then went back to whatever she was doing.

One day we had a trash fire going—yes, it was so rural where I grew up, you had to burn your own trash because the county wouldn't pick it up—when the toy farmer drove his tractor over to me again and started acting up. I'd had enough, so I grabbed it and threw it into the fire. Let me tell you, that little farmer began screaming for his life as the plastic began to melt. I should have rescued him, but I was too freaked out to move.

My next encounter came when I was in third grade. The bus used to drop me off at my grandmother's after school, even though it would often be several hours before she'd make it back home from her job in the school cafeteria.

One of my favorite ways to pass the time was to hang out in the huge field behind her house. I'd stand out there by myself and act like I was putting on a rock-and-roll concert for an imaginary audience. This was before I'd discovered hip-hop, so I was really into being a rock star. I'd play air guitar and pretend I was Michael J. Fox riding on top of that van in *Teen Wolf*.

One day I was in the middle of a mean guitar solo when a

black flying saucer suddenly appeared above the trees that lined the yard. It looked exactly like the generic flying saucer that you would always see on TV and in movies: a black disk with a little round bump coming out of the top.

The saucer hovered over the trees for a moment without making any noise. Then, just as suddenly as it'd appeared, it zipped off and was gone. I'd never seen a flying saucer before, but I wasn't scared. Why should I have been? People are afraid of what they don't understand. But even at that early age, I was already fully aware that nonhuman life existed in the universe. If anything, seeing the saucer was just another confirmation of what I'd already known.

Another supernormal presence in my life has been Hags, who are a major part of southern African-American folklore. Hags are female spirits or witches who come into your bedroom while you're asleep and sit on your chest until right before dawn (they don't like sunlight). When they've got you, you literally can't move. Some doctors try to call this condition "sleep paralysis," but in South Carolina we know better: it just means you got a visit from the Hags!

Almost everyone I know in South Carolina has had the Hags come to them at least once or twice. Some folks try to keep them out by sprinkling salt by their doors, because it's said a Hag will try to pick up every grain and run out of time before the sun comes up. Another trick is to leave a straw broom by the door because a Hag will get distracted trying to count all its straws.

Growing up there was an old lady in my neighborhood who used to catch Hags. She never told me how she did it, but when I asked her what they looked like, she said they were small shadowy figures that had the shape of a woman's body. I didn't totally believe her, until the Hags finally came for me one night when I was a teenager. I woke up out of a deep sleep to see a little shadowy bitch doing a dance on my chest. I tried to brush her off, but I couldn't move a muscle. Then out of the corner of my eye I saw three more little female shadows waiting for their turn to jump on me. Over the course of what seemed like hours they all took turns giving me lap dances on my chest until they finally split right before dawn. It truly felt like I'd had a train run on me by a bunch of Hags.

Some of you are probably thinking, "Charlamagne, would you please stop it with these Hags and UFOs? No one believes in this shit."

Well, to that I'd like to say that, number one: I don't care if you believe me. I experienced all of these encounters (plus a few more), so I don't need anyone's validation. Besides, why would I lie and open myself up to ridicule for no reason?

Second, a lot of people *do* believe in the sort of paranormal activity I'm describing. Not only because they've experienced it themselves but also because Hags and other supernormal beings are directly rooted in the cultures the slaves brought to this country hundreds of years ago.

In many parts of West Africa, there's nothing strange about being visited by Hags. Just as there's nothing strange about the concept of talking to your dead ancestors. For generations and generations, the West Africans I'm descended from have believed that there's no separation between the spiritual realm and our day-to-day lives.

Growing up in Moncks Corner, it wasn't unusual to hear adults talking about communicating with the dead. I can often remember my grandmother mentioning that she'd spoken to my dead grandfather in a dream. "Yes, he came to me last night and warned me someone might die today," she might say, "so I want you to be extra careful today."

Talk like that felt normal. It even felt comfortable. I liked knowing that the spirits of my ancestors were out there, looking out for me, sending me advice through dreams and visions.

Julia and Larry's Son

As a kid you can get so focused on your parents being your providers that it's easy to forget they had a life before you were born. I've noticed the same dynamic with my eldest daughter, who has never asked many questions about my past. The other day I casually mentioned something that happened while I was in jail and her jaw dropped. "What?" she blurted out. "You went to *jail*?" For a second you could see her thinking, "I don't know who this guy is, because my daddy would never do anything that would land him in jail!" I can't lie, I liked that the idea of me being locked up was mind-blowing to her. But I also made a mental note that it was time to start teaching her our family history—the so-called good and the so-called bad.

As to my own parents, I do know that my mother, Julia Ann Ford, is a beautiful woman, physically, mentally, and spiritually. She was born and raised in the Moncks Corner area. Her father died before I was born, so I don't know much about him. My grandmother Rosa Lee Ford was a lunch lady in our school district for many years. My mom grew up with a sister and a brother, though he sadly drowned when he was around seventeen.

After high school, my mother attended South Carolina State University, an HBCU in Orangeburg, which is roughly forty-five minutes farther inland past Moncks Corner. After graduating, she started working as an English teacher in Charleston, where she somehow got caught up with a character named Larry McKelvey, aka my pops. They got married and had a daughter, my older sister, Teresa. After Teresa there was a miscarriage and then came me, followed by my younger brothers, Julian, BJ, and then my sister Ashley. At some point my father also had my half sisters, Tara and Sara, but we didn't know about them until after my parents split up.

Like I mentioned, my mother is a Jehovah's Witness. She doesn't drink or smoke or carry on. But she married my pops, so there had to be an adventurous streak in there somewhere. My first glimpse of it came one day when I was over at my grandmother's house looking at an old picture of my mother, my aunt Lo, and some other folks. After glancing at the picture, my grandmother threw some shade my mother's way, saying, "My, my, my . . . look how short Julia's dress is compared to everyone else's." When she said that, it hit me: my mild-mannered mother must have had a wild side when she was young!

As for my father, there was never any question about his wild side. He stands about five five, and like a lot of little dudes with big personalities, was constantly living life to the fullest.

Everyone in Moncks Corner knew my father as "Cowboy." They called him that because he is a rabid Dallas Cowboys fan. So much that he has "six time Super Bowl Champion Dallas Cowboys" tattooed on his arm. Mind you, as I'm writing this they've actually only won five. He figured he could speak (or in this case, draw) that sixth ring into existence, but we're still waiting. Once, my mother brought me a Washington Redskins sweatshirt after they won the Super Bowl. When my father came home and saw I had a sweatshirt from the Cowboys' most-hated rivals, he took it out in the front yard and treated it like my plastic tractor: threw it in the fire.

My father didn't love the Cowboys because he was from Dallas, or even Texas. Nope, his people had been in South Carolina for as long as anyone could remember. He loved the Cowboys because during the seventies they were winners and had the pretty cheerleaders. They were America's team. My father was drawn to that energy. When Jay Z was on *The Breakfast Club* he told me that his father had a similar attraction to the 'Boys.

"It's really my pop's fault," he said after I asked him why he repped the Cowboys instead of the Giants or the Jets like everyone else from Brooklyn. "[My father] grew up in that whole era, those guys who wanted that Cowboys lifestyle. All those guys doing coke, you know."

"My pops was definitely on coke." I laughed.

"I got the whole thing pegged," said Jay. "I can give you the whole profile. . . . He have an Afro?"

"He absolutely had an Afro."

"I *know* he was a Cowboys fan," said Jay.

It was true. For a certain kind of black guy in the seventies, the Cowboys represented a dream they were chasing.

It's no surprise my father was attracted to their flashy image. He always prides himself on being the best-dressed person around, even though he usually looks country as hell. Just to give you an idea, he wore an all-red leather outfit (shirt, jacket, pants, shoes, *and* hat) last time he took his wife out for Valentine's Day. Imagine what a pimp would look like in a small town in South Carolina. What you're seeing is my pops.

Dressed like a fool or not, around Moncks Corner my father was undisputedly the Man. Everyone loved Mac (another one of his nicknames, short for McKelvey). If my dad was on the scene, that meant things were popping. During the eighties and nineties he ran a bunch of nightclubs, including one called the Zebra. When R & B artists like Clarence Carter, Tyrone Davis, or Millie

Jackson came through town, they would often play a set at the Zebra. The legendary George Clinton even made an appearance one time. (I bet my father paid him in coke.)

My father would make a point to show the artists a good time while they were in town; to this day he claims he sniffed coke with Rick James and Teena Marie. He's probably lying, but since neither of them are here to dispute it, we'll let him have that. . . .

When he wasn't throwing concerts at the Zebra, my father was working several other jobs. For a while he had a fish market on Main Street called Mac's Seafood. I used to work there when I was little, sweeping up, helping customers, and putting stuff back on the shelves at the end of the day.

His steadiest job—legally at least—was working as a contractor. He was great with his hands and could build houses from the ground up. His dream was to build homes in the area and then flip them for a profit, but he struggled with drugs and alcohol, which tripped him up before he could get his construction empire off the ground.

In a word, my father was a hustler. If you needed anything in Moncks Corner, you saw Larry McKelvey. Some shrimp for a fish fry? See Larry. A waitressing job at one of his clubs? See Larry. New roof on your house? See Larry. A little coke for the weekend? See Larry for that too.

My father was a big talker, but he could always back it up. For the most part I never saw him get into any real beef, but I do remember one night my father walked briskly into the trailer and whispered something into my mother's ear. All I could make out was "We tied him up."

Next thing I know, my father is on the phone trying to explain to some guys why they can't find their friend: turns out my father had gotten into a fight with him—a dude as "big as motherfuckin' Hulk Hogan" as he later described it. Because my father was out-sized, he hit the guy with the brass knuckles he always carried and knocked him out. My father didn't know what to do with his knocked-out foe, so he tied him up, drove to our trailer, and called the guy's friends to explain what happened. They must have come and picked him up peacefully because I never heard about the guy again. It was because of that situation that I started carrying a set of brass knuckles myself. Old habits die hard, and I'm still known to have a pair on me from time to time.

While it was cool to have a father who was the "street mayor" of our town, a lot of pressure came with it. Everywhere I went, I'd inevitably hear, "There go Cowboy's son." You can't have much anonymity in a small town when your dad has one of the big-gest personalities. Especially as his oldest son. It's hard to play the background when your father is always lit. Of course, playing the background is what a kid, even one with a big mouth like mine, often wants to do.

Many times I felt my father was friends with everyone in Moncks Corner except for yours truly. Growing up, I always wanted him to be my buddy, because that was his relationship with my cousins who were around the same age as me. With them, my father was the Big Homie, a steady stream of advice, belly laughs, and back-slaps. With me, he was more serious. Instead of laughs and back-slaps, I got lectured and slapped upside my head.

Looking back, I can see he was tough on me because he didn't want me to make the same mistakes that he had. So even though *I* wanted my pops to be one of the homies, *he* knew he wasn't here for that. He was here to be my father and that's exactly what I needed.

Transcend Your Circumstances

It ain't where you're from, it's where you're at.
—Eric B. and Rakim, "I Know You Got Soul"

When the God Rakim first spit those legendary bars, most people assumed he was speaking on physical locations. It didn't matter if you were from the Bronx or Brooklyn, the suburbs or the streets, if you were down with hip-hop, then in Rakim's eyes you were good.

There's tremendous value in that message. Yet as I grew to appreciate the song over the years, I realized there were layers to Rakim's lyrics: he wasn't only speaking about locations on a map, but a state of mind too.

In other words, the place where you were born, or the circumstances you were born into, don't have to define you. You can be born in a Moncks Corner, but have a New York City mind-set. You can grow up in a housing project in Chicago, or a trailer park in Louisiana, and still have the mentality of someone who was raised in LA.

I'm speaking here to all the people, especially young ones, who feel trapped by their circumstances. Who feel they must move to an Atlanta, a New York, or a Los Angeles in order to prosper.

Ultimately, you might have to make that move. I did. But before you do, you must focus on where your mentality is *where you're at.*

Too many people who grow up in a proverbial small pond fall into the trap of believing that they'll never achieve success where they're at. As a result, they end up settling. "What's it matter that I dropped out of high school? There are no good jobs around here anyway," they'll rationalize. "So what, I got a baby before I got a degree?" they'll say. "It's not like my mother went to college either. . . ."

I understand how easy it can be to sink into that mind-set. I doubt most people reading this book grew up in a town where the prospects of "making it" seemed any more daunting. If you were lucky in Moncks Corner, like my mother-in-law, Ms. Patty, you could get a job at the Gates factory, which made timing belts for cars. Before it closed in 2008, it employed maybe a couple hundred people. Or you could work for Berkeley County, like my mother did. After that, the next biggest employer was probably McDonald's. It's no wonder so many people turned to selling drugs; there just wasn't much legal money to be had.

That feeling of hopelessness, of opportunity always being outside of your grasp, can be depressing. I saw it take its toll on a lot of people, including many of my cousins and friends. When my father warned me not to fall into the trap of spending "the rest of your life sitting drunk under a tree," he wasn't using it as a metaphor. I would literally see my cousins—guys who as teenagers dressed fly, had game with the ladies, and excelled in sports—wasting away their days sitting under a tree for shade, sipping on cheap liquor and talking about the good ol' days. Except they weren't even out of their twenties yet, and their dreams were already dead. A guy drinking under a tree in Moncks Corner could just as easily be someone smoking a blunt on a park bench in the Bronx or drinking their lunch in a bar in Houston. A person I describe as "under a tree" represents anyone who has decided it'll never "happen" for them, so why even bother trying?

Personally, I never, ever in my life thought that my journey was going to end in Moncks Corner. I might have been raised in a small pond, but I was convinced that my hustle and determination were going to make me a fish that was going to swim on to wider waters. Even when I was really fucking up, I always believed that there was something greater out there for me. And how did I know that? How was I sure of it?

Because all the incredible books I was reading and inspirational music I was listening to told me so!!!

The Beauty of Books

If I've had any advantage in this life, it's that I was encouraged to read. From an early age, my mother always made sure she had a book in my face. One of the first ones I remember her giving me was from the Jehovah's Witnesses' *The Watchtower* publications called *My Book of Bible Stories*. I read those tales over and over again.

Around the same time I started reading *The Watchtower*, my mother made another great move by enrolling me in the Book It! program at my school, Whitesville Elementary. The program was sponsored by Pizza Hut and the idea was every time you read four books, you would get a free personal-pan pizza. Recently, I read a study that claimed this program didn't actually increase or decrease a person's motivation for reading. I would like to take this opportunity to tell whoever wrote that study to please SHUT THE FUCK UP FOREVER.

I can promise you that the Book It! program motivated the hell out of me when it came to reading. Maybe I was predisposed because I looked like a Teenage Mutant Ninja Turtle, but I used to love Pizza Hut. Nothing was more exciting than going to Pizza

Hut on a Friday night, showing them my reading certificate, and being rewarded with a personal-pan pizza.

Another savvy thing my mother did was encourage me to read books about people I didn't seem to have anything in common with (not that there were a ton of books about little black boys growing up in the rural South anyway that weren't about slaves). She wanted books to help introduce me to worlds that might otherwise seem foreign. As a result, I read a lot of Judy Blume and Beverly Cleary. I read so many of them that after a while I started believing that I knew everything about women, especially little girls. To this day I still think about how if Ramona Quimby had grown up in this era they would have loaded her up on Ritalin and killed all her creativity and imagination.

My mother might have had me reading books about little white girls, but my father was giving me a super black reading list. From an early age, he'd been exposing me to books like *The Autobiography of Malcolm X*, or *Message to the Blackman in America* by Elijah Muhammad. At first I wasn't interested.

But as I got a little older, a force came into my life that made me want to pick up all those books my father had been recommending. That made me believe that instead of being a fish stuck in a small pond, I was actually a god in control of my own universe.

That force was hip-hop.

The Microphone Fiend

As a kid, R & B was the dominant music heard in our home. My mother loved the Supremes (she still plays them for my daughter today), while my father was into soul and funk, especially James Brown. The Godfather of Soul was born in Barnwell, South Carolina, and I think my father always felt a connection with him because of that. My dad used to have this black Datsun pickup truck and he would drive around Moncks Corner playing song after song of James Brown. From the old stuff like "Cold Sweat" and "Say It Loud" to the funky shit like "Doing It to Death" and "I'm a Greedy Man," my father loooooved every groove James ever recorded. He even managed to crash James's funeral in Augusta, Georgia, talking his way onto the stage by acting like he was a part of the family. In a way, he was.

The same way my father couldn't get enough James Brown, I developed a similar love affair with hip-hop. Like all true hip-hop junkies, I can still clearly remember the time I got my first hit. I was with my cousin Tyrone McKelvey at my uncle Harris and aunt Lottie's house when Tyrone announced, "I got a new song I'm going to let you hear." As if he was about to let me in on a big secret. He stuck in the tape and soon I was transfixed by a bass line that felt like it was reaching out of the speakers and punching me in the chest. Then came a deep voice that was at once both harder *and* slicker than anything I'd ever heard before.

> Thinking of a master plan
> 'Cause ain't nothin' but sweat inside my hand

When I heard Rakim spit those opening lines, it was like a whole new world had opened up before me. The song sampled the soul sound of my father's generation ("Don't Look Any Further" from The Temptations' Dennis Edwards), but Rakim's voice sounded like it was speaking directly to *me*. He was describing a struggle I was already seeing around me—not enough money to buy groceries or pay the rent—but in a way that sounded empowering. Rakim might have only had sweat inside his hand, but his voice was so self-assured and intelligent that you just *knew* it was only a matter of time before he got his hands on some money again. In fact, the song was called "Paid in Full." He wasn't just going to get paid, he was going to get *paid in full*.

In those three minutes my life was transformed forever. From that moment on I was all in on this hip-hop thing, soaking up every cassingle (remember those?), cassette, and CD I could get my hands on. In the early nineties, that meant listening to a lot of New York legends like Biggie, Nas, Wu-Tang, and my personal favorites, Mobb Deep.

Studying their lyrics, I began to notice references to places that I'd never heard of before. "What is this Queensbridge Nas speaks of?" I'd ask myself. "I don't know it, but if it birthed Nas, it must be popping."

Wu-Tang kept referencing a "Shaolin." "Is that where all the gods go to build?" I wondered.

And Biggie kept talking about "BK." I didn't know if it was Burger King or some other place, but if he was referencing it, I wanted to check it out.

I had the same reaction to Outkast and Goodie Mob rapping about Atlanta or Tupac shouting out LA. I'd never set foot in California, but "To Live and Die in L.A." described the city with so much energy that Pac made me feel I'd been there. When I did make it to LA for the first time years later, thanks to Tupac I hit the ground with the confidence of someone who'd grown up in South Central.

My crew and I loved those songs so much that eventually we started naming spots around Moncks Corner after the places we'd hear shouted out. Highway Six, a notorious drug corridor, became "Shaolin" after Wu-Tang's nickname for Staten Island. The neighborhood of Whitesville became "Brownsville," after M.O.P.'s Brooklyn stomping grounds. A house where we sold dope became "Queensbridge," after the home of Nas and Mobb Deep.

A lot of folks in the media at the time were calling hip-hop a cancer, a negative influence on African-American youth. They said it promoted violence and was misogynistic. They may have been right, but it was having a different influence on me. The truth was that hip-hop wasn't just helping me come up with corny nicknames for places around Moncks Corner. It was sparking my interest in history; it was whetting my appetite for knowledge (definitely more than it was being sparked in school).

As I pored over the lyrics of groups like Public Enemy or Wu-Tang Clan, the messages of black consciousness my father had been pushing on me started to feel more relevant. When I heard Public Enemy say, "Farrakhan's a prophet and I think you ought to listen to," or Biggie say that he was "deep like the mind of Farrakhan," the dots began to connect.

Thanks to hip-hop, I started devouring books off my father's reading list, books like *Message to the Blackman in America*, which exposed systematic racism, and Akil's *From Niggas to God*, which expanded on the Five Percenter teachings I'd heard referenced in many songs. *The Seat of the Soul* by Gary Zukav and *The 48 Laws of Power*, Robert Greene's classic that was quoted by so many rappers, also helped me become more strategic in my thinking.

People don't realize how a man's whole life can be changed by one book.

—Malcolm X

The combined effect of these books and music on my mentality was extremely powerful. Imagine me as a teenager: I'm lying on my bed in our trailer late at night. Occasionally I'll hear a car kicking up pebbles as it drives down our dirt road. The only other sounds are crickets and bullfrogs outside my window. I'm truly stuck out in the middle of nowhere. A million miles away from where the action is.

But in my busted CD Walkman, a piece of tape holding down the battery hatch, a whole other world is forming. Wu-Tang Clan's "C.R.E.A.M." starts to play softly through the headphones, just loud enough that I can hear it without waking up my mom in the next room:

> Leave it up to me while I be living proof
> To kick the truth to the young black youth
> But Shorty's running wild, smoking sess, drinking beer
> And ain't trying to hear what I'm kicking in his ear

As Inspectah Deck spits those rhymes over a relentless, driving RZA production, my mind is far away from the cornfields, dirt roads, and swamps outside my window. Nope, I'm weaving through the streets of New York City in a kitted-out Jeep, flying past bodegas and housing projects. Instead of a small-town country boy, I feel like a rap superhero. Capable of leaping over my small pond in a single bound and landing whereever I damned well please.

That's the confidence I always got from hip-hop. When Rakim said he was "born to be the sole controller of the universe / Besides the part of the map I hit first" that power came through the speakers and went directly into my soul. Yes, the map might say I was stuck in Moncks Corner for now, but my home was about to be the cosmos.

With hip-hop and books empowering me, the excuse "I'm from this small-ass town" simply wasn't going to be a good enough reason for me *not* to make it. I'd learned that from Malcolm X to Method Man, from Louis Farrakhan to the Notorious B.I.G., so many of my heroes had grown up in circumstances as bad, if not worse, than mine. If you let society tell it, none of them should have achieved what they did.

But they *had* made it. They *had* become legends. Because someone had planted the seed in their minds that they were bigger than whatever environment could have easily held them down. Just like they had instilled that sense of confidence in me.

Which is why I have to say: Thank you to Rakim for planting the seed in my mind that *it ain't where you're from* physically, but *where you're at* mentally that allows someone to transcend their circumstances. And then thank you to the Wu-Tangs, the Mobb Deeps and the Nas of the world for watering that seed until it blossomed into a confident young man who was determined to transcend whatever barriers life seemed to have put in front of him.

Beyond Your Zone

In order to chase your dreams to their end, you must be very focused on getting inspiration where it's available. Take books: just by the fact that you're reading these pages, you obviously respect the value of the written word. Make sure, however, that you continue to explore books that don't seem to directly connect with your experience. If you're a young black woman, read up on some of the experiences of Asian men. If you're a white guy, pick up a book about the struggle of black women, or the immigrant experience. If you're into sports, read a book about science. Or if you mainly read self-help books, check out a historical novel. As I learned from my mother, there is incredible power in subjects that don't seem to pertain to you.

One of the best books I read recently is Gary Vaynerchuk's *Jab, Jab, Jab, Right Hook*, a guide to how to get your story across on social media. On the surface, I wouldn't seem to have that much in common with Gary: He was born in Russia and as a kid moved to New Jersey, where his parents opened a liquor store. He did poorly in school (OK, maybe we do have something in common) and spent most of his time helping out around their shop or selling baseball cards. After college, he took over the family business and, through a combination of social media savvy, aggressive pricing, and all-around hustle, transformed it from a $3 million to $50 million business in just over five years.

Gary doesn't look like me, he didn't grow up in a trailer, he wasn't raised in the same religion as me, hell, he didn't even start off speaking the same language as me, but his story still spoke directly to me. It motivated the shit out of me to keep hustling every day, and when I interviewed him on *The Breakfast Club* and my podcast *The Brilliant Idiots*, a lot of people said they were some of our most motivational episodes ever.

Exploring people and ideas outside your comfort zone is one area where hip-hop has been, unfortunately, very weak. As a culture, we don't allow ourselves a chance to grow. If something doesn't look like "us," or sound like "us," we have a tendency to dismiss it out of hand.

I grew up as black as you can get: you ain't getting any blacker than Larry McKelvey's son. But I still REFUSE to have a limited cultural experience. If something seems authentic and interesting, I'm going to check it out. Whether on the surface it appears to be "hip-hop" or not. I'm never going to dismiss anything until I explore whether it might have some value for me.

One year I was at the iHeartRadio Music Awards and they had a tribute to Freddie Mercury and Queen, who I admittedly didn't know that much about. When I saw them onstage playing "Another One Bites the Dust," I said, "Oh shit! These guys were white?" "Another One Bites the Dust" used to have the Zebra rocking, so I assumed they were black. My dad, Mr. Black Power, probably knew they were white, but that didn't stop him from playing them in his club. If a song rocks, it rocks. Just as if a book is interesting, it's interesting. Never stunt your own growth by dismissing something just because it doesn't feel familiar.

The Holy Ground of Walmart

Another mistake people with small pond mind-sets make is not being motivated by the success stories taking place right in front of them.

I've always had the opposite mentality. Growing up, I looked for *every* possible connection between myself and someone successful, no matter how tenuous the link might seem. I'll never forget flipping through the TV one afternoon after school and landing on BET's *Rap City*. The host Big Tigger was introducing DJ B-Lord as a guest on the show. "Live from North Carolina, it's B-Lord," Tigger said before B quickly corrected him with "No, I'm from South Carolina."

It was a seemingly insignificant moment, a couple of seconds on a video show. But it hit me like a lightning bolt. "Wow," I remember thinking. "That DJ on a national TV show just said he was from South Carolina." Someone from my state was a guest on the same show that Method Man, Raekwon, and Mobb Deep had all been on. The artists I'd been worshipping. With the simple words, "No, I'm from South Carolina," suddenly a direct path from Moncks Corner to the rest of the world opened up before me. "If B-Lord can make it, I can do something too," I told myself. And I never lost that faith.

I got the same surge of confidence the first time I heard Wu-Tang's Inspectah Deck rap, "I smoke on the mic like Smokin' Joe Frazier." Why? Because I knew Joe Frazier was from Beaufort, South Carolina. Philly might try to claim him, but Smokin' Joe was ours. My father kept a picture of him fighting Muhammad Ali in our trailer and always reminded me he was a Carolina boy. So hearing him shouted out in one of my favorite songs was like putting another battery in my back. "Great people are born here," I figured. "If he made it, I can make it too."

If one person that looks like you made it, then you can too.

—Gary Vaynerchuk on *The Brilliant Idiots*

I was also inspired by Ryan and Doug Stewart, who were multi-sports stars in Moncks Corner. Ryan won a football scholarship to Georgia Tech and ended up getting drafted by the Detroit Lions, playing in the NFL for five years. From there he and Doug started a sports radio show in Atlanta called *Two Live Stews* (one of the all-time great show names) and then started popping up on ESPN. Whenever I'd see them on ESPN's *First Take* (one of my favorite shows), I'd think, "Man, I watched those guys come up. If people respect their opinions on TV, then there's no reason they can't respect mine."

Seeing local athletes get college scholarships always motivated me. From 1995 to 2000, it felt like there was a steady stream of guys from Moncks Corner who were getting a free education thanks to their football skills. Rusty Williams got a scholarship to Auburn. My cousin Tory Liferidge to Duke. My other cousin Mal Lawyer to Clemson. Yet another cousin Kinta Palmer to Penn State. Courtney Brown, who is from Alvin, the next town over from Moncks Corner, also went to Penn State and then became the number one pick in the NFL draft. Sports were never my thing, so there was no chance I was going to get that sort of ticket out of town. Still, watching so many of my peers head out to college made me think, "I've got to do better too." It wasn't limited to sports either. When my girlfriend (now my wife), Mook Mook, graduated in 2000, she went to the University of South Carolina in Columbia. Knowing that my mother had graduated college back in her day motivated me too. Being aware of all that success made me think, "I can't be a bum. I gotta do something too."

I would even find inspiration in places as unlikely as Walmart. Growing up, if it was late at night and me and my homeboys were tired of sitting around playing video games, we'd go down to Walmart to look at shit. I thank God for twenty-four-hour Walmarts, because in a small town, even just wandering the aisles let me feel like I was ending my night on a high. As pathetic as that might sound to some of you who grew up in real cities, it was a big deal to me. I can say Walmart became my place of worship to a larger world.

That sense of being a portal to opportunity became even more significant after I learned about the owners of the chain, the Walton Family. The guy who started the company, Sam Walton, was from a small town just like me. In fact, the town he was born in, Kingfisher, Oklahoma, had a population of only around twenty-five hundred people, making it a smaller pond than Moncks Corner. No easy feat.

When I read Sam Walton's story, I just figured, "If this guy from the middle of nowhere could make his dreams come true, why couldn't I?" I didn't care that Sam Walton was a white man. Or that he was passionate about retail, which has never been an area of interest to me. I just knew he had come from a small town and built something national. Something with a legacy. That was more than enough for me.

Embrace Your Core

While it's important to rise above your roots and transcend your circumstances, it is also key that no matter where life takes you, you must never get detached from those roots. You can go from swimming in the smallest pond to controlling the oceans like Poseidon, but if you lose touch with your core, you're gonna find yourself adrift. Make no mistake about it, Moncks Corner is my core. And as any real trainer will tell you, when your core isn't strong, everything else is going to fall apart.

For instance, I'm having a great run in this media game, but there are absolutely still times when I become unsure of myself. Times when I feel confused about what moves I should be making. When I feel like I'm missing opportunities that I can't see. When I feel like my energy is blocked and I'm stuck in a rut.

Every one of us feels this from time to time.

How you handle those feelings is what will set you apart. When I'm stuck, my solution isn't to leave my house in New Jersey and go party in Manhattan. I don't try to make myself feel better by hanging out with fake industry people who are going to tell me how great I am all night. Or a bunch of IG models who only want to be around me because I'm a little famous.

No, when I'm stuck, I reconnect with my core. That means getting on a plane to Charleston and then heading straight to Moncks Corner. I will literally drive to my mom's house and go sleep in my old bedroom.

The room is basically how I left it. There's still a closet full of fading old *The Source*, *XXL*, and *Blaze* magazines. The pages I used to study, like Muslims study the Quran, or Jews the Torah. I'll pick them up and read fading articles about Ghostface Killah, my favorite MC, or Mobb Deep's Prodigy just to remind myself of the energy I used to get from those pages. When I can reconnect with the dreams my younger self used to have, whatever little drama or doubt that was getting me down quickly becomes irrelevant.

But I'm not done. After recharging at my mother's house, I'll drive to my late grandmother Rosa Lee Ford's house (God bless the dead). Nobody lives there anymore, but I'll still sit on her porch and soak up all that house's great energy. I'll meditate and pray and soon I'll feel like I'm talking to my grandmother again. It feels very natural, since as I mentioned, my grandmother always used to say she communicated with my dead grandfather. Having a similar chat with her gives me a peaceful feeling.

After we talk, I'll open up the front door and go sit inside her empty house. (I don't do it every trip because there's a big bolt on the door and it can be a hassle to get the key.) If you've ever entered an empty house, you know you're greeted by tremendous energy the moment you step across the threshold. It freaks some people out, but I embrace it. I love to revisit all my beautiful memories and reconnect with that kid who was so full of dreams. It never fails to get me back on point.

When the roots are deep there is no reason to fear the wind.

—African Proverb

It doesn't matter whether you're in media, law, sales, or education. Between Twitter, Instagram, Snapchat or whatever else comes next, all of our minds are cluttered these days. All of us feel overwhelmed by the pace of life. Knocked off-balance by the never-ending stream of information we read, watch, and listen to every day.

In order to get your equilibrium right, you must return to your core. If you can still physically go back, jump in the car or on a plane and get there ASAP. Lie in your old bed and reconnect with your old dreams. Sit on your front porch and remember how you felt as a young man or woman. If your relatives aren't around anymore, close your eyes and talk to your grandma, or your grandfather, or the auntie who raised you. Celebrate that the street you might live on now is nicer, but also embrace that dirt road you grew up on. Appreciate that all your power emanates from that dirt and that you wouldn't have it any other way. You'll probably shed a few tears, but they'll be empowering. Not painful.

Whether you grew up in a trailer in a dusty Southern town, a housing project in Queens, or even a mansion in LA, understand that the dreams you had lying in your old bed, or sitting on your old stoop, are what got you where you are today. And that losing touch with them is the only thing that can stop you from transcending your circumstances.

PYP
(Pick Your Passion, Poison,
or Procrastination)

There are three primary "P's" to choose from in life: (1) Passion, which leads to prosperity. (2) Poison, which leads to pain. (3) Procrastination, which doesn't lead anywhere at all, because you sit around waiting for things to just magically happen. Please don't pick "P's" numbers 2 and 3. Instead of hoping you'll be successful, follow your passion and make conscious decisions that will help you realize your destiny.

"Destiny is not a matter of chance, it's a matter of choice." That's a quote from the nineteenth-century American orator William Jennings Bryan. Or so I'm told. I guess I heard it at some point in high school, though I can't say when for sure, given how high I was during most of my classes. No matter how that quote got into my head, I'm grateful I held on to it, because it changed the course of my life.

Remember those Choose Your Own Adventure books from back in the day that allowed you to pick between different outcomes? I loved them because if you chose a story line that led to you getting eaten by a shark or cut in half from a transdimensional portal, you could just go back a few pages and start over again. In life, second and third chances often aren't an option. If you pick the wrong adventure too many times, there's no coming back.

A book about my teenage years could have easily been called *Choose Your Own Fuckup*. Most of the choices I made during that time had me headed straight toward one of the three dead ends my father kept warning me about.

I was caught up in building street cred during my teenage years. And I'm not proud of all the dumb shit I did. All these years later, I can report that there is not one major purchase I've ever been able to make using street cred. No dealership has ever accepted street cred for a car, and no resort has ever let me book a room with an ocean view using street cred. When I go see my banker, she's never asked me if I was interested in getting better interest on my "gangsta."

This is why I get so frustrated when I see young men giving themselves titles like "Trap Niggas," "D Boys," "Real Street Niggas," "Savages," and "Goons." It's as if we call ourselves everything *but* men. Real men protect and provide for their families by any legal means necessary. Did you catch that? By Any LEGAL Means Necessary.

I shake my head at these kids, but back in the day I was making the same mistakes. I was as dumb as any D Boy, as stupid as any Savage, as greedy as any Goon.

Yet here I am today.

That's why when you read yet another story about kids wildin' out in Chicago, or acting like a bunch of damned fools somewhere (OK, everywhere) in Florida, just remember that I was once that stupid too. Maybe even worse.

That's why if you take one thing away from these stories, don't let it be, "Man, Charlamagne was bad when he was a kid." Instead, let it be, "As bad as he was, Charlamagne still managed to turn it around."

Then remember that all these other young thugs out here, no matter how lost they might seem, can make similar changes in their lives. As long as they accept responsibility for their decisions. Just like I did.

Nerd Life

I might have ended my school days as a thug, but I started off as a sensitive-ass square. That's right, I would not stop crying the day my mother dropped me off for first grade at Memminger Elementary in downtown Charleston. I walked around bawling because I was surrounded by kids I didn't know, but things got better the second day, and by the end of my first week I was back in my comfort zone. After a week or so, I'd established myself as one of the stars of the class. The school even selected me and another little girl to take a foreign language class, an honor that was rarely bestowed back then. It made me feel special.

The kids in the class gravitated toward me because I was smart and extremely verbal. After school I would hold court by the playground and keep the other kids in stitches by running my mouth about kindergarten life—which girls my friends had crushes on, comic books I'd read, and little impressions of our teachers. Even back then, I got a rush from being the center of attention and keeping people entertained.

By second grade we had moved to Moncks Corner, where I continued taking French and Spanish. Soon they had me in the accelerated class and I'd gained a reputation as one of the "bright kids" in our school.

My only weakness was that even though I was very verbal, I had a strange fear of talking in front of the class. Then I learned a trick—if I scrawled out a couple words about what I wanted to say ahead of time, I became more comfortable. Once I started doing that, you couldn't keep me out of the spotlight. I even starred in our school's production *Stone Soup*.

I can honestly say in elementary school I was everything I want my own kids to be today: a funny, hardworking, respected nerd who loved learning. Appreciated by the teachers and popular with the other kids.

Then I got to Berkeley Middle School for sixth grade and things began to change. And not for the better.

In elementary school the classes hadn't been grouped according to ability, but for middle school they broke us up in tracks. "A" and "C" were the accelerated classes, while "B" and "F" were for the regular kids and "D" seemed to stand for "delinquent."

I was in "A," which definitely didn't stand for "African-American," as there were only a handful of black kids in both accelerated classes. I can even name all of them some twenty-five years later: JoJo Smith, Teresa Grant, Jasmine Monroe, Denise Gibbs, Tameka Haynes, and Danielle Dixon. All the other black kids were in "B" or "D."

As a result, I started hanging with the nerdy white kids who were in my advanced classes. My best buddies were two white guys, Connor and Wyatt (did I even have to mention they were white with names like that?). I spent almost all my time between classes or at recess with those two and their friends.

There's an action shot of us goofing around in our sixth-grade yearbook that pretty much captures that period. I've got big

Coke-bottle glasses and a fanny pack on, which was my standard getup in those days. When I was older and caught up in the thug lifestyle, I used to HATE seeing that picture because it told an undeniable truth about me: I was a fucking nerd.

Even though my nerd credentials were impeccable, I couldn't help but notice that my friendship with the white kids seemed to have its limits. We were thick like thieves at school, but when the afternoon bell rang we'd go our separate ways. They'd have playdates, sleepovers, and birthday parties with their other white friends, but I never seemed to be invited. To this day, I don't know if they didn't want me over at their houses or if the resistance was coming from their parents.

I lived in a trailer with my Jehovah's Witness mother and my Jheri-curled father. Their parents were middle-class white people whose fathers probably wore polo shirts and Dockers. My world might have seemed too foreign to them to connect with. Whatever the reason, I can remember thinking, "I don't really belong with these kids. They're not my people." That left me with a gnawing desire to be part of something. If the white nerds weren't ready to fully embrace me, I was going to chase that feeling of fitting in.

Wherever it took me.

The Thug Life

My transition from nerd to thug started with an innocent comment about Bell Biv DeVoe.

I was at my aunt's house in New Jersey, hanging out with my sister Teresa and my cousin Rachelle. We were watching TV when the video for BBD's hit "Poison" came on.

"Ronnie's so cute," declared Rachelle as he strutted on-screen rocking an Africa medallion, a full-length black leather coat, and a high-top fade.

"No, Michael's the cute one," countered Teresa.

I just wanted to be down, so I took my sister's side.

"Yeah, Michael's definitely the cute one!" I said with enthusiasm.

The moment I said, "cute," they both whipped around and looked at me like I'd just announced that black lives don't matter.

"Daddy come here!" screamed my sister, causing my father to rush into the room. "'Nard* just said one of those boys in Bell Biv DeVoe is cute!!!"

This was way before the days of gender fluidity, trans rights, or acceptance of any sort of behavior that could be interpreted as gay. Even if those concepts had been popular back then, my father still wouldn't have cared. There was no way his eldest son was going to go around calling male R & B singers cute.

"Get the hell away from these girls!" he barked and then dragged me to my aunt's backyard. My older cousins Ty and John were already out there playing football—where in my father's eyes I should have been all along. He told them what I'd said and then left it up to them to deal with their pussy-ass cousin. For the next three hours, they treated *me* like the football. They kicked me, punched me, and dragged me all over that yard.

My father wasn't done with me though. When we got back to Moncks Corner, he made it his business to make sure that I was spending the rest of the summer with "real niggas" like my cousins. It was time to beat the influence of the nerdy white boys out of me before I became too soft.

There was, however, a glitch in my father's plan. I didn't *like* my cousins. Mainly because they used to beat the shit out of me.

*Another one of my nicknames, short for Lenard.

It wasn't just the episode in Jersey either. *Every time* I'd see them, they'd tackle me, body-slam me, put me in a sleeper hold, or slap me in the back of my neck. Who wants to constantly deal with that?

My cousins didn't like me either. They'd seen me doing well in school, strutting around with my fanny pack, reading books, and hanging out with the white boys. Mind you, there were other black kids in our school with glasses and fanny packs (they were poppin' back then). But those other kids weren't *Larry McKelvey's* son.

Uncle Larry's son being a teacher's pet and a good student was an affront to them. So if they saw me with Connor and Wyatt, they'd tease me, calling me "Mr. Magoo," a "white boy," and, of course, "Urkel." Anything that might demoralize or embarrass me.

My father never outright told me he was behind the bullying, but I believe he was. The way I see it, even though my cousins legitimately didn't like me, they still had too much respect for my father as a street dude to lay a finger on me. Let alone brazenly bully me in public. My father had to have given them the green light.

My father probably figured it was a positive kind of intimidation. You know, the type of bullying that happens when your family is full of future convicts and they want you to stop wasting your life trying to be a good kid who gets straight As and Bs so you can come hang with them and work on being a future convict too.

If that was their plan, it sure as hell worked. Connor, Wyatt, and the other white kids weren't interested in hanging out with me if it meant having to deal with a bunch of older black kids who seemed hell-bent on slapping and punching their friend Larry. My cousins must have seemed like ISIS to them. The white boys already didn't want to hang outside of school, and soon they were steering clear of me in the cafeteria and playground too because they were scared. I can't blame them—I was scared too.

For a kid who had become accustomed to being the center of attention, finding myself without a group of friends was depressing. When it became clear my white friends weren't going to hang out with me anymore, I faced a choice: I could hang with my cousins, or I could have *no* friends at all. So I started rolling with my cousins, even though they continued to bully me.

One of their favorite games was knocking off my glasses. It was as if my glasses represented everything—good grades, white friends, and a bright future—that they hated. I once read that during the cultural revolution in China, wearing glasses often got people killed because they were a symbol of elitism. My cousins didn't know nothing about China, but they instinctively had a similar reaction to me wearing glasses.

That meant every time I saw my cousins there would be a smack, a push, or a trip and *bam!* My glasses would be on the ground. After a while the frames got bent completely out of shape and one of the lenses kept popping out. I had to walk around with tape on them just to keep everything in place.

One morning I was out in front of the school when my cousins Brandon and Cameron rolled up. "Yo, what's up, Larry," called out Cameron. Before I could answer, he gave me a hard shove and my glasses flew off. When they hit the ground, one of the lenses shattered into a thousand pieces.

Staring at the broken glasses on the sidewalk while my cousins laughed at me, I realized I was tired. Tired of being bullied. Tired of not having friends. Tired of always looking over my shoulder.

"Fuck this smart shit," I told myself. "I gotta be down with them guys if I'm going to survive."

This time, I wasn't getting my glasses fixed. My days as Mr. Magoo were over. I was casting my lot with my thug-ass cousins. Which is when the real bullshit began.

School Daze

My first concession to the thug life was hiding my intelligence. I suspect a lot of kids do this when they find themselves in an environment that doesn't value academic achievement and learning. They'd rather blend in by acting stupid than stand out by seeming smart. So in my case, the teacher's pet who'd always raised his hand in class and volunteered to do extra work suddenly became the class clown. I'd crack jokes, pass notes, make funny noises, and throw stuff when the teacher wasn't (or was) looking.

Despite having been such an advanced student in elementary school, no one stepped in and encouraged me to do better. I was fairly new to Berkeley Middle, so the teachers there weren't familiar with the nerdy Larry who'd been studying French in elementary school. I was doing such a convincing impression of a knucklehead that they had no reason to believe that I was capable of more.

It's tempting to look back and ask, "Why didn't my mother try to protect me? She should have kept me away from those dudes." First off, she simply didn't know. It's not like I went running to her with my drama. I also believe this was a tough time for my family. My father was going through his battles with drugs and alcohol, plus he was starting to step out on my mother a lot. For her part, my mother was doing the best she could. There wasn't much time to focus on why Larry was acting up in school.

I managed to pass sixth grade, and when seventh grade rolled around I was completely focused: on being as big a pain in the ass as possible. Just as I'd gotten addicted to being the positive center of attention in elementary school, in middle school I'd discovered the attention goes to the funny, disruptive kids. Armed with that information, I had only one objective every time I stepped into school: create some "good laughs!"

The term "good laugh" became something of a messed-up mantra for me and my cousin Kwame, who also went to Berkeley. We'd walk around doing dumb shit, and if we could get someone to crack up, we'd yell, "good laugh, good laugh, good laugh" to each other in an idiotic voice. Imagine a black, less mature version of Beavis and Butt-Head.

Nothing was off-limits in our quest for a "good laugh." I mean *nothing*. For example, we noticed that our seventh-grade teacher (I'll call him Mr. Walrus because that's what he was shaped like) had a particularly large set of testicles. Whenever he sat down, his balls would bunch up in his pants and form an inviting target. So one day Kwame climbed down under his desk, snuck up on Mr Walrus, and stabbed him in the balls with a pencil. Not with the eraser side either. When the pencil pierced his pouch, Mr. Walrus gave a wild scream and kicked his desk over. Kwame and I had bolted from the room before Mr. Walrus could catch us, yelling, "Good laugh, good laugh," as we ran down the hallway.

Another time, Kwame stuck his finger in his underwear, got a little doodie on his finger, and then walked up to a substitute teacher. "Um, I think you've got something on your face," he told her. "Where?" she asked innocently. Kwame then ran his tainted finger under her nose. "Right there!" he cackled, and then ran out of the classroom. Definitely a "good laugh."

Frankly, I'm embarrassed to even tell those stories, but I want you to really understand how obnoxious and disrespectful we were. We were exactly the type of kids I DON'T want my own children to turn into. Or even be around.

Needless to say I failed seventh grade and had to go to summer school. To their credit, a few of the teachers saw that I wasn't as stupid as my actions suggested and encouraged me to get my act together. "Larry, you're only choosing to play dumb," my seventh-grade math teacher, Mrs. Gibbs, told me. "It might be funny to you now, but it's going to hurt you in the long run."

I knew she was right, especially the "choosing" part, but I still didn't listen. I had convinced myself that being a class clown was the only way I was going to not just survive but thrive at Berkeley Middle School. Instead of holding back, I actually doubled down on my bad behavior.

Fun Fact: Berkeley Middle School is where TV host Stephen Colbert's brother Jay Colbert used to teach seventh-grade social studies. I remember thinking Mr. Colbert was cool because one day he and some other teachers came to school with their clothes on backward and performed "Jump" by Kris Kross.

We pronounced his name "Col-burt"—not the French pronunciation, "Cole-bear," that Stephen uses today. I guess Stephen decided to jazz it up for TV, and I don't blame him. By the way, what's up with guys from South Carolina taking French names as their handles? (*Charlemagne* is French for "Charles the Great" by the way.)

Going to summer school between seventh and eighth grades didn't put a dent in my delinquency. If anything, my behavior got worse in eighth grade because that's when alcohol got introduced into the mix.

It started when my friend Jamal—RIP—began smuggling forties into school. Eighth fucking grade, can you believe it? And he wasn't alone. Caleb, who is now a stone alcoholic, would break out mini liquor bottles on the bus that we'd drink before we got to school.

One time I was in Ms. Baylor's social studies class and showed my cousin Kwame a bottle of vodka Caleb had given me. "I'm going to drink this right here," announced Kwame. "Naw, just wait till recess," I told him. "Fuck that," said Kwame, and took a big swig, making zero attempt to be subtle. Of course, Ms. Baylor saw everything. We got pulled out of class and sent to the principal's office, where the bottle was discovered. For punishment Kwame and I were put in this program called SKIP, which was basically a teenager version of AA. I'd sit in a circle and have to tell the group, "Hi, my name is Larry, and I have a problem with alcohol."

I wasn't alone. Jamal would often bring a forty to recess and we would stand around the school yard sneaking sips of Olde English while other kids were playing football or basketball, and be completely messed up before it was time to go back to class. What the hell was wrong with us?

Just in case you have any doubt that the bad choices you make as a kid can mess you up forever, let me tell you what happened to Jamal. When we were teenagers he got busted with a concealed weapon. Then he caught a couple cocaine convictions. Finally, in 2007, he was arrested for strangling a woman to death with her pajama pants. They gave him a thirty-year bid, which he was serving until he killed himself in jail in 2014. I can't say for sure things would have turned out different for Jamal if we hadn't been getting wasted during eighth-grade recess, but I can say that lifestyle was setting me up to ruin my own life.

The administration could see that I was troubled. After a handful of incidents, they declared that I needed to either see an in-school therapist or be transferred. I agreed to talk to the therapist, but I only viewed the sessions as something I had to put up with until the administration stopped bothering me.

"Do you hear voices, Larry?" the therapist asked me one day.*

"Yes," I replied. "I definitely do."

"What do they sound like?"

"They sound a lot like you, and they keep asking me do I hear voices."

Thanks to that kind of attitude, I ended up failing eighth grade too. Time for another trip to summer school, which was the only way to prevent being left back a grade. This time, however, my father wasn't trying to fork over the summer school tuition. "If Lenard wants to keep on being an idiot, let him get left back," he told my mother and me. "He can spend next year getting teased for being stupid. Maybe being embarrassed will wake him up." My mother wasn't taking as hard a line—she thought it was important for me to graduate with my class. Taking advantage of the split in their ranks, I put on an earnest face and promised, "Sorry, I'll take it seriously this time." My father finally relented and put me in summer school. I managed to pass, and in the fall I was ready to enter Berkeley High School.

Good ol' Berkeley High School. I can say that the seed for every poor disciplinary choice I made in my adult life was planted at Berkeley. Its halls were filled with future thugs, drug dealers, and even murderers. You might wonder how a small-town school could produce so many delinquents. Well, when I entered Berkeley High, "being hard" was the thing to be. Maybe in the sixties civil rights would have been the popular movement, or black power in the seventies. But in the nineties it was the thug life.

I give hip-hop credit for inspiring me to read more and be more

---

*In school, people would always mispronounce my name as "Leonard," so after a while I was like "just call me Larry." My parents could never understand why at school I was known as Larry.

socially conscious, but it also needs to be said that hip-hop's influence wasn't all positive. We were a bunch of country kids shaped by violent movies like *Menace II Society*, *Boyz n the Hood*, and *Juice*, as well as aggressive music like Mobb Deep, UGK, the Geto Boys, and Onyx. When we heard Onyx yell, "Throw your guns in the air," we took it literally. We didn't have guns right then, but the seed was planted in our heads. It wouldn't take long for it to grow, either.

Hip-hop movies had a major impact on us too. When *Juice* came out, everyone talked about how fly Tupac looked when he tucked a .38 pistol into his 40 Below Timberland boots. So of course me and my boys also wanted .38s and Timbs to manifest all of Pac's swag. Same thing when *Menace II Society* was big. The movie might have been about the quest to get out of the ghetto, but we ignored that story line. We were too gassed off how cool Larenz Tate's O-Dog character looked packing a nine-millimeter pistol. Soon we were all trying to cop one of those as well.

Hip-hop definitely got me hype for my first fight in high school. My cousin Brian Washington and I were standing in line in the cafeteria when this upperclassman cut our spot. Despite only being a freshman, I told the guy, "Yo, you can't do that." He was a street dude, and rolled with a crew of thugs, so of course he immediately turned around and started talking shit to us.

What he didn't know was that morning I had been listening to Redman's "Time 4 Sum Aksion" on my Sony Walkman. That song was so hype that Mike Tyson even used to enter the ring to it.

As this upperclassman was talking shit to us, all I could hear in my head was, "Time for some action! Time . . . time . . . time for some action!" Without a word, I just cocked back and punched the dude dead in his nose. He stumbled and tried to grab me as he fell, but couldn't hold on. I'd put him on his ass. He tried to get up and fight back, but the teachers came rushing over to break it up as Brian and I slipped away.

Once we were out of the cafeteria, Brian began celebrating like I had just hit the game-winning shot in game seven of the NBA finals. "I knew you had it in you!" he yelled as he bounced up and down next to me. Brian was one of the cousins who used to terrorize me, so his approval was almost like a perverse version of Dell Curry beaming with pride after his son Steph won the MVP of the NBA.

I'd like to say that deep down I wish I hadn't hit that guy, or knew it was stupid to walk around with a .38 tucked in my boots, but . . . nope! Trust and believe I *loved* that feeling of Brian hyping me up. I loved knowing that the other kids in school would look at me in awe because I knocked out an upperclassman thug, or would want to be my friend because I packed a pistol. I loved that attention so much that all I wanted to do was cause more trouble.

I didn't have to look far to find it. Kids were fighting in the halls, bringing guns to school, and smoking weed in the parking lot. The administration seemed powerless to rein it all in. They tried handing out three-day suspensions for fighting, but kids would just ignore them and show up for school anyway. The inmates were truly running the asylum at Berkeley High School.

The worst of the thugs was the "Hit Squad," a crew of kids who borrowed the name of the popular early nineties rap crew featuring EPMD, Das EFX, Redman, and K-Solo. The Berkeley High Hit Squad wasn't about making music, however. They would literally go around the school hitting people. They were making memes of knocking kids out before memes even existed. Every couple of days they would pick someone at random and let it be known that person was going to get jumped at the end of school. Sure enough, as soon as the final bell rang the Hit Squad would be waiting to hand out the fade to their unlucky victim. They were such a menace that the local paper, *The Berkeley Independent*, wrote an article about how their reign of terrror was so bad that kids were staying home from school rather than deal with them.

The Hit Squad never gave me any problems because a few of my cousins from Kittsfield were in the crew. It also helped that I was able to strike up a friendship with their leader, a kid we called Steel (because that's what it seemed like his hands where made of). Steel admired the Afro I was rocking at the time and I always made him laugh, so I never had to worry that my name was going to get called.

I managed to make it through the ninth grade, but sophomore year got off to a bad start. I helped set off this huge brawl in the cafeteria and beat up a kid pretty badly with one of those Master Locks that we used for our lockers. The school couldn't really look the other way on me beating a kid with a lock, so I was suspended for ten days.

A few things happened during my suspension that have stuck with me forever. First, my pops forced me to cut my Afro. A lot of people in town used to call me "Snoop Dogg" because I copied his signature look of Chuck Taylor sneakers and an Afro. My father never paid much attention to it until it was in the news that Snoop had caught a murder charge. On the first day of my suspension my father grabbed me and announced, "Oh, you think you Snoop? You won't be Snoop in my house! 'Cause next thing you know, y'all have a murder case too!"

"I'm not trying to look like Snoop!" I protested. "I'm trying to look like Redman!" It was a huge distinction to me, but my father didn't even know what a "Redman" was. He thought I was out of my mind.

He marched me straight down to the barbershop and told them to chop off that 'fro. As the barber put the clippers on me, my big fear was that without the Afro the girls at Berkeley weren't going to like me anymore. My hair had been my signature look, the source of my swagger. Without it I might be a nerd again! Thankfully, I came to find out that, if anything, my fresh fade made me even more popular with the girls. (Yes, I had a hairline back then.)

The other lasting memory of that suspension was being forced to dig ditches for my father. When I got suspended, my pops was building the foundation for a ranch-style house that he planned to move our family into. Someone needed to dig ditches and spread huge piles of dirt across the foundation, which had to be at least two thousand square feet. Who do you think ended up getting the job? Yep, the dumb-ass kid who'd just been suspended for ten days.

Even though shoveling dirt under the South Carolina sun was backbreaking work, my father refused to lift a finger to help. Instead, he'd stand under the shade of a tree and lecture me about what I had to look forward to if I didn't straighten up. "This fun to you?" he'd ask as I'd strike the ground with my shovel. "Is this how you want to spend the rest of your life? Out in the sun digging ditches? Carrying dirt? Because this is what you have to look forward to right now. You're either going to dig ditches or end up in one of those holes permanently because you will be buried dead in it."

Nothing gets through to a hardheaded teenage boy like manual labor. Words—be they threats or encouragement—go in one ear and out the other. Those ten days of shoveling dirt got my full attention.

In the movies, after the son spends ten days digging ditches, he realizes the errors of his ways and gets his act together once and for all. It would have been nice if that's what happened, but my life wasn't following a movie script. I sincerely wanted to do better, but it still wouldn't be long until I screwed up again.

Once I was back in school, it became clear that my suspension wasn't an anomaly—the administration was cracking down. Over the summer, the school district, having wisely come to the conclusion that Berkeley High was out of control, fired all the old administration. The district then brought in a whole new team whose sole purpose was to clean up the school. Ben Hodges became the principal, Sadie Brown was his assistant, and neither of them were playing. At all. The first thing they did was take a hard stance on fighting. One fight, as I'd found out, led to an automatic suspension. Fighting three times resulted in an automatic expulsion. They also got serious about guns. If you got caught with one at school it meant an automatic expulsion and an arrest record.

Instead of sitting in his office with his head in the sand like some of his predecessors, Mr. Hodges was a physical presence on campus. He rolled around like a cop—even sporting a walkie-talkie—looking for bad kids to bust. As the year progressed, a lot of the guys I hung with were expelled and assigned to night school, which was a punishment even the toughest thugs wanted to avoid.

Here's why: if you were expelled, the school district could legally bar you from events like football and basketball games. That might not seem like a big deal, but remember we're talking about Moncks Corner. There really wasn't anything for teenagers to do except go to high school football and basketball games. Those games were the catalysts of our social lives. Folks would spend their entire weeks debating which outfits or pair of sneakers they were going to wear to the game that weekend. When that got taken away, even the grimiest goons would start looking for ways to get back *into* school.

In addition to being quicker with the expulsions, Mr. Hodges also started paying out cash rewards to those willing to turn in fellow students with guns and drugs. And I was more than happy to help out. Yes, ladies and ghettomen, you read that right: I was certified scum who betrayed my fellow students for money. In fact, the only thing that kept me from getting expelled was that Mr. Hodges and Sadie Brown cut me some slack for being such a reliable rat.

The saddest thing is, I didn't feel bad because I never ratted out the "real gangstas." Instead, I had a policy of only turning in dorks who were trying to be down. Since we thugs were the coolest clique in school, other kids would bring in guns and drugs to school hoping to impress us. I'd check out whatever they had, act like I cared, and then drop a dime on them. I would justify it to myself by saying, "That dude was a clown anyway; it's not like I told on a real G." Remember when at the end of *Paid in Full* Cam'ron's character, Rico, said he'd give up some people in DC, but he wasn't snitching on anyone from Harlem? That was my mentality. Selective snitching wasn't real snitching.

Despite being one of their top informants, eventually the administration at Berkeley had enough of me. I forget the exact incident that stamped my ticket out of there, but I do remember that Sadie Brown did hatch a plan to help me. Instead of being expelled and sent to night school like many of my friends, Ms. Brown got me transferred to Stratford High in Goose Creek, where my mother was teaching. It was a great idea in theory—no way this kid will keep acting a fool with his mother watching over him. Sadly, at that point it didn't matter where I was at physically because I was completely lost mentally. So exit Berkeley High School, enter Stratford High.

• • •

Getting transferred away from my friends was supposed to be a punishment, but I was in heaven at Stratford. The school had some of the most beautiful girls I had ever seen, many of them from "well-off" families. If most of the kids at Berkeley High lived in trailers and single-story ranch-style houses around Moncks Corner, it seemed like most kids at Stratford lived in big brick houses on cul-de-sacs. Going to Stratford was like being handed a set of keys to a different world.

It turned out that there was nothing those preppy girls loved more than a faux hood nigga like myself. Evidently, I seemed more dangerous and exciting than the preppy dudes at Stratford. I ended up dating one girl from Stratford whose father was a meteorologist and whose mother was the head of a bank. Her code on my pager was 90210 because she reminded me of the privileged chicks you would see on that show. They didn't have black folk like that in Moncks Corner. The situation was so full of opportunity that after a few weeks I started scheming on ways to get all my boys who had gotten kicked out of Berkeley into Stratford so we could fuck all the girls in the school together.

Our plan didn't work (you couldn't get into Stratford without an address in Goose Creek), so we settled for the next best thing, which was going to all of Stratford's football and basketball games. When we'd roll into the stands, the girls would start buzzing. Teachers and parents can warn you about your choices all they want, but if a bunch of teenage girls sweat your style and treat you like a star, that's what's going to matter to you most. Transferring to Stratford might have been intended to wean me off the thug life, but, if anything, it made being a thug even more attractive to me.

No Remorse

As you might imagine, the guys in Goose Creek didn't appreciate my presence in their preppy paradise. "Who this motherfucker think he is?" they'd say. "Who said he could come around here like he's the shit?" I didn't pay them any mind though. Knowing they couldn't stand seeing me ride around their nice neighborhoods blasting Mobb Deep and M.O.P. only made me want to do it even more.

The tension came to a head one Sunday afternoon when me and two of my boys—Zeke and a guy we called DT—were parked in Goose Creek kicking it to some girls on the sidewalk. Just then two black guys from the neighborhood rode by in a Jeep. Clearly they didn't like what they saw. We exchanged a couple of "what's up?"s Then I decided to have a little "fun" with them. I started walking toward their Jeep, copying Ice Cube in *Boyz n the Hood* when he yelled, "We got a problem here?" while lifting up his shirt to reveal his gat. It was an iconic scene, but when I did it, the .38 I was packing was tucked in so low they couldn't actually see it. As a result, they didn't react, and a crisis, it seemed, was averted.

The guys drove off and we left to go to McDonald's. After we'd gotten our food, a few minutes later they pulled up next to us again. Only now what seemed to be one of their big brothers was driving. They must have picked him up for some muscle. Big bro leaned out the window and yelled, "Yeah, what's up now? Y'all still got a problem?"

Before I could say anything, my boy Zeke, who was in the passenger seat of our car, rolled down his window and pointed a .25-caliber pistol at their car. Everyone in the Jeep's eyes got real big. A look of sheer terror that I'll never forget. Mobb Deep coined the term "shook ones" and that perfectly described how those dudes looked in that moment. Shook.

In the next moment two shots rang out.

Pow! Pow!

After the bullets flew, we shouted "Queensbridge!" or something equally corny. Then DT hit the gas and we sped away without looking back.

Here's the really sad part: even though we'd just opened fire in the middle of the day on a major thoroughfare filled with people coming back from church, we weren't particularly worried. We didn't place an anonymous call to 911 to say there might be a couple of kids who'd just been shot on College Park Road in Ladson. We didn't start hashing out a desperate plan to get rid of the gun, or hide our car. We didn't start cooking up alibis we could use if the cops came looking for us.

You know what we *did* do? We drove back to Moncks Corner and laughed about what had just happened. "Yo, did you see those niggas' faces when you pulled out the hammer?" "Word, they looked scared shitless!" Then we ate our McDonald's. I promise you, we were barely even thinking about it an hour afterward. It was a momentary thrill—wow, we finally shot our gun at someone—for some directionless kids. No more, no less.

All that changed the next day. I was in my second-period class at Stratford when what looked like most of Goose Creek's police force burst into the room. They scooped me up and marched me back to the principal's office, the whole time asking me, "Where's the gun? Where's the gun?" I didn't answer at first, not because I was playing it cool, but because I honestly had no idea what they were talking about.

When we got to the office I looked through the glass and could see the two younger kids from the Jeep sitting in there. It was only then I understood why the cops had come for me.

Once I'd processed what was happening, the first thing that popped into my mind was "THOSE FUCKING SNITCHES!" I was outraged that they had called the cops over a little harmless gunplay. What suckers! That's how lost I was. Those kids could have easily been shot or killed. OF COURSE they called the cops on us.

When the kids saw me, one of them said, "Yeah, he was in the car." With that the cops threw me in cuffs and dragged me out to a cruiser in front of the entire school. You might think that getting led out of school in handcuffs would have woken me up a bit or made me realize the severity of the situation. But it didn't faze me one bit. I had no real sense that I'd done anything wrong, so what should I be scared of?

Once I got down to the police station, I learned that I'd be facing assault and battery with intent to kill. Even though no one had been hit, the bullet was embedded in the headrest behind the front passenger seat. I don't know if Zeke was aiming to miss, but basically he hit the only empty seat in the car. Any other one and we would have likely been looking at a murder rap.

I heard the charges against us, but I still figured I'd be out of jail by nightfall and back in class the next day. That's the mind-set I'd developed over all those years of getting in trouble at school. You do something stupid, serve a little suspension, say you're sorry, and then get right back to it. I couldn't see why this would be any different. There was a big football game coming up the next weekend and I told myself, "As long as I'm out before the game, I'll be good."

I put on my orange jumpsuit and waited for someone to come and get me. A day went past. Then another. And another. Finally

I got word that my father had shown up. "About time," I thought. "He's going to bail me out and I'll be able to make the game." But my pops killed that dream real quick when I was finally taken to him.

"Boy, you are in some serious fucking trouble," he told me.

"I know, I know," I replied, trying my best to sound remorseful. "So, you gonna get me out?"

"Fuck no! You're going to sit here!"

"What you mean 'sit here'? The game is this weekend!"

"Forget that game. Forget the whole damn season. Forget football," my father told me. "You ain't going nowhere! You gonna sit in this goddamn jail until you decide to get your act together."

Once my father got it through my thick skull that I wasn't getting out anytime soon, I settled into the routine of jailhouse life. The worst part was the food. Three nasty meals a day you only ate because there weren't any other options. The Berkeley County jail didn't even have a commissary back then, so I used to spend a lot of time on the phone with my mother and siblings trying to convince them to smuggle in some M&Ms for me.

I slept in what they called a "pod cell," a big room housing eighteen other guys. It was disgusting—there were only three showers and three toilets for all of us to share. Definitely no place for a teenage boy.

What probably saved me was that one of my cellmates was none other than my old buddy Darnell—yep, the same guy who'd tried to strangle me a few years earlier. When I walked into that pod the first time and saw Darnell sitting there, I figured I was a dead man. But rather than pick up the ass whipping where he'd left it off, Darnell actually gave me props. "I always respected that when I ran up on you, you didn't lie about what you said," he told me. "I liked that you owned it."

We actually ended up being cool, in large part because we both shared an interest in the Five Percenters. On more than a few occasions we had each other's back, which was important, given that we were both teenagers surrounded by men in their twenties or thirties.

The only time I had any drama was when I got into a fight with an older dude named Walt. We got into an argument about something stupid. I think Walt just woke up that day pissed off to be in jail. (And who could blame him?) Later that day me and some of my boys jumped him in our cell. I thought there might have been some repercussions with the correction officers, but for whatever reason, nothing ever came of it.

My days mainly consisted of spending hours in my pod reading books, debating about rappers, or even spitting a few rhymes myself with my fellow inmates banging on the sides of our bunks for a beat. The only thing I had to look forward to was my next court date. I was in that jail for almost three months until my lawyer was able to get my charge of assault and battery with intent to kill reduced to pointing and presenting a firearm. Even though I hadn't shot the gun, I refused to say who did. These were my boys, not some nerds at school. I was going to operate by the code of the streets, so in the end, we all got the same charge.

You're probably thinking after three months behind bars, I was ready to turn my life around. After three months of eating hard grits every day, hiding behind trash cans when it was time to take a shit (they didn't have doors on the toilet stalls), and sleeping next to dudes jerking off, I'd be excited to get my life back on track. Excited to get away from those thugs once and for all. To return to my nerd roots and start realizing my potential again.

Nope.

Instead, all I could think about was how great it was going to be to get back on the streets. Since I hadn't snitched, I knew my street cred would be sky-high when I got out. I felt like a soldier who'd just gotten back from fighting for his country and was about to get a ticker tape parade.

I knew the perfect setting for my triumphant return would be Berkeley's football game the Friday night after I was released. My father must have sensed what I was planning, because he specifically told me not to go to that game. He knew I'd be strutting around like a peacock, instead of lying low, which is what you should do when you're a high school student who just finished spending three months behind bars for almost killing someone.

Ignoring my father's instructions, I not only went to the game but also came up with the bright idea of getting high as fuck with my friend Jerrell beforehand. Jerrell Garnett—God bless the dead—is and was my brother. He was one of the first street dudes in Moncks Corner to show me love and always had my back. I hadn't smoked any weed while I was locked up, so my tolerance was low. As soon as I set foot in the stadium, I started panicking. Was everyone looking at us? Did the teachers know I was high? What about that security guard?

Instead of a returning hero, I felt like a freak. After a while I couldn't take it anymore, so we went back to Jerrell's house.

Jerrell's house had become our hangout spot after his mother had gotten married and moved out of town. Jerrell and his older brother Stacks inherited the house and started selling weed out it. After that business took off, the brothers decided to add crack to their menu.

It was the last place I should have been chillin' at fresh out of jail, but Jerrell was my boy and I felt comfortable there. After regaling him with some jailhouse stories, we decided to spark up another blunt. We were about halfway through it when my father's black Datsun pulled up in front of the house. Being a hustler himself, my father knew damn well what went on there. I was caught red-handed.

There was no point in trying to talk my way out of it, so I just walked down to the car and silently got in. My father was calm at first and pulled off like everything was cool. After driving in silence for a few minutes, suddenly he turned and without warning punched me dead in my face. My head smacked against the glass with a resounding *bam!* I covered up, expecting more blows. Instead, he just let me have it verbally. "I paid all this money to get you out and you told me you were going to change," he yelled. "But you're already back out here doing the same old dumb shit. You've only been out a few days and you're showing up high at football games. And now I catch you in this dope house! Are you out of your mind?" My father just gripped the steering wheel and stared ahead before turning to me again and saying, "You're going to end up right back in that jail. And I promise you, boy, next time I'm not getting you out!"

He knew me too well.

Moving Packs

South Carolina isn't known for producing a lot of major drug dealers, but all the exploits you heard about Big Meech and the Black Mafia Family doing in Detroit and Atlanta in the nineties, folks were doing it even bigger in my home state. Trust me.

Remember how I said that Charleston's port had been a major distribution point for many different commodities, like cotton, rice, and slaves? Well, by the mid-1990s, the entrepreneurial-minded people of Charleston had figured out another product that they could bring in through the harbor: cocaine.

The biggest distributor in the whole state was actually a guy from Moncks Corner named Calvin Washington. Calvin worked as a longshoreman at the Charleston port and somehow linked up with a guy from Panama who had connections. Together they allegedly figured out how to use Calvin's access to smuggle major weight off the boats and into the streets.

Calvin had Berkeley County BOOMING until 2007, when the feds finally caught him unloading three thousand pounds of coke. That's a street value of over 100 million dollars—newspapers called it the largest bust in South Carolina history. So when I say there was a lot of coke in the streets, I'm not exaggerating.

Calvin's people lived in a nearby town called Cordesville and it seemed like all of them worked in his organization. Their kids went to school with us and dressed pretty much how you'd expect coke dons' kids to dress: lots of gold chains, brand-new Jordans, fresh jeans, and creamy leather jackets. I can remember one of them pulling up to school in eighth grade in a brand-new Ford Explorer with rims on it. The young lady wasn't even old enough to have a license, but she was driving one of the nicest cars in town.

Calvin would get the weight in Charleston and then bring it out to the countryside, where he'd break it down into smaller pack-ages. Then his people would hit off local dudes—maybe my pops was one of them—with packs that they could sell on the street. Not surprising for an area where there wasn't much in the way of opportunity, a lot of folks wanted to be down.

I never knew where my father was moving his packs, but the

younger kids I knew sold dope on an infamous stretch of country road called Highway Six. To the locals, Highway Six was synonymous with trouble. My grandmother used to tell me she had dreams I'd be killed on that road.

She had good reason to be fearful, because I saw a lot of young men die on those streets courtesy of the drug game, including John Arnold, a street legend from that era. John stood only around five foot six but was also cock diesel and did not play games at all. I remember one night I went to McDonald's with John and his cousin Patrick. John just walked in, went behind the counter, and started helping himself to some Big Macs and fries. The staff knew better than to try to stop him.

I heard another time he drove up on a motorcycle to confront some dope boys who had threatened his nephew. Those boys were all packin', but John pulled right up to them and announced, "If anyone here messes with my nephew again, I'm coming back up here and killing every last one of y'all." Those boys could have shot him up on the spot, but his reputation was so fierce that they didn't dare challenge him.

John was mythical in his stature, but true to my dad's prediction, the streets eventually caught up with even him. Word was someone shot him in the back and killed him as he drove away from a drug deal. He was probably only eighteen or nineteen years old.

Another infamous story from the time was about a guy named Pooh, also a big dealer in the area. He died racing his sports car down in Charleston. When he crashed, the car split in half and his dirty money went flying all over the road.

At first, I was content to watch the dope game from the sidelines. I would be at Jerrell's, just smoking weed and playing video games while the other guys conducted their business around me.

But after a couple of months watching them put money in their pockets, I started to question why I was holding back. Why be there if I wasn't going to get paid too?

I decided to check myself into the game, and Jerrell was more than happy to show me how to play. The first thing he did was give me a fifty-dollar slab of crack. When I broke it up, it came out to about five rocks, which was worth $100. Once I sold them all, I'd made fifty dollars' profit.

After a couple of weeks of fifty-dollar slabs, I graduated to a "quarter spoon." It was basically seven grams of crack that, when split up correctly, would earn you about a hundred dollars off every gram of crack you produced. So if you spent $250 on your initial pack, with a little bit of cooking, you could end up earning around $600 to $700 for your trouble. Not bad for a high school kid.

The most weight I ever got up to was a half ounce, which was fourteen grams of crack. Generally, though, I would stick to quarter spoons and try to sell at least three of those a week. I wasn't too flashy with my profits, only making a couple of decent-size purchases. One time this hustler from New York City came to Moncks Corner trying to move stolen Rolexes. I was skeptical if they were real, but a friend told me, "If it's real, it won't tick." The guy's watches definitely didn't tick, so I bought a Rainbow model off him for about a grand.

The most profit I ever had in my pocket at the end of the week was $3,500. At the time I was dating a young lady and I wanted to show off, so I took her and her roommate on a shopping spree at the mall. Since I was feeling like a big shot, I told both of them, "Here's some cash. Go get whatever y'all want." They didn't hold back, and by the end of the afternoon I was damn near broke again. In an era filled with stupid decisions, that one still stands out to me. What was I thinking?

When I first began selling dope, sometimes the fiends would ask what my name was (even crackheads have manners down South). I was afraid if I said "Larry" they would say, "Oh, ain't you Larry and Julia's son?" and somehow word would get back to my father. So whenever someone asked, I'd say instead, "My name is Charles."

Soon all my boys started calling me "Charlie." In time, that turned into "Charlie Chronic" because we were smoking so much weed. My homeboy started calling himself "Matthew Marijuana," and we called our little crew "the Infamous Buddha Heads." Corny, I know. But trust me, at the time it was hot.

Once, during a stint in night school, I was reading a book that mentioned the famous French king Charles the Great, or Charlemagne, as he was known in French. I learned he was a renowned warrior but also was famous for spreading education and religion. That sounded very cool to me. Since I was already going by "Charles," I figured why not spice it up and start calling myself Charlemagne? I decided to add "Tha God," to the end of it instead of "the Great," because the Five Percenters believe that we're all gods. Then, for a final twist, I misspelled it Charlamagne instead of Charlemagne. (Basically, I wrote it the way I pronounced it.) It might seem confusing now, but it all seemed to make sense at the time. The moral of the story is this is why you don't stick with nicknames you gave yourself as a stoned teenager.

Jerrell and Stack's mother's name was Queen Esther, so we began calling their house "Queensbridge," a dual homage to her and Mobb Deep. Another wack name, I know.

One Friday I was hanging out at Queensbridge selling a little dope with my buddy Juan, who had just come home from doing a bid. I'd run through my stash and was ready to leave but my replacements hadn't shown up yet. I knew where their stashes were, however, so I decided to stick around and sell some of their stuff too.

Not long after that a black Trans Am pulled up in front of the house. Juan looked out the window, sized up the car, and said, "That could be the police." "Word?" I said, and got ready to run. Just then, a white guy stepped out of the Trans and immediately I relaxed. It was a dude named Chad who'd gone to Berkeley High with me and had a huge scar on his head from where he'd once tried to shoot himself. He was a pretty steady weed customer and I'd have recognized him anywhere.

"That's no police, that's just Chad," I said, exhaling.

"Well, Chad must be working for the police," replied Juan, his OG senses still on alert.

"Naw, Chad's cool," I said. "He's here all the time."

"All right," replied Juan. "As long as you vouch for him, we're good."

Chad walked up to the house, and I greeted him through the window.

"Chad, my man, what's the word!"

"Yo, Larry! Everything's good. Can you hit me off with a couple bags of smoke?"

"No doubt," I said, passing him the weed through the window. He handed me back the money, we said peace, and Chad went on his way.

Later that night a bunch of us were sitting around the house, playing video games, smoking weed, talking shit, basically doing whatever trap boys do on a Friday night. I had a crack vial in my pocket, so when a car pulled up to the front of the house, I jumped up, ready for a sale. Before I could get out the door, another car pulled up. Followed by another. And another.

While I was still trying to process what was happening, Juan called out, "It's the police!" This time there wasn't any question in his voice. He was stating a fact.

Everybody started scattering throughout the house, flushing dope down the toilet and trying to jump out windows. Then the police started kicking down the door. It was my first time in a situation like that and all I could think of was the Goodie Mob's song "Dirty South":

> One to da two da three da four
> Dem dirty Red Dogs done hit the door
> And they got everybody on they hands and knees
> And they ain't gonna leave until they find them keys

That's pretty much how it went down. I managed to flush my crack down the toilet, but moments later I was on the living room floor on my hands and knees. One of the cops asked me what my name was. "Lenard McKelvey," I mumbled. "Oh," he replied. "We got a warrant for you."

I should have listened to Juan: Chad *was* working undercover. And since they already had a warrant for me, evidently they'd been watching the house for a while. Off I went to jail along with some of the other dudes who had been selling in the house with me.

As soon as we got to the jail and they put us in the cold tank, I started throwing up. Some thug, right? Being locked up again made me physically ill. Since I'd only recently gotten out on the weapon charge, I figured this time they were going to throw me under the jail. I was really screwed this time.

Despite my fears, the next day I found out that not only had my father been able to bail me out, but he had also hired a lawyer who managed to get me probation for the weed charge I was facing.

I'd gotten locked up on a Friday and by Monday morning I was on my way back home. I wasn't totally in the clear though. As soon as I walked in the door my mother tried to beat me with a belt. "Don't even waste your time trying to beat some sense into this fool," my father said, stepping between us. "He ain't shit. Just kick his stupid ass out instead." Before she could even issue the ultimatum, I was already out the door and headed back to Jerrell's. In my mind I was a street guy. And street guys didn't take orders, let alone whippings from their mother.

A few days later the bust made the *Independent*. The reporter wrote something to the effect of "The dealers had a sophisticated operation which included a drive-through window through which buyers could purchase drugs." They had it dead wrong, of course—our "sophisticated operation" was just me selling Chad weed out the window because I was too lazy to get up from my video game and meet him outside.

It might have been an exaggeration, but that article made my street cred skyrocket. I wasn't just a dope boy: I was part of a sophisticated drug ring. What member of a drug ring lives at his home where he isn't "respected"? What head of a drug ring lets his father put his hands on him? What head of a drug ring bothers going to high school?

Not this one. Nope, you couldn't tell me I wasn't a REAL nigga in them Moncks Corner streets. And I was . . . a REAL STUPID nigga. One who couldn't see that his choices were leading him further and further down a dead-end path.

The Power of God

I'm not proud about much from that time in my life, but one thing I can say I never did was ask God to look the other way when it came to my sins. I've always believed God gives us the freedom of choice when it comes to our actions. We can choose to submit to the God in us, which is our higher selves, or we can choose to submit to the devil in us, which is our lower selves.

Future once rapped, "Fuck what you heard / God blessin' all the trap niggas." I love Future, but I have to say he got that one wrong; fuck what you heard, God is *not* blessing none of you trap niggas. Why would God bless you for ruining the community? You really think pumping poison to the people is worth you being blessed? Man, God is sending each and every one of you trap niggas' prayers to his spam folder; he don't even receive those emails.

Nevertheless, trap niggas always seem to think God is going to cosign their BS. I remember my friend Zeke called me from jail one time and said, "Man, do that thing you be doing for me." I asked him what he was talking about. "That thing you be doing when you talking to God." "You mean praying?" I asked. "Yeah, do that for me if you can." I couldn't believe Zeke didn't even know how to pray. In this case, I did pray for him because Zeke was my guy, but I also told him God had nothing to do with this situation. What he really needed was a lawyer and bail.

I had another homeboy who told me about a time he was trafficking guns from South Carolina to New Jersey. While he was driving through Virginia he found himself on one of those dark backcountry roads. If you have ever made that road trip you know Virginia has some scary back roads where you can see the mountains and it feels like Bigfoot is going to jump out in front of your car at any moment.

Well, my boy didn't see Bigfoot, but he did see something much scarier: a state trooper pull up behind him. Ever been driving a car full of illegal guns while smoking weed and the police get behind you? No? Well, it creates optimum paranoia. You know once the cop hits those blue lights, pulls you over, and asks to search the vehicle, it's a wrap.

My friend is a pastor's kid (the irony, right?), but his reaction to that cop getting behind him was to pull out his gun and cock it. When I asked him why, he explained he knew he had to kill the cop in order to get away. "Nigga, what?" I asked, but he was dead serious. He wasn't going to prison.

My boy told me that after he pulled his gun, he said a prayer to God. Seconds later the cop hit his lights. Miraculously, instead of pulling him over, the cop just passed him and sped off to whatever emergency he was responding to.

Here's the thing: my boy told that story as a testimony to God's power. In his twisted mind, God answered his prayer and made the cop drive past him. When he told me that, I looked him dead in his eye and said, "Man, if you don't shut your dumb ass up! God wasn't looking out for you, he was looking out for the cop!"

My boy probably got confused because he thought he was communicating with God when he was really chopping it up with the devil. That's an easy mistake to make because the DEVIL is the one who makes the most noise. God doesn't make a big fuss—if anything, he damn near whispers. You either listen or you don't.

Everything good that happens to you is because of God; everything bad that happens to you is on you because you made the choice *not* to recognize the power of God in you. It was your choice. That's why I hate when people say they "found God." Man,

God was never lost. *You* were. There was never a missing person's report out for our creator.

Like Father, Like Son

My relationship with God might have remained rock solid, but my relationship with my pops was crumbling. His warnings were clear, but I wasn't listening. One of the reasons was because he wasn't exactly following a straight and narrow path, either.

For starters, his cheating on my mother had been getting more flagrant. Eventually it would come out that he'd had a second family on the side, but at the time all I knew was that things were really bad between my parents.

My father had always been my authority, and I listen to his guidance to this day. Still, seeing him hurt my mother weakened his stature in my eyes. If you're trying to get a point across to a knucklehead teenage boy, you've got to show and prove by actions and deeds. Your example is what gets through to a teenager. Not words.

Unfortunately, my father's examples almost completely contradicted everything he had been telling me. He'd tell me not to sell coke because I'd end up in jail, but he was out there moving it himself. He'd tell me don't hang out with street dudes, but he was one of the biggest street dudes in the area. It's no wonder my attitude toward him became "Whatever, man."

Our issues came to a head one day after the cops pulled my father over in Kittsfield and found a little coke in his car. They must have decided he was some sort of kingpin, because they then showed up at my mother's house with a search warrant. I happened to be home and told my mother she didn't have to sign the warrant. While I was trying to calm her down, the cops started shouting they were going to come back later and kick down the door. Despite my protests, she caved and let them in.

The reason I didn't want those cops inside was because I happened to have a vial of crack on me. When the cops started banging on the door, I'd stuffed it in the pocket of a coat that was hanging in my closet. Once the cops were inside, they started tearing through the entire house, including the closet. When they pulled out the coat, I figured I was a goner. But unbeknownst to me, the pocket had a hole in it and the vial had fallen in the jacket lining, where in their rush the cops somehow missed it. I breathed a silent sigh of relief.

My reprise was short-lived. Inside one of our trash cans the cops found a little plastic lunch bag I'd used to carry the crack before I'd put it in the vial. There weren't even any rocks left in the bag, just some residual dust. That was enough for the cops though. They weren't about to leave the house without an arrest (my father evidently didn't have anything stashed there), so back to Berkeley County jail I went.

Guess who was sitting in the cell when I got there? Yep, my pops. Now, when they brought me in, did he ask, "What happened?" or "Are you all right?" Nope. The first and only thing he said was, "Listen, boy, do not say nothing all weekend. Not a word!" It was a Friday and for the next three days we just stared at each other. No one uttered a single word. I later found out he insisted on silence because he was convinced our cell was bugged.

When Monday came, they had to let us both out, since between us they'd found less than a gram of coke. Cowboy and Son weren't kingpins after all. Outside the jailhouse, we didn't have an emotional embrace or a heart-to-heart talk. Instead, we started bickering over whose fault it was that we'd been busted.

"You're paying for your own lawyer this time!" my father scolded me.

"What?" I shot back. "I only got caught because they had a search warrant for you!"

"Yeah," he replied. "But you shouldn't have had anything in the house anyway. This is on you!"

That's what our relationship had deteriorated to: a father and his teenage son arguing over whose fault it was that they'd both been arrested on the same day.

Pick Your "P"

Even though our weekend in jail represented the height of dysfunction, I still give my father a lot of the credit for helping me get out of the hole I dug for myself as a young man. Given some of the situations that I've gotten myself into, that might seem like a surprise. And it's true, at the time, my father felt like one of my biggest enemies. He screamed on me. He threatened me. He whooped my ass more than one time.

The one thing he never did, however, was give up on me. No matter how many times he swore he wouldn't bail me out again, the next time I got locked up, he'd be there with the money. No matter how many times he called me out, or even tried to knock me out, once the emotions had cooled, he would be there by my side, pushing me to make something out of myself.

It's not easy to stand in front of your son after the two of you have spent the weekend in jail and say, "Boy, you need to get your life together!" but my father did it. No matter how messy his own affairs were, he'd look me dead in the eye and say, "*You* need to do better! Don't do what I do, do what I say!"

My father probably didn't know William Jennings Bryan from will.i.am, but he sure as hell understood the concept of "destiny is not a matter of chance, it is a matter of choice."

Every lecture, every threat, and every pep talk was based around the simple principle that life wasn't just *happening* to me. I wasn't being pulled along by some invisible force that I had no control over. No one forced me to sip a forty at recess. No one told me to punch that kid in the cafeteria, or to smack the other kid with a lock. No one made me walk up on that Jeep. Just as no one forced me to sell weed to Chad, or start hanging with the dope boys at Jerrell's. Each and every one of those situations resulted from a choice that I made. He beat that concept into my head (figuratively and literally) until I finally came to understand it as fact.

Be miserable. Or motivate yourself. Whatever has to be done, it's always your choice.

—Wayne Dyer

Today, I've taken that concept and turned it into a maxim I call PYP: Pick Your Poison, Procrastination, or Passion. It reflects my belief that we have three basic choices in how we approach our lives.

We can pick our poison, which is doing the dumb shit that might make us a little bit of money or temporarily feel like a big shot, but in the long run will destroy our lives. The devil is always pushing the poison on us. For me, the poison was selling drugs. For others, it could be doing drugs. It could be gambling, chasing money, or constant cheating. There are a lot of poisons to pick from out there.

We can pick our procrastinations, which are those choices that aren't as obviously negative as our poisons but still don't take us where we need to go. When I was acting crazy in school, drinking forties and yelling "good laugh," that was a form of procrastination. I hadn't graduated into pure thugdom yet, but I wasn't pursuing my potential either.

The danger of procrastination is that we can get stuck in it for our entire lives. Even after we start our careers, we can get caught up in a cycle of choices that don't poison our lives but don't propel them either. Staying at a job that you don't care deeply about for fifteen years reflects this sort of choice. As does staying in a romantic relationship where the spark has been gone for a long time. Those are choices. You can always find a new job if you're prepared to hustle and make sacrifices. You can always find new love if you're prepared to be fearless and take life as it comes. A lot of people *choose* not to make those choices. They'd rather wait for the chance they'll fulfill their destiny than actually choose to grab it.

Our other choice is passion. One of the reasons I always refer to myself as a member of the "Pinkett-Smith-Winfrey-Knowles-Carter" family is because those are examples of five powerful black people who have always picked their passion in life. Individuals who never let the circumstances of their situations dictate how they were going to live their lives. They never settled. They always went for what mattered to them. Those are the people I strive to emulate.

When I was young, my passion was learning. I felt energized and fulfilled when I was reading a book, or addressing a class.

Then I got disconnected from my passion. My life, and the lives of the people around me, suffered greatly because of it.

It wouldn't be until I weaned myself off the poison that was drug dealing and street life once and for all that I would be able to recognize the passion that would refocus and transform my life:

The radio.

Fuck Your Dreams

The truth might hurt, but it's always helpful. Nobody wants to hear they're fat as fuck and need to lose weight, or they're not as talented at something as they think they are. But just because they're lying to themselves doesn't mean that you have to lie too. It doesn't benefit you or the person you're talking to when you sugarcoat your words. You have to tell people what they need to hear, as opposed to what they want to hear. And if you are the person getting that harsh dose of reality, then make sure you accept it.

By the time I was eighteen, I'd already racked up quite the thug's résumé: multiple trips to summer school, expulsions from two high schools, and three arrests.

In the movies, any one of those situations could have been the one that finally got me "scared straight." But like I said earlier, this isn't the movies. This is real life. And in real life, the most important changes often don't happen overnight. They take place slowly, not over the course of scenes, but over the course of months, sometimes even years.

Ironically, it would be my cousins, the very guys who pulled me into the thug life, who would slowly inspire me to get out of it. Not because they were setting a better example themselves. Instead,

75

over time I became so disgusted with their decline that I became determined not to end up like them myself.

In particular, watching my cousin Lamar fall off affected me deeply. When I was fourteen or fifteen, Lamar seemed like the coolest dude in town. He was a talented barber, and people from all over Berkeley County would flock to our hood just to have him cut their hair. Through his barber business (and selling a little dope on the side), Lamar always had money in his pocket and a beautiful woman by his side. If that wasn't enough, he could also dance and dress his ass off.

I'll never forget going to visit him in Myrtle Beach, where he and his girl Jayla were staying at a fancy hotel with an ocean view called the Captain's Quarters. Jayla had a beautiful face, fat ass, big boobs—the type of woman a horny teenager like myself could only dream of. "Man, all I want to do when I'm older is stay in a room like this with a girl like that!" I told myself. That scene at the Captain's Quarters came to represent the epitome of success to me. A few years later when I started making a little money, one of the first things I did was book a room there with Mook Mook.

Unfortunately, by the time I'd graduated to the Captain's Quarters Lamar had broken Law Number 4 of Biggie's "Ten Crack Commandments": "Never get high on your own supply." Once Lamar started hitting the pipe, his world fell apart quickly. Soon the barber who would never have dreamed of stepping outside without a fresh lineup was letting his hair wolf. The guy who always dressed fly was wearing the same sweatpants and T-shirts for days at a time. Folks stopped coming for haircuts, and Jayla left him, as did all the other girls he was messing with. He was only in his early twenties, but it was already clear to me that his life was never going to amount to anything.

I saw something similar happen to my cousin Malik. He'd

always been fly, respected by the guys and popular with the ladies. Then he started smoking crack too. Soon he was another basehead wandering around with his dreads unkempt, his clothes a mess, and asking people if he could borrow five dollars.

My cousin Anthony was yet another walking warning. To be fair, Anthony had the deck stacked against him because his father was a crackhead. Despite that, his grandmother and mother worked very hard trying to raise him right. He was a good football player in high school who also had a reputation of being a bit of a pretty boy. He always seemed to have a nice ride and a good-looking girlfriend. Anthony didn't go to college, but after high school he got a solid job fixing air conditioners that kept good (and legal) money in his pocket.

Over time, unfortunately, it became clear that Anthony liked to drink and smoke weed a little too much. OK, waaay too much. It didn't help that Anthony was an angry drunk who would get into fights after a couple drinks. To make matters worse, he lost most of his teeth after he crashed his ATV four-wheeler, which of course he was riding drunk. Today he's in his thirties and is a mess. His teeth are mostly gone and his beard is completely gray. He looks like he's fifty. Yet he still keeps on drinking and smoking like he did when he was eighteen. When I think of "drunk under a tree," I think of Anthony.

Watching my cousins fall apart in front of my eyes terrified me. As badly as I wanted to be like them when I was younger, by the time I was eighteen or nineteen I *didn't* want to be like them just as badly.

Even worse, the rest of my family was starting to view me with the same sort of disgust with which I had come to view Anthony, Malik, and Lamar. I learned that the summer I turned eighteen, when my aunt Mudda announced that she was going to visit our family in Jersey. "Cool, I'm going to come too," I volunteered. It never occurred to me she'd have an issue with that. But she shot it down quick, telling me, "I'm sorry, baby, but I want no problems with no drugs or nothing." She was right to say it, but it truly hurt my feelings and made me think, "Dang, that's how y'all look at me?"

Another time I was bragging about this girl I was trying to talk to, one of the "Valley girls" from Stratford. Dana, one of my favorite cousins, overheard me and let me have it. "You really think a girl like *that* is going to want to be with somebody like *you*?" she asked with a snort, before adding, "'Nard, you're exactly what TLC be talking about in that song: a scrub! You're on a fast track to nowhere. Why would she even mess with you?" Dana called me a scrub with complete conviction too. Hearing that from someone in my family, especially a cousin I was close with, was like a smack in the face. One I desperately needed.

In addition to being disgusted by watching my cousins go from ballers to bums, there were two particular incidents that helped me finally come to the realization that I didn't want to live a criminal lifestyle anymore.

The first incident was after I'd begun buying my coke from this crazy dude named Clarence.

One of the major problems with dealing drugs—outside of the obvious legal and ethical issues—is that it makes you extremely paranoid. Everything is lovely when the money first starts coming in, but after a few months you start to become secretive, distrustful, and greedy. And that's only if you're not dipping into your own stash. Once you start doing that, there's no coming back.

I never did coke or crack myself, but I was smoking way too much weed, which only heightened my paranoia. The first way it affected me was that it made me decide I needed my own coke source—I was so paranoid I didn't want to share dealers with anyone else I knew. So I got down with crazy Clarence. At first he was great, always having a package ready to go whenever I needed to re-up. But it also became clear he could be reckless and impulsive.

One time I was back at my mom's house when Clarence and some other dudes showed up at 7:00 a.m. looking for some money I owed. And in case I didn't get the message that they wanted to get paid, they brought a couple of guns with them to drive the point home. Not the kind of drama I should be bringing to my mother's house. I managed to talk Clarence down, but it was a tense scene.

My father happened to be there and as soon as Clarence and his crew left he asked, "What the fuck did those boys want?" I tried to tell him they were looking for some video games they'd left with me, but my pops was too street savvy to fall for that. "Bullshit," he said. "No one is coming for video games at seven in the morning. Whatever it is, those boys are going to blow your fucking brains out if you're not careful!"

A few weeks later I found myself in an even worse situation with Clarence, as hard as it might be to believe it can get much worse than an armed drug dealer showing up at your mother's door early in the morning.

Once again I'd found myself owing Clarence money, and once again he wanted me to pay up. Only this time he wanted me to go on a little drive with him to settle our debt. I didn't really have a choice, so I met Clarence at the appointed time and jumped in his ride.

"Where we going?" I asked as he pulled off.

"To rob this nigga's crib that owes me some bread," Clarence replied matter-of-factly. "Hit this blunt," he added, passing me some weed.

My heart sank. The last thing I wanted to be doing was breaking into what I was sure was another drug dealer's home with Clarence. How did we know the dealer wasn't going to be home? Was I going to get shot the moment I walked in the door? Were the police going to catch us on the way out? As we smoked, I became more and more paranoid. I had to think of a way out of the situation.

"You ever do something like this before?" Clarence asked, taking another drag of the weed.

"Yup," I lied, trying to sound as calm as possible. "I ran into some nigga's crib one time, but no one was home."

I wanted to dampen Clarence's enthusiasm for our mission. "It turned out to be a big waste of time," I continued. "When we got in there, we found his safe, but it was empty. Usually the niggas who you would think have mad money actually don't have anything in there. They usually keep it somewhere else."

"Yeah, you probably right," Clarence said.

We arrived at the house. "Now listen," Clarence instructed me. "I'm going to park, then we walk up to the front door and kick it down. We gonna get dude down on the floor and then get the money."

"Fuck that!" I thought to myself. I had to talk him out of this plan.

"Look, there's a light on," I said pointing at the house. "That means he's home. Suppose he's in there with some other dudes and they got guns. They might shoot us when we come through the door."

Clarence evidently hadn't considered that scenario. "Yeah, that's true," he said. "Lemme drive around the block a few times and feel it out."

At least I'd bought myself a couple of minutes. As we pulled around the corner I saw the headlights of a car approaching from the other direction. "Yo, that's the cops!" I yelled, though truthfully I couldn't tell what sort of car it was.

When Clarence heard that he began to hit the gas, but I told him to slow down. "If you speed, they'll get suspicious and pull us over," I told him. "Just be cool and they won't suspect nothing."

"Good call," Clarence told me, taking his foot off the gas. "Man, fuck this. Let's do this another night!"

"Word," I said calmly, though inside my mind was screaming, "WOOOOO!"

I'd manage to outfox Clarence, but I didn't ever want to find myself in a spot like that again. The lifestyle was getting very old, fast.

In those days, I used to keep my crack in plastic tubes I'd buy at a fishing tackle store. They were meant to hold bait, but I realized they were perfect for drugs because they were airtight and waterproof. That way I could throw them in the bushes or even toss them in the water if I thought the cops were coming. The guys in that bait and tackle shop must have thought I was one serious fisherman for all those tubes that I bought.

One day when I was at Jerrell's house, I somehow got it in my head that the cops were about to raid his place.* So I took a half ounce I was planning to sell and hid it in his backyard.

---

*Post-traumatic stress disorder is real. Hopefully you haven't experienced it, but being the subject of a drug raid is like being attacked by an army. I was paranoid for a long time after that.

That night I came back to Jerrell's to hang out with him and his cousin Vincent. Vincent was a real character. For starters he was mentally challenged. He literally rode the short bus. But to make up for what he lacked in brainpower, God had blessed Vincent with one of the biggest dicks in the entire universe. Seriously, this kid was the size of a Pringles can.

How did I know that? Vincent was an unapologetic exhibitionist. It's a crime he never got into porn. Vincent would whip that thing out any chance he got and then chase people around singing, "I'm fuck ya girl, yo. . . ." He particularly loved tormenting Anthony. "Crackhead's son, I'ma fuck your girl," he'd sing out to Anthony, swinging his giant dick in two hands.

The night in question, Jerrell, Vincent, and I were drinking and smoking and got pretty wasted. My paranoia softened by the booze, I decided it was finally safe to go retrieve my dope. But when I went to the spot I thought I'd left it at, I couldn't find it. I even got down on my hands and knees to search, but the crack was nowhere to be found.

My paranoia came roaring back. How could it be missing? Had someone already taken it? That must be it. I decided the someone was probably Vincent. He was my guy, but he had been there when I stashed it earlier. He must have come back during the day when no one was looking to grab it. "That crazy big-dicked bastard," I fumed. "I can't believe he did me like that."

I was frantic. How should I confront Vincent? Should I just yoke him up and demand to know where the dope was? Should I tell Jerrell and then the two of us could jump him? Or maybe Jerrell was in on it? Maybe they were both playing me. . . .

As my paranoia hit a fever pitch, I had a revelation: *Something was seriously wrong with me.*

Only someone who had completely lost his way would be

drunkenly crawling around in the dark looking for crack while convincing himself that he'd been outsmarted by an autistic kid with a porno-sized penis.

I felt like I'd hit rock bottom. "This is ridiculous," I thought to myself. "I'm acting insane. I'm questioning my brothers who I know have my back. This drug world is too cut throat. I don't want this to be my life anymore."

I let the whole thing go and returned to drinking with Jerrell and Vincent. I never did find the dope, but that pathetic scene did start to wake me up to how out of control my life had become.

The other turning point happened a few years later when I had already started to get into radio. Even though I was finally pursuing my passion, I was also still hanging around with my street dudes. I wanted to have it both ways, but the universe was about to let me know that wasn't an option.

I learned that once and for all on June 8, 2001. I'd decided to throw a party to celebrate my cousin Kinta Palmer getting a football scholarship to Penn State. I rented a cabin at a place called Short Stay on nearby Lake Moultrie and invited a whole gang of people to come over and party. The night started off great— lots of drinking, smoking, dancing, and bullshitting. But at some point one of the girls passed out and when she woke up later that night, she claimed that some of the dudes at the party had sexually assaulted her. I wasn't there at the time—I'd left to go get some weed—and when I finally heard about what had happened, the entire party had cleared out.

Apparently she'd gone into a dark room with some guys to have sex and when she'd started to protest, one of them said, "Relax, it's Charlamagne."

After I heard that rumor, I asked my homeboys who had been

there. "Did anyone touch this girl sexually? Did someone use my name?" They all swore to me up and down that nothing had happened.

Early the next morning my phone rang and I expected it to be about the fallout from the party. Instead, it was my friend Boobie, who delivered the chilling message, "Yo, Scrap is dead." Scrap was Jerrell's cousin, someone I considered a big brother. Turns out he had died after driving home from a club drunk, hitting some railroad tracks at a high speed, and flipping his car over.

I couldn't process the information. I needed to get out of the house and talk to someone, so I headed over to Kittsfield, where my cousins always hung out. When I got there, sure enough they were literally sitting under a tree. I jumped out of the car and started yelling, "Yo, Scrap is dead. He's dead!" My cousins just looked at me and said, "Yeah, Kinta is in jail too."

"What?" I asked. "What's he in jail for?"

"Man, you didn't hear? They said he raped a girl at that party last night."

When I heard that, I was doubly devastated. Kinta was about to go to Penn State, one of the most powerful football programs in the country. He had a chance of ending up in the NFL if things broke his way. I knew he hadn't been involved, but just the accusation alone could derail his dreams before they'd even begun.

I hopped back in my car and drove straight to the police station to help clear Kinta's name. When I got there, I told the officer at the desk that the whole party had been my idea. "I rented the cabin, I bought the alcohol, I went out to get weed, I invited the girls; that was all my doing," I told her. "I take full responsibility. Kinta didn't set any of that up. And I know he didn't touch that girl." The officer listened to my confession, took a statement, and then said, "OK, well, thank you for coming down here and sharing that. I'll let you know if we need anything else from you."

Before I left though, the cop hit me with a surprise; Kinta hadn't been arrested for anything. Turned out my cousins had made the whole story up just to mess with me because they hadn't been invited to the party. I'd like to say I was shocked they'd do that, but I could believe it all too well. My older cousins had always hated on Kinta and myself because we were younger and going places. Rather than cheer us on, they got more satisfaction out of trying to trip us up.

The police did come and arrest me a few weeks later in connection to the assault. They took a couple of blood and hair samples but released me the same day. Eventually the criminal sexual charges were dropped, but I was hit with a charge of contributing to the delinquency of a minor because I'd brought the alcohol to the party.

The previous stints in jail hadn't affected me, but that one, as brief as it was, definitely did. Deeply. As crazy as it may sound, forget about shooting at people, forget about drugs—this was a possible rape charge. That caught my attention.

It was all too much. I had people possibly lying to girls, using my name to sexually assault women. I had people possibly stealing dope from me. Not to mention forcing me to go on home invasions where God knows what might happen. CLEARLY I needed some new friends.

"I'm done with this lifestyle," I told myself with finality. "I'm done with all this street shit. The lies, the drama, the danger, the death. I'm not going to make it if I try to keep one foot in the street. It's going to suck me in and I'm never going to get out."

Yes, I'd said those words before.

This time I meant them.

The Witness Dream

Like a lot of people who find themselves disillusioned with the street lifestyle, I thought religion might help me get into a better mental and spiritual space. Since I'd grown up a Jehovah's Witness, that congregation seemed like a logical place to look for a fresh start.

I'd stopped going to Kingdom Hall (which is like the Witness equivalent of church) when I was thirteen or fourteen, but as my life started to spiral out of control, my mother and several of my aunts kept encouraging me to give it another try. I wanted to make them happy, but I was apprehensive.

The truth is, despite being raised in it, I'd never felt a strong connection with the faith. And even with my love for books, I actively hated going to book study on Thursday nights because it meant I'd have to miss *The Cosby Show* and *A Different World*. It sucked to go into school on Friday morning and everybody would be buzzing about what had happened with Lisa Bonet the night before, but I didn't know what they were talking about. On very rare occasions we'd get to stay home on a Thursday and I can remember how incredibly excited I was just to be able to catch one of those shows.

Plus, being a Witness made me feel left out at school. If you're not familiar with the faith, Witnesses also don't observe Christmas, Halloween, Father's Day, or any other holiday. Whenever there was a celebration in school, we couldn't be part of it. Most of the kids had no idea why we'd always be off to the side during Christmas plays or Halloween parades. Or why we couldn't even make cards for Mother's Day or Father's Day.

To my pop's credit, he understood the awkward position we

were in. Every year he'd make sure to pick up Christmas gifts for us, even if we weren't celebrating the holiday. I remember one year it was a Nintendo; another year it was a pair of Hi-Tec boots. Not the knockoffs I'd asked my mother to buy me at Payless but the official Hi-Tecs that all the cool kids were rocking. I might not have gotten them on Christmas morning, but I got them. That way the first day all the kids came back from break and were bragging about whatever they'd gotten for Christmas, I could chime in with, "Oh yeah, I got that new Nintendo too," and not feel completely left out. My father understood moments like those can be important to a kid.

That's why my biggest beef with the Witnesses is that I didn't like how they treated my father. When he was struggling with drugs and really needed support, I felt like they turned their backs on him. One night, one of the brothers (similar to a deacon in a Baptist church) stood up and announced, "Larry McKelvey is being dis-fellowshipped from the Kingdom Hall of Jehovah's Witnesses." After that, no one was allowed to talk to him while he was on the premises.

The theory is that the shame of being isolated will motivate you to correct whatever mistakes you've made, but I thought the whole concept was wack. If someone is going through a rough period, help them. Don't ostracize them and make them feel even worse about themselves.

Their methods weren't always as severe as de-fellowshipping someone. When I was particularly troubled as a teenager, some of the elders from the Kingdom Hall would come study with me at my mother's house. I remember I was studying with one of the elders and I asked him about Deuteronomy 14:8, which states, "And the pig, because it parts the hoof but does not chew the cud, is unclean for you. Their flesh you shall not eat, and their carcasses you shall not touch." When I asked how come then we still ate pig, he replied, "Well, that's from the Old Testament. We think if you pray over the food, it's fine to eat." Being the smart-ass that I am, I said, "Well, the Bible also says you shouldn't have sex before marriage. So if I pray over the pussy, then I can fuck it, right?" Sounded like a perfectly logical question to me, but I do remember him squeezing my hands extra tight when he prayed with me later on that night.

Despite moments like that, I did return to the hall to both make my mother happy and to see if I could find some motivation to help me turn my life around. It took only a few services, however, before I decided that being a Witness wasn't the answer for me. I respect that the faith has lent a lot of stability and support to my mother's life. I don't know if she would have made it through some of those tough times without the community having her back.

It wasn't going to have the same impact on my life. I don't think there is any organized religion that is the answer for me. I've taken valuable lessons from many organized groups—the Witnesses, the Nation of Islam, the Five Percenters, just to name a few. At the end of the day, however, I'm a spiritual person. Not a religious one.

Having said that, I do believe that in order to be truly successful in this world, you need to have a close relationship with God. I'm not telling you that you have to go out and convert to Islam, get baptized in the name of Christianity, or become a Jehovah's Witness. But you do have to have *some* type of spiritual foundation.

I'm always shocked when I run into people who don't believe in God. I'll even ask them, "How can you not believe that there's a power greater than you who's engineering this whole system of things?" Usually they'll tell me something like, "Man, God is just some mythical fairy tale. God is no different than Santa Claus, the Easter Bunny, or the Tooth Fairy."

I disagree wholeheartedly, but that mind-set is honestly one of the reasons I don't sell that junk about holiday headliners to my daughters. Maybe it's the Witness influence on me, but to this day I'm not a fan of holidays. I think it's a mistake to hype your kids on Santa Claus, the Easter Bunny, and the Tooth Fairy on one hand, and then try to sell them on God with the other. When they get older and realize Santa and the Easter Bunny aren't real, it becomes too easy for them to dismiss God as well. "So you were lying to me about everybody else, but this God character is real?" they'll say. "Yeah, right." And then they'll miss out on the affirmation, confidence, and faith that religion can provide when they're older and really need it.

True Love, False Dream

I might have been raised a Witness, but my true religion was hip-hop. Hip-hop culture was where I found inspiration, direction, and community.

Ever since my cousin Ty had put on that Rakim record, hip-hop had become the driving force in my life. When I was out in the streets, hip-hop is what helped me dream. When I was in jail, it was what helped me pass the time and stay positive. Hip-hop dictated every aspect of my lifestyle: what I wore, what I drove, what I ate, how I rapped to females and dealt with other males.

Being so heavily involved in the culture, it was only natural I decided I wanted to be a rapper myself. Let's face it, almost every guy in the hood thinks he can be the next Jay Z or Lil Wayne. Especially if you have the gift of gab, like I did. When you see guys who came from backgrounds like yours popping champagne on yachts, driving around in the flyest cars, and wearing expensive jewelry, it's easy to fall into the trap of thinking, "Hey, I can do that too."

I didn't just fall into that trap, I dove into it headfirst. I started off like most kids do, just rhyming in the lunchroom or on front stoops with my friends, making up new lyrics to popular songs. Especially after I smoked a little weed, rapping was the way I wanted to express myself.

My partner in rhyme was Jerrell. In many ways, our mutual love for hip-hop is what brought us together as friends. One of the first times I was ever over at his house we were smoking weed and some of the other dudes there were like, "Yo, Larry, kick something for us." I ran down whatever little rap I was working on at the time and Jerrell liked it. From that point onward, we were always talking hip-hop together.

A lot of people have a corny rap name buried deep in their closets, but few were cornier than mine, "Dizzy Van Winkle." I used "Dizzy" because, once, one of my boys called me "Dizzy Ass." I looked up the definition of "Dizzy" and saw that it meant "mentally confused." For some reason I liked that. The "Van Winkle" was a play on the idea of having been asleep for years and finally waking up. Stupid, I know. But when you're seventeen years old and have smoked a couple of blunts it sorta makes sense.

One of the earliest raps I wrote was inspired by the original version of Biggie's classic "One More Chance." My not so classic rap went:

> Girl, you got plenty more dicks to suck
> You're about to choke
> I don't give a fuck
> You gonna suck my dick until I nut
> You got plenty more balls to lick

Aww shit
Suck it, girl
Just like you're sucking on a mint
Plenty more salads to toss
Open those cheeks like it's butt floss.

What can I tell you? I was wack.

Even though I'm a natural talker, it never fully translated to rapping. No matter what sort of beat I was rhyming over—classic boom-bap, up-tempo, slow, or Dirty South bounce—I'd struggle to stay in the pocket. I practiced and practiced but could never completely get in sync with the beat.

Jerrell, on the other hand, could rap his ass off. He *lived* in the pocket. He always stayed on top of the beat, slipping in and out of the rhythm the way a great surfer rides a wave.

After messing around for a few years, when we were about seventeen Jerrell came to me and said, "Yo, let's actually do this. Let's go get a record deal." He didn't have to tell me twice—being a rapper is what I'd been dreaming of too. To cement our commitment, I got a tattoo of Wolverine from the X-Men holding a microphone on my arm. Wolverine was one of my favorite X-Men characters, a natural loner who didn't mind being part of a team when needed. Wolverine also had healing powers, which I felt I possessed emotionally as well. I felt like I could bounce back quick from things. I felt like I was going to be Wolverine on the microphone.

There weren't many opportunities for rappers in a place like Moncks Corner. But there was a group of guys in the area who started a label, TNT Records. "I know these guys," my pops told me one time when I mentioned looking for a deal. "If you're really serious about this thing, I can introduce you to them."

TNT was short for "Tabby and Tyrone," and it turned out to be backed by the OG Calvin Washington. Of course I wanted to be down, so with my father's introduction I went over to their studios in North Charleston.

There was a gang of rappers milling around the studio looking to get signed, but Calvin went out of his way to show me more respect than the others. I hadn't done anything as an MC to earn that sort of respect so I was surprised at the time, but I later came to understand it was my father's influence.

Nothing popped off right away, but I kept in contact with TNT over the next few months and it seemed like they were interested in signing me to a deal. Then one night I went over to the studio and as I started to pull into the parking lot, I saw FBI agents swarming all over that place. There were white dudes in dark Windbreakers everywhere! I didn't even slow down, just kept on driving and never looked back.

Even though it never landed me a deal, hanging out at their studio led to one of the most important conversations of my life. During a session one night I met a rapper named Willie Will who was also an overnight jock at the local hip-hop radio station Z93 Jamz. I had just graduated from night school and was looking for opportunities, so I asked him how he got put on at the station. "I just started with an internship," he told me. "How hard is it to get one?" I asked. "Ah, it ain't nothin'," he replied. "Just go down there and tell them you want to intern. They'll have you fill out a couple of papers and probably give you something on the spot." I was a little skeptical about how interested a radio station would be in a recent night school graduate who'd already been arrested twice, but I didn't have anything to lose. So one day Mook Mook drove me to the station and it turned out Willie was right. I had a couple of conversations, filled out a few forms, and *bam!* I was an intern at Z93 Jamz.

After interning at Jamz for a few months, I noticed that the station had a good relationship with a local rap label named Never So Deep Records, which was making a lot of noise. It was run by a middle-aged guy named Dr. Robert Evans and his son Robert Junior, or DJ Bless, who was also the in-house producer. Even though the TNT situation hadn't worked out, I was still clinging to my dream of making it as a rapper, so I decided to go over to Never So Deep and introduce myself.

I was a little wary because a local rapper I knew named Infinity the Ghetto Child had told me he thought something about Dr. Evans and Bless's energy was off. Even though he was signed to their label, he didn't really like Dr. Evans and Bless. I was prepared not to like them too, but after meeting them in person I had the exact opposite impression. Their studio had a real family vibe to me, and everyone treated me with respect and warmth. Plus, there was no denying that DJ Bless's tracks were absolute fire.

Unfortunately, by the time I linked up with Never So Deep, Jerrell was too caught up in the streets to really focus on rapping.* Since Jerrell was distracted, Willie Will and I decided to form a group called the Street Lordz. Dr. Evans and Bless were interested in working with us, so we recorded about four records with them. Willie and I were trash as rappers but Bless's production was so great that it seemed like we might be able to make something happen despite our limitations.

The more time I spent around Dr. Evans and Bless, I began to suspect that it wasn't their energy that Infinity didn't like but their

---

*Ironically, Jerrell would return to rapping years later and it would end up costing him his life. In 2013 he was recording in a studio in a mobile home when a gunman came looking for someone else. Jerrell was apparently in the vocal booth with his headphones on and didn't hear what was going on. The gunman sprayed up the place, and now my partner is dead.

work ethic. They were disciplined in a way that I hadn't experienced before in a hip-hop setting. The studio cultivated a healthy, professional environment because neither of the Evanses smoked or drank. In fact, I can remember being in the lobby drinking a Ballantine Ale and Dr. Evans walked over and asked, "Yo, can you get that shit out of here for me?" That doesn't happen too often. In addition to no drinking, Dr. Evans also didn't allow any weed smoking or chasing girls. Guys like Infinity didn't appreciate that—they wanted to come to the studio, get high, spit their rhymes, and have a party.

I'd never really met anyone like Dr. Evans before and wanted to learn more about him. I came to find out he was from Queens, he'd been an NYPD cop for over a decade before getting his medical license and then moving down to South Carolina to help his son run Never So Deep.

They might have come down south to make music, but the scene at Never So Deep was about much more than beats and rhymes. Dr. Evans and Bless practiced vee arnis jitsu every day and even had a dojo in the back of the studio. Dr. Evans made us work out and watch what we ate. He was also a heavy reader and put me on to impactful books like *The Art of War* and taught me about historical figures I'd been sleeping on, like Denmark Vesey.

He preached that in order to reach our full potential, both our bodies and our minds needed to be sharp. Being around his positive, focused energy had me looking at life in a different way. He was becoming an incredible mentor to me. One who was about to give me the most important career advice I'd ever receive.

Birth of the Radio Guy

I was interning in Jamz's promotions department, but I didn't really care that much about learning the promo game. Instead, what had me excited was that the internship allowed me to hang out with Willie Will while he did his overnight shifts. Technically I wasn't supposed to be sitting in during his shifts, but I wasn't going to let a small detail like the lack of permission slow me down. If I had waited for that invitation to come to the studio, I might still be waiting. I wanted to see what an overnight shift was like, so I just showed up and basically never left.

Once I was in the room, I never tried to muscle my way onto the mic, but I made my presence felt. I'd crack little jokes to keep Willie loose, cut out newspaper articles for him to talk about, pass him notes on funny things he could say about artists, and generally keep the energy upbeat.

After a few months of playing the background, people began to notice I was having a positive impact on Willie's show. Ron White, who was the music director at the time, approached me at one of the station's outdoor events. "I hear you popping up now and then on Willie's show," he told me. "Would you be interested in having a spot on air yourself?" he asked me. "Hell yeah," I quickly replied.

Ron was prepared to give me a shot, but I had to prove myself first. I started off doing voice tracking for Sunday mornings. That meant the station would record me hosting a show earlier in the week and then play it back on Sunday mornings, which was a slow shift since most people were either asleep or in church.

I quickly passed the "sounds good on the mic" test, but I apparently failed the "able to create appropriate content for a Sunday morning" one. Ron moved me to Saturday nights, which fit me better. Once I'd cut my teeth doing that, I started filling in for Willie when he was traveling, or for other jocks when they couldn't make their shifts. It was an unexpected position to be in, but I had an advantage working in my favor—I didn't "know" radio. No one had taught me the "right" way to do anything. I didn't work at my college radio station. I hadn't even gone to college. I hadn't attended a technical institute that instructed me on how to work the boards or set up the mics. I was a blank slate. I literally walked off a dirt road and up into the station.

The only thing I knew how to do was run my big-ass mouth. So that's what I did. I got in front of the mic and talked. I didn't know about liners, or positioning statements, or how to come in and out of commercial breaks. I just stated my opinions. "Yeah, that's the new Nelly song 'E.I.,'" I might say. "Damn, that record is wack." I talked to my listeners the way I talked to my friends.

It might not have been the most sophisticated approach, but it worked. From almost the first shift I hosted, people would let me know they liked how I sounded. In particular I remember getting a call from Tessa Spencer, who at the time was the cohost of the big morning show in Charleston, ironically also called *The Breakfast Club*. They were local celebrities, hosting parties and appearing on TV commercials. "You sound great on air," Tessa told me. "Like you've done this before." To me, Tessa represented the pinnacle of success. To hear her say I sounded good was a tremendous confidence boost.

Being on air gave me a sense of freedom that I'd never experienced before. Some folks clam up or get nervous when it's time to go live, but I got a rush from knowing I could connect with thousands of people. I loved that I could make someone out there laugh or get pissed off. Just knowing that I was connecting was an incredible experience. For years I'd been looking for that sense of belonging, and in radio I had finally found it. But even though the rest of the world could see me growing into my gift, I was still focused on getting a deal for my rap groups. I'd become very inspired by how Ludacris came up (for those of you who don't know, he was a rapper who'd gotten a deal thanks in large part to his success as a radio DJ). I made the mistake of thinking Luda's path was the same one that I had to follow.

The person who finally helped me clear off my lenses and see my future clearly was Dr. Evans. As soon as I'd gotten on air, he recognized that I'd found my actual calling. He started schooling me on great African-American DJs like Petey Greene in DC and Frankie Crocker in New York City. Guys who didn't just play records but had made their reputation off their wit and opinions. He told me I possessed some of the same talent he'd heard in them.

I appreciated the compliments, but I believed my future still lay in being a rapper. One day he finally pulled me aside and said, "Listen, Charlamagne, I know your dream is to be a famous rapper, but fuck that dream. You're just not that good.

"You are, however, *great* at being a radio jock," he continued. "Focus on that instead. And if you still want to be involved in hip-hop, learn the behind-the-scenes skills of running a label. Because it's never going to happen for you as a rapper. You need to dead that dream."

When Dr. Evans told me that, it was as if a giant weight had been lifted off my shoulders. As I've said, deep down I never felt comfortable rapping. Every time I went into the studio to spit a verse, I'd get a little tight and anxious. I'd overthink instead of just being natural. I'd try to be hard instead of just being myself. The exact opposite of how I felt talking on the radio.

That's why I didn't put up a fight with Dr. Evans when he dashed my dream. I didn't get offended and say, "Are you crazy? That last Dizzy Van Winkle verse was fire!" Rather, I calmly replied, "You're right. I'm done."

Simple as that.

I was through with rapping and ready to dedicate my talents to the radio.

Fuck Your Dream (If It's Not Really Yours)

I'm incredibly grateful that in Dr. Evans I had a mentor who was honest enough to tell me "fuck your dream." It sounds strange, thanking someone for announcing "you suck," but it's the type of mentorship that's desperately needed. Especially in the African-American community.

Everybody wants to be successful in life. That's the goal whether you're black, white, Spanish, Asian, or Martian. Still, a young black person growing up in America is going to have a slightly more narrow view on how to obtain that success. That's because when we see examples of success that look like us, they are usually in sports and entertainment.

It's no surprise that growing up everybody wanted to be the next Jay Z, the next Oprah, or the next Michael Jordan, just as now people want to be the next Drake, the next Issa Rae, or the next Steph Curry. Don't get me wrong, those are tremendous people to emulate, but the problem is most people simply aren't born with the specific talents necessary to excel in those fields. You might have been born with a gene that makes you predisposed to be able to build a stem cell, or design a skyscraper, but you'll never realize that if you waste your time trying to spit rhymes like Jay Z or shoot threes like Steph. Jay himself said, "Remind yourself / Nobody built like you / You designed yourself!" That should be our collective mentality. Design yourself. Construct your own dream. We have to stop thinking that just because we see something working spectacularly for someone else, that's the only path available to us!

I was lucky because my father never pushed me to follow the same dreams as everyone else. My cousins were getting football scholarships to places like Clemson, Penn State, and Alabama, but my father helped me look beyond sports. He might say, "You need to get in the weight room and get a little buff," just so I'd be able to handle myself, but he never made me feel that the football field was my only chance to make it. "Think about being a doctor, a lawyer, or an engineer," he'd encourage me. Just as my mother was always pushing me to read books that would make me think about worlds and lifestyles that I wouldn't otherwise encounter in my day to day life.

Even with that sort of constant encouragement, I *still* gravitated to one of the stereotypical dreams for kids in my community: rapping. Thankfully Dr. Evans woke me up, but not enough young people have a presence like that in their lives. Instead, they spend years and years chasing their "dream" of being a rapper, even though the world keeps telling them it's not for them. It really breaks my heart to think of all the people who could have been great engineers, architects, doctors, and lawyers but never even considered those dreams, let alone chased them. All because the entertainment game looks so glamorous.

The De-motivational Speaker

In response to this epidemic of "false dream" chasing in the African-American community, I try to use my voice and platform to be what I call a de-motivational speaker. Ever since I first got on the radio, I've been approached by a steady stream of people who are looking for help in breaking into the entertainment industry. They might send me a link to their mixtape or ask me to listen to their podcast or check out their new song.

For a long time, I'd make an honest effort to listen, but I'd rarely hear anything that would capture my attention. A few years ago I decided that I was finished being fake in those situations. First, being fake just goes against my basic nature. Second, I wasn't doing these people any favors by passively encouraging them to waste their time. Taking a page from Dr. Evans, I vowed that if I saw a person following *someone else's* dream, I'd let them know. What they did with that information was their call, but I'd at least be candid with them.

One example: a couple of years ago I was asked to host a talent show at Penn State. Before the show even started, I knew what I was going to see: a lot of rappers. We were at an institution of higher learning filled with state-of-the-art facilities and brilliant professors, but I knew I was going to be asked to judge a lot of students chasing the same dream my cousins and I chased back on the dirt roads of Moncks Corner.

So before the performers started, I addressed the crowd:

"I want to make one thing clear: I am a de-motivational speaker. My job tonight is to get all you students on your proper career path. You guys already have a great plan, which is being at one of the best universities in the country. You guys are majoring in all these amazing fields, like agriculture, engineering, criminal justice, and economics. Yet some of you still have pipe dreams of being a rapper. And I'm here to tell you: fuck your dreams!

"So if anyone gets up on this stage tonight and is anything less than the next Jay Z or Nicki Minaj, please boo the shit out of them.

Please hurt their feelings. Please make them feel so bad that they'll never think of wasting their time on rapping again and will head right back to the library where they belong. Maybe then they can find the cure for AIDS, or figure out a new way to grow crops like they're supposed to, instead of wasting their talents on this played-out dream."

The crowd laughed, but I was dead serious. Sure enough, one of the first performers up was a wannabe rapper. He had long dreads, wore fatigues, and smelled like weed as he walked past me.

"This guy ain't a rapper," I announced. "He gotta be y'all's weed man."

The crowd went wild. Evidently, I'd nailed it.

He shot me a dirty look and then proceeded to spit a terrible rhyme. I let him finish and then decided it was time to dead his misplaced dream.

I started by going in on his appearance. "Nigga out here looking like one version of ten different rappers," I told him as the crowd howled. "Nigga look like 2Chainz, Ace Hood, Cash Out . . . fuck out of here!" The guy immediately rushed back onstage and started shouting at me like he wanted to fight before security hustled him off. "See, this is why nobody likes rappers," I said. "That's why rappers can't make it in life."

I later found out the reason he wanted to fight was because he felt I was "snitchin'" on him with the "weed man" comment. He was in fact one of the campus weed dealers and had already caught a charge. The kid was clearly delusional. I'd never even met him before and simply made a general observation based on his appearance. If anything, he'd snitched on himself by overreacting to the comment.

Yes, I was rough on the kid, but he needed it. Hopefully he went back to his dorm after the show and reconsidered how he was spending his college career. If he thought, "Man, maybe this rapping thing isn't for me after all," then I did my job. Because he was terrible. Some kids on campus might have told him he was nice, but they probably just wanted free weed. There was no scenario where that guy was ever getting a record deal. He had, however, demonstrated a hustler's mentality. Maybe he could apply some of his entrepreneurial instinct to an internship on Wall Street, or a sales job in the advertising world.

And to be clear, I don't just go around discouraging college students. No, I offer my de-motivational speaking services free of charge to *anyone* I see chasing the wrong dream.

Take Musiq Soulchild, an incredibly gifted R & B singer who has made some classic joints like "Love," which I used to rock my daughter to sleep to. But despite his undeniable talent, Musiq never quite reached the level of commercial success he deserves. A few years ago he decided that the way for him to finally break through was to reinvent himself as a rapper named "The Husel." It was a terrible idea, one that didn't reflect Musiq's true dream of being a classic R & B singer.

"I can't respect the Husel," I began the interview when he came on *The Breakfast Club*. "Musiq Soulchild is a great R & B singer. Why conform to what these kids are doing today?"

Musiq responded that he wanted to be a rapper because he was bored of singing. I wasn't buying it. We argued back and forth about the validity of the project, with Musiq finally conceding that the concept was rooted in his desire to make more money. To me, that confirmed my suspicion he wasn't chasing his true dream. He was chasing the money. So it was time to properly demotivate him.

"You're an amazing artist," I reminded him. "That's why I don't like seeing you conform to such a gimmick!"

"It might not be for you," Musiq shot back.

"I don't think it is, dog," I replied. "I don't think it's for you either. . . . I don't want you to feel like you're not appreciated as Musiq Soulchild. Because you are appreciated!"

Musiq and I eventually agreed to disagree on Husel, but it seems the public was on my side. I never heard any talk about that album. To me, that's the universe letting Musiq know he was chasing a false dream and should have stuck to his true calling, which is making beautiful, stirring love songs. If he releases another album filled with songs like that, I'll be the first to pick it up.

Sometimes you have the right dream but the wrong approach. If that's the case, then you still need a de-motivational speech. I had to give one to T-Pain when he came on a show I was hosting in Columbia, South Carolina. T-Pain was promoting his debut single "I'm Sprung," which featured him using the auto-tune program he'd end up making infamous.

Back then Auto-Tune was only something I knew from my pop's Roger Troutman records, so I was curious about why T-Pain was using it. I asked him to sing the song live without any Auto-Tune, and to his credit he accepted my challenge. Unfortunately, he sounded like trash.

Instead of trying to play it off, or, even worse, tell him he sounded good, I kept it 100. "That was terrible," I told him. "You really need to work on improving your voice."

T-Pain didn't appreciate my honesty. He even called me a few days later to cuss me out. "Stop playing that clip," he told me after it went viral. "You're fucking with my money." But I held my ground. "Sorry, man," I told him. "It's for your own good. You've got to learn how to sing for real."

Thankfully T-Pain took my advice to heart. A couple of years later he appeared on the Wendy Williams show and said that my de-motivational speech is what inspired him to stop relying on Auto-Tune and start focusing on his art.

"I want to thank Charlamagne," he said. "If it wasn't for him, I wouldn't be in the position I am now. He made me take my craft seriously. I stopped smoking and really started working on my vocal technique."

I was happy to help. Today T-Pain and I are good friends and are even working together on several TV projects.

The T-Pain example is critical, because there are going to be people who tell you "Fuck your dreams" when in fact you are on the right path. When you have found your actual gift.

I had a moment like that once with my cousin aunt (the only reason I call her a "cousin aunt" was because she was like my parents' cousin, but she was actually my cousin's aunt. So I would call her "Aunt Penny" like my cousins did, even though she was actually closer to a cousin to me. Make sense? Of course it doesn't. So let's just say "Aunt Penny").

Anyway, I remember being in her kitchen with all my younger cousins around the time I was doing overnights at Jamz. I was drunk and pontificating about my life plans, about how I was going to be as big as Tom Joyner, Doug Banks, Angie Martinez, Big Tigger, or any of the radio personalities who were poppin' at the time. Yes, I was running my mouth, but I was also trying to speak my success into fruition.

Aunt Penny heard me from the other room and stuck her head into the kitchen to add her two cents: "Larry, you shouldn't put your goals so high, because when you don't achieve them you will be disappointed."

I literally heard a record scratch when she said that. I took a moment, then looked at my cousin aunt and declared, "That's the dumbest shit I ever heard in my life." I almost always show respect for my elders, but that comment had me hot.

"Don't dream too big," is a very poisonous thought to put into the mind of a young person: if you look at her own kids today, or her nephews and nieces, none of them are doing much with their lives. Probably because they listened to her advice. This is why it's critical that you be able to tell the difference between someone telling you "Fuck your dreams" in order to get you on the right path or simply telling you "Fuck your dreams" because they've already given up on their own.

I trusted Dr. Evans because I knew he had taken the time to observe me, to see what I was capable of. Plus, he was an accomplished individual in his own right. He was someone who strove to get the most out of life. Someone who chose pursuing passion over procrastination. Those are the types of people you want to listen to.

The key is to remember that no matter who you are, or where you come from, your dream *is* out there. Try to think of life as a big-ass Christmas tree. Then think of God as our collective father, who has made sure to put one gift under that tree for each of his children.

Don't try to grab someone else's gift, no matter how shiny or cool it might look. You're not ever going to find lasting success that way. Keep on rooting around under that giant tree until you find the gift with *your* name on it.

And if I catch you playing with someone else's gift, I'm going to let you know about it. I'm going to hit you with a de-motivational speech because that's what you need. Sometimes I'll see people write online that I'm a "dream killer" or a pessimistic person. Those are just knee-jerk reactions. The fact is I'm extremely optimistic. I have complete faith that as long as you follow YOUR dream, you're going to find success.

There Are No Losses,
Only Lessons

You should give zero fucks about any perceived losses in life as long as you learn something from them. Always look for the lesson in any situation you think didn't go your way. Understand that your plan isn't necessarily also God's plan for you.

My friend Donnell Rawlings (aka "Ashy Larry" from *Chappelle's Show*) once told me that you don't become a true star in radio until you've been fired three times. Well, by that measure I must be doing pretty well, because I've been fired four times.

Some of you are probably thinking, "Yes, but you deserved all those pink slips because of your foul-ass mouth." That might be the perception, but I've never actually been fired for anything I did on the air. There aren't any stories of me getting people to have sex in church, like Opie and Anthony. Or getting in trouble for making fun of tsunami victims like Miss Jones did. Or threatening to put mayonnaise in the crack of a four-year-old girl's butt and take a bite out of it, like Star threatened Envy's daughter. Nope. Nothing like that.

And as far as off-the-air behavior, I consider myself a model employee. Almost to a person, I know my colleagues have respected and enjoyed working with me.

That's one of the reasons why when I look back at those firings, none of them felt devastating to me. There was never a moment when I felt like getting let go was a death sentence to my career. I always remained optimistic that I was going to bounce back, because I subscribe to the concept that "there are no losses in life, only lessons."

When you get fired, instead of getting mad at your employer or getting down on yourself, the best thing you can do is say, "Thank you for the opportunity" and keep it moving. Then, once you've given yourself a day or two to get past whatever emotions you might be feeling, take a calm, cool, and collected look at the reasons behind your termination. Even if you were told (like I often was) that your employer was simply "going in another direction," something motivated that. Figure out what it was, so you know what missteps to avoid at your next job. And most important, believe that there *will* be a next job.

A lot of folks want to plan out their career step-by-step. "First I'm going to get a position at this company, then I'm going to move on to a bigger place," they'll say. "From there I'm going to take an executive job at . . ." They've got their whole career, from intern to manager to executive to CEO, scripted out before they take their first step. It's great to have a vision for what you want to accomplish, but very rarely do people's blueprint for themselves go exactly according to plan. So please, never, ever give up because things aren't going the way that *you* planned them at first.

When I'm moving full steam toward my goals and suddenly I get knocked off my path, I don't get flustered or despondent. I just have the confidence that I'm going to be redirected to the next opportunity. Which is why I like to call getting fired an act of "divine misdirection."

I've learned that I can map out all the moves I want, but ultimately God's GPS is better than whatever navigation app I've downloaded.

Leaving Z93 Jamz

There was a growing buzz about my on-air presence, but I still couldn't land a full-time slot on Z93 Jamz. It was a heritage station (one that has been running the same format for decades), which meant that it had more money, more promotion, more history, and a bigger signal than its competitors. Z93 Jamz was, and remains, the big dog in the Charleston region. As a result, jocks rarely left because there was really no place better to go.

I still had my internship in the promotions department and the occasional overnight shift, but I was hungry for more. I wanted to figure out a way to move up the ladder, so I started questioning all the full-time jocks about their journeys, looking for insights into what they'd done to get ahead. One thing I noticed was that they all had mass communications degrees. It occurred to me that my lack of a degree could be holding me back.

To enhance my résumé, I decided to enroll in a communications program at Trident Technical College in Charleston. It seemed like a good idea but I didn't even make it through the first class. "Why am I here?" I asked myself, looking around at my fellow students. Most of them had barely set foot in a radio station, let alone hosted their own show, like I had. "I've been winning by following my instincts," I told myself. "So why now should I listen to someone else's advice on the 'right' way to do this?" There was no good answer to that question, so I walked out of the class and never went back. I realized I was hustling backward at that school. I already had the *privilege* of working at a radio station. Instead of waiting for an instructor to tell me the right way to be on the air, I needed to exercise my privilege and figure it out on my own.

I did learn one thing that day: no amount of classroom instruction can ever match the experience you'll get from actually performing a job.

Nothing that is worth knowing can be taught.
—Oscar Wilde

Back at Jamz, I settled into a groove of helping out with promotions and grabbing whatever air shifts I could. Around that time there was a female listener named Jamaica who used to call into all the male jocks and talk real freaky to them. She had a very sexy voice and people would always get a kick out of her calls. Then one day I got hit up off the air by some folks who knew Jamaica and alerted me to the fact that "she" was actually a "he." They even passed along her government name.

The next time Jamaica called during one of my shifts I confronted her and said, "Hey, Jamaica, isn't it true that your name is really such and such. . . ." Jamaica wasn't happy about being outed and called up Jamz to complain about me. She spoke to the program director (PD), a guy named Terry Base, and told him she was going to sue the station. Instead of telling Jamaica, "Hey, I don't see what Charlamagne did wrong," Terry overreacted and took away my shift, relegating me to liners. (For those of you who don't know the term, liners means recording scripts for the time, weather, and introducing the next song.) Technically I was still on air, but I'd lost the platform to express my personality. Having to read off a script? That was the worst thing that could happen to me. I went from being impatient to downright miserable.

But as has often been the case in my career, what seemed to be a dead end was actually God setting me up for my next winning move. A new station called Hot 98.9 was launched in Charleston to compete with Jamz. It didn't have nearly the signal strength as Jamz, but it was looking to make a splash in the market. They'd heard me on Jamz and offered me my own nightly show, seven to midnight, every Monday through Saturday.

On paper, staying with Jamz would have been the safe bet, even if it meant being stuck on liners for a while. Jamz still had the best reputation in the area and chances were eventually something would have opened up for me. Safe bets, however, have never appealed to me. I quietly agreed to a deal with Hot, which wasn't a betrayal because Jamz had never committed to me full-time. Few things I'd ever done at that point in my life had felt better than walking into Terry Base's office and handing in my resignation letter. I didn't tell him why I was leaving, but he probably figured it out when Hot started running promos for my new show later that day.

Some people at Jamz said I was a fool for leaving, but I didn't give it a second thought. Besides being productive and improving my craft, I was also getting a real paycheck for the first time in my life. Granted, my salary was only $19K a year, but when your employment history includes Taco Bell and selling crack, just saying you have a salary makes you feel like the man.

• • •

My program director at Hot was George Cook, who remains a friend and mentor to this day. Back then George was just another young radio guy trying to figure things out on the fly. His idea was for me to host a nighttime show that had the feel of a morning show. George's reasoning was that since the late, great Doug Banks was syndicated on Hot in the mornings, it was important for the station to have a local show heavy on talk on at night. I loved the concept. Taking calls and talking to people was my passion because it was the best way to stay connected to the streets. Looking back, interacting with callers on the radio was one of the precursors to social media. And there's no doubt radio personalities are the original catfish. If I had a dollar for every time someone tells me, "Man, you don't look the way you sound. . . ."

My signature segment was called "Hate O'Clock." I would open up the phones and say, "Hot 98.9, holla if you hating" and people would just vent about whatever was bothering them. Someone might hate on a shirt someone at their school was wearing. On 9/11 everyone called in hating on bin Laden. They'd even call in and hate on me. I used to love it.

Another feature I started was called "Lyrical Warfare," which gave would-be rappers an opportunity to call up the station and spit a freestyle. If they were dope, I'd give them props. If they were wack, I'd play a sound effect that said, "You are Ba . . . Ba . . . Boonky . . . Ba . . . Boonky . . ." People still quote that sound effect in Charleston to this day. I remember one guy called in who was doing way too much DMX-style grunting during his rap. When he was done, I told him it sounded like he was having rough gay sex with Hulk Hogan.

I've always believed in the balance in ratchetness and righteousness, so around 11:00 p.m. I would wind things down with a segment called "Charlamagne Tha God Thug Love Status." I would play nothing but slow songs and talk directly to the ladies in the audience, making sure to end the show on a positive note.

That balance was a hit, and within a couple of months I took the show from number fourteen to number two in the market. I was still living with my mama, but suddenly I was a bit of a celebrity in Charleston, which was a new experience to me. Yes, I had been popular in high school. But being well-known in an actual city? On the radio? That was virgin territory. And I didn't know how to handle it.

Messed Up by "Fame"

I won't even try to sugarcoat it, I let my newfound "fame" get to my head. And by "fame," I'm not talking about making a lot of money, driving a fancy car, or appearing on TV. For a twenty-something-year-old radio jock in South Carolina, fame was seeing your name on the marquee of a club for the first time. Or when you walk into a party, everybody acts like you're a celebrity instead of a radio personality making $19K a year.

Pretty tame stuff, but that was more than enough to get me gassed. I didn't have much money, but I had the ability to make or break people socially, and I took advantage of that.

One moment that illustrates how shitty my head was started at Night Life, a club in Kingstree, a town just outside of Moncks Corner, where I was hosting a party. My name was on the marquee in big letters: CHARLAMAGNE THA GOD. There was already a line outside, and soon as I got out of the car people mobbed me and started showing me love. I felt like a movie star, or a rapper with a hit single in heavy rotation. One of the people crowding around me was a beautiful young woman named Jubilee. One of my homeboys asked her, "What's up for tonight?" and without blinking she said, "I'm going to do whatever Charlamagne wants me to do." I'll never forget those words.

We ended up taking this young lady back to Moncks Corner later that night. When I say she "fucked the team," she fucked the team. She had sex with at least six of my homeboys. That was Saturday night. But we weren't done. That Monday night I was doing an on-site broadcast from a club in Charleston called the Diplomat. A local rap trio was hanging out there and I told them, "I got this girl here, she'll give you head for fifty dollars." Jubilee was with it. I made 150 bucks that night. Yes, it was all consensual, but I was behaving like a piece of shit. I'd gotten a taste of power and couldn't handle it. As the saying goes, "Power corrupts, absolute power corrupts absolutely."

My ratings on Hot 98.9 kept being strong, but trouble was headed my way. The station brought in a consultant named Michael Newman, who also consulted for Hot 97 in New York, at the time the biggest hip-hop station in the country. Michael wasn't feeling my style and tried to give me some notes. In my heightened arrogance, instead of taking his advice, I told him, "Send my air check to someone who will get it. I know they'll love this on Hot 97 in New York!" Michael wasn't with it, but I got George Cook to vouch for me and Michael finally relented. He sent my air check to Hot's legendary PD Tracy Cloherty, who proceeded to trash it. "Why is he screaming all the time?" was one of her notes.

Michael had always thought I was too ghetto, so he used Tracy's reaction to take me down several notches. To my understanding, he recommended to George that I be fired from Hot 98.9 if I didn't change my ways. I caught wind of what he proposed and confronted him. "Some white dude from who knows where is not going to tell me how to talk to my people in Charleston," I told him. Of course Michael really wanted me gone after that. He kept pushing George to let me go, and when he wouldn't, they decided to let George go instead. He was replaced by a DJ named Corey Hill.

Corey was a popular radio personality, someone I had grown up listening to on the station 100.9. Despite my respect for his track record, Corey and I got off to a bad start. Corey was an incredible on-air talent, but that was the problem. He was a radio personality. I didn't want a fellow jock to be my boss, especially one I knew I was better than.

One of Corey's first moves was to make me get rid of all the features—preproduced bits or scripted segments—in my show. The very elements that had made me so popular. That meant "Hate O'Clock" and "Lyrical Warfare" were all gone. It felt similar to when Terry put me on liners at Jamz. Without my features, I felt powerless. The job started to feel like work again, instead of fun. Looking back, I can see I had been leaning on features too much. I hadn't learned how to trust my ability to carry a show on my own without any props. But Corey hadn't taken away my features to help me develop into a better on-air personality. He was really trying to get me the fuck out of there.

Things came to a head quickly. I had gone to Miami one weekend and came back on Monday. Before my shift, Corey called me at home and told me, "Don't come in to work until we talk." "Am I suspended?" I asked him. "What did I do?" "Oh, it's nothing," he replied. "Just wait to hear back from me."

Three days went by before Cliff Fletcher, the general manager of the station, called and asked me why I hadn't been coming into work. "Corey told me to stay home until he talked to me," I explained. This was news to Cliff. "Why didn't you call me when that happened?" he asked. "Now we need to talk." So Cliff and I went out to lunch, where he explained that he needed me and Corey to work things out. Cliff's research showed that the station's ratings spiked when I was on but then would flatten out again after my shift. Cliff said this showed the station needed to build around my energy.

After I said I'd try to work things out, Cliff went back to the station to see if Corey would agree to the truce. While Corey conceded that my show was popular, he said he still didn't think I was a good fit for the station. His big thing was that I was too out of control. When pressed for an example, he claimed I'd said "Suck my big black dick" on the air. I knew that wasn't true because (A) I don't have a big dick, (B) I don't believe in lying, and (C) if I had talked about my dick, it would have been in a much wittier fashion than that.

Despite all the accusations, Corey and I agreed to bury the hatchet. But then a week or so later I got a voice mail from Corey saying the station had "decided to move in another direction."

There it was, my first firing.

I'd barely been on the air for a year, and already I was out of the game.

I've talked about the importance of not giving a fuck, but the truth is, I gave a huge fuck when I got that voice mail from Corey. I was getting canned from a job that I loved, a job that had become central to my identity. I felt I needed that job. Especially coming from where I'd been.

I was worried my radio career was over before it had ever really gotten started. There was even a DJ on Z93 Jamz named DJ Cass (I used to clown him and call him "DJ Ass") who openly gloated at my demise. He and Corey were friends, and as soon as I got canned, he went on air and started sending subliminal shots my way, saying, "Somebody just got fired in this town. Y'all know who it is. And you will probably never hear that guy on the radio again."

After I got fired, I fell into the classic trap of blaming the "haters" for what had happened to me. "I know Corey Hill, Michael Newman, and DJ Cass were behind this; they got me fired," I'd mutter to myself.

And they probably were. But the situation was still clearly *my* fault.

Once I calmed down and did some self-evaluation, I was able to see the lesson in my "loss":

I needed to humble myself.

I'd abused the power and position that came from being a local celebrity. I was putting out terrible energy into the world, and true to the laws of Karma, it didn't take long for that energy to return to me.

I also learned another critical lesson from that situation: never say "I'm not ready" when faced with an opportunity. When George Cook had been let go, Cliff Fletcher had asked if I'd have any interest in the PD job. I told him no, because I didn't think I could do it. Later, after I told Dr. Evans that I'd potentially passed on the job, he let me have it.

"Why?" he asked incredulously.

"Because I'm . . . I'm . . . I'm just starting in radio," I stuttered. "I don't know how to be no program director."

"If I ever hear you say what you *can't* do again, I'll slap the shit outta you!" he said, before adding, "Listen to me, you son of a bitch: when there's an opportunity, you take it. You grab it now and we'll figure out how to be a PD later. Never tell me or another person what you can't do. How do you even know you can't do it?" When he explained it to me like that, I knew he was speaking pure gospel.

I wasn't the only person who learned from the situation. The station learned that when you have a hot radio personality, let that person cook instead of trying to dampen their flame. You see, after I was fired, over the next year, the station's numbers fell off so hard that the parent company eventually had to switch formats. When it was all said and done, *nobody* had a job.

A pessimist sees the difficulty in every opportunity; an optimist sees the opportunity in every difficulty.
—Winston Churchill

Despite so many missteps at the time, almost everyone involved eventually got themselves back on track. Today George Cook is the director of operations and brand manager of K104 in Dallas, one of the most respected stations in the country. Corey Hill, who I'm happy to say is my guy now, is making moves as DJ Hustle Simmons, hosting shows in Boston and Myrtle Beach. DJ Cass is still on Z93 Jamz in Charleston. Roughly fifteen years later, I think he finally got a full-time slot.*

Looking back, I can see that God had actually sent me a sign that getting fired from Hot wasn't going to be more than a bump on my road to success. A friend of mine named Neek hosted middays at Hot 103.9 in Columbia (more on that station later). She was also a God-fearing woman who would often go to the same church as me. Her faith supported me one day when I was wondering when I would get a call up to a bigger radio market. "Charlamagne, you just have to pay attention to signs," Neek told me.

---

*No need to tell me I'm petty. I already know.

"God always shows you signs. In fact, when you leave this radio station today and drive home, the first license plate you see on another car might tell you exactly where you're going to wind up. It might sound crazy, but God will be planting a seed in your mind so you can fertilize it by constantly thinking about it and working toward it."

Heading home later that day, Neek's words suddenly popped back into my head. So I looked at a truck passing me and saw the license plate read "New Jersey." "There's no radio stations in New Jersey," I told myself, trying to downplay the moment. But then my mind immediately fired back, "True, but that's only because everyone in New Jersey is listening to the New York stations. So I must be going to New York." As much as I wanted to have faith, I dismissed the idea: as a young radio personality in South Carolina, it seemed inconceivable to ever land in the number one market in the country. It wasn't that I didn't believe in my talent—I did—it's just that I thought New York would be too hard to break into.

I couldn't see it at the time because I wasn't properly recognizing the power of God in me. I wasn't cognizant of God's ability to make the impossible possible. As if taking a radio jock from South Carolina to New York City was somehow above his pay grade. Man, that's light work for God.

Remember, when God plants something in your spirit, embrace where that energy takes you. Don't make the mistake of fixating on what's *not* going to happen, think about all that *will* happen because you are following a plan laid out by the creator.

In my case, before I could take a bite of the Big Apple, that divine misdirection would lead me one hundred miles up the road to Columbia, South Carolina, where I would be offered the advice that foreshadowed me eventually being in NYC.

The Big DM

After I was let go from Hot, I had no idea what to do with myself. There weren't many other options in the way of urban radio in Charleston. Thankfully, Dr. Evans came to my rescue with a game-changing suggestion.

"You need to put together an album," he declared after I shared my uncertainty with him.

"What do you mean?" I asked. I had heard of DJs doing albums before, like DJ Clue, Funkmaster Flex, and Greg Street. What was the value in a jock doing an album though? What I needed to do was get back on the air.

Then Dr. Evans broke down his vision for me. "Take some songs from Never So Deep artists and put a bunch of skits between them. Structure it like a radio show. Do talk breaks between the songs like you're on air. Give the skits all the energy that you had on the radio. That way, people won't forget about you. You'll be keeping the buzz you had on Hot fresh in people's minds."

I trusted Dr. Evans, so I got to work on what would ultimately be called *Charlamagne Tha God Presents Concrete Champ: The Radio Show*. The album featured twelve songs produced by Never So Deep with short interviews and talk breaks I recorded in between each track. Just to give you an idea of how out there the album was, we had one skit where a girl tried to mix my cum with pancake batter. Yep, you read that right. We pressed up three thousand CDs of *Concrete Champ*s and distributed them to record stores and radio stations all over South Carolina.

Dr. Evans's instincts proved correct again. The album eventually made it into the hands of a brother named Mike Love, who was the PD of a station called the Big DM in Columbia, South

Carolina. Mike liked what he heard so much that he offered me a job doing weekends at the station.

Getting a job at the Big DM was a major blessing. Not only did it get me back on the air, but as an added bonus Mook Mook was attending the University of South Carolina in Columbia at the time. Now, I had a personal *and* professional reason to be in the city.

Columbia was my first taste of working in a big city. If you're from Los Angeles or New York you might take issue with that description, but trust me, Columbia was boomin' back then.

I feel one of the reasons people sleep on Columbia is because they don't realize it is a college town. In addition to the University of South Carolina, it's also home to Benedict College and Allen University. Colleges mean there's plenty of young women, and where there are young women, there will also be plenty of young men looking to party. Plus, Columbia is only three or four hours away from Atlanta, so it was an easy destination for rappers, promoters, and hustlers looking to build their base outside of the ATL.

The Big DM is where I met several future stars for the first time. One Saturday night an unsigned rapper from Atlanta came by the station looking to play me his music. He had already put out one album, *I'm Serious,* on LaFace before getting dropped due to poor sales. Now he was out on the streets in Columbia trying to drum up support of his independent single "24's."

Of course, that rapper was T.I.

When I first met T.I., he was rocking regular jeans and a dirty gray Champion hoodie. He might have looked fresh out the trap, but he still had all the aura of the mega star he is today. I played "24's" on the air that night and soon T.I. was a constant presence in the city, holding court in the clubs and screwing almost all our women (or so it seemed). Columbia became like a second home to T.I., as he later acknowledged in the DJ Khaled track "We Takin' Over," where he rapped, "Started in Atlanta, then I spread out with it [to] South Carolina . . ." When I heard that shout-out, I was proud T.I. had remembered all the early love we gave him in Columbia.

Another Atlanta rapper who paid his dues in Columbia was Young Jeezy. When Jeezy first showed up in Columbia looking to build a buzz, he wasn't signed to Def Jam yet. I remember, my man Fatz brought him to perform at a club called the Main Event with another artist from Atlanta named Big Country. Only fifty or sixty people showed up that night, but Jeezy still put on a high-energy show, which I respected. Jeezy didn't get discouraged and kept grinding, eventually dropping his classic mixtape *Trap or Die*. Then the world realized his talent. So that when he played the Main Event a year later, over three thousand people packed into the club, with another thousand on the street outside trying to get in. There is no artist from anywhere in that region, especially Atlanta, who didn't come through Columbia and build their buzz.

Same with Killer Mike and 2Chainz. Both those guys would spend a lot of time in Columbia doing performances before they broke nationally. Columbia was also the home of professional athletes like the NBA star Jermaine O'Neal and the NFL star Duce Staley. There was a lot of energy in Columbia and I fed off it.

The drug game was absolutely boomin' in Columbia during that period, which meant there were lots of dealers who needed ways to "clean" their money. One of their favorite methods was throwing parties at the city's various clubs. They'd book the artists and hire me and one of my best friends to this day, DJ Frosty, to host the affairs. This was the height of the trap era, so as you can imagine parties thrown by Southern drug dealers tended to get crazy. One of the biggest issues was that Kappas from the local colleges would show up to these parties wearing their traditional red colors and throwing up their hand signs, which pissed off the local Blood members who were also in the spot. The Bloods didn't understand the Kappas were just a frat and thought they were trying to invade their turf. I saw a lot of stupid shit go down over that misunderstanding.

On the air I was really finding my groove. I'd brought back my "Hate O'Clock" segment and also introduced a new character called the Concrete Ghetto Chick, played by my good friend Ashley James. Columbia loved it and our ratings were poppin'. It seemed I'd found a new home.

Then radio politics tripped me up. Before switching to hip-hop, The Big DM had been an adult contemporary station. Despite the strong ratings my individual show was getting, the station's parent company, Inner City Broadcasting, decided that it wanted to switch back to adult contemporary. My segments had worked really well coming between Clipse or Ludacris records. That type of content wasn't going to fit too well between Earth, Wind & Fire or Eddie Levert.

Once the switch was announced, Mike Love kept it real with me and explained there wouldn't be a role for me at the new Big DM. But, he added, I should hold tight in Columbia because something else was cooking. In a few weeks it came out that Inner City had bought Columbia's Hot 103.9, a hip-hop station that had previously been the Big DM's most heated local competitor. Just like that, my skill set was back in demand. I went from competing with Hot 103.9 in the ratings to being one of the new faces of their station. Bill Black, who worked at Hot 103.9, described it as similar to when the wrestler Bill Goldberg suddenly switched from the WCW to the WWE overnight.

Personally, I wasn't too concerned with what station I was working on as long as I was on the air and allowed to do my thing. And the new Hot 103.9 was definitely letting me cook. In the past I had focused on features out of necessity—there simply weren't that many good interviews to be had. Once I was on Hot, that began to change. They became a power in the marketplace, and every established artist who came through town made sure to pay us a visit.

My first interview to go viral (before going viral was a thing) was with Buffie the Body on Hot. If you don't remember Buffie, she was a video vixen who was infamous for being one of the first "celebrities" to get ass implants. I asked Buffie about what her plan would be when she got older, when her looks started to fade and gravity set in. She didn't appreciate the question and ended up getting so mad that she threw a CD at me as she walked out of the studio. A lot of websites and blogs ran the interview, giving me my first taste of national exposure. In fact, my homeboy Van Lathan of TMZ recently told me that interview is what put me on his radar. He recalled that after Buffie told me to shut up because I was "just a local radio personality in Columbia," I fired back that "My mouth is going to take me farther than your butt." And if you check the scoreboard, I think most people would admit what I said has come to pass. It might have seemed like a bold prediction at the time, but I feel it's another example of how you can speak things into existence.

Another memorable guest was a young Trey Songz, who I messed with by saying things like, "Listen, you're no Omarion." Even though it was one of Trey's first interviews, he didn't get flustered and laughed off my jokes. I'll always remember at the end of the interview, he told me that I had some of the same qualities as Star and Bucwild, who were ruling the airways in New York at that time. "You need to be in New York too," he told me. Salutes to Trey for planting that seed in my head.

My favorite interview from my time in Columbia was with Minister Louis Farrakhan. The minister had come to town to hold a press junket for the Millions More Movement. At that time I was doing youth ministry at Mosque Number 38 in Columbia, so I was granted the privilege of attending the junket at a local hotel.

Since I had grown up reading so much material from the Nation of Islam and watching Minister Farrakhan's videotapes, I was hyped to be in the same room with him. Too hyped, in fact. I was very aggressive and tried to turn the junket into my own personal conversation with the minister. As soon as they opened up the floor to questions, my hand shot up and I shouted out, "Minister Farrakhan, can you give any advice on how to balance Islam and hip-hop?" The minster gave a very thoughtful reply and once he was finished my hand shot up again: "Minister Farrakhan, can you speak about why we need socially redeeming value in music?" He answered my question and then my hand shot up one more time.

Before I could shout out another question, Minister Farrakhan cut me off. "Brother, you just wait," he said with a kind smile. "I'm going to talk to you afterward." I figured he just said that to shut me up, but true to his word, one of his aides came up to me afterward and led me to a room where the minister was waiting. The minister patiently sat with me as I was able to ask him the rest of my questions. I was also able to present him with a document I'd written for Columbia's *The State* newspaper called "The Ten Commandments of Hip-Hop," which was my attempt to bring a little consciousness to the culture. When I was done, the minister sized me up and said, "Young man, I believe that you are more than what you appear to be to other people." That was a pivotal moment for me. Knowing that a wise elder like Minister Farra-khan saw my potential gave me immense confidence that I was on the right path.

I ended up playing my interview with the minister on my show, which didn't sit well with everyone at the station. Chris Connors, who was my PD at Hot, pulled me aside and said "some people" might not like the interview. He also hinted that "those people" also might not appreciate it when I wore my T-shirt with a picture of Minister Farrakhan around the station. I assumed he was talking about this fat-ass, redneck, white devil, Boss Hogg–looking super-visor we had named Steve. "The hell with those people," I told him, and proudly continued to wear the shirt every chance I got.

The Wendy Williams Experience

Inner City Broadcasting had been founded in 1970 as one of the first African-American-owned radio networks. The station's pri-mary owners were the famed Harlem power broker Percy Sut-ton and Clarence Jones, who had published the *Amsterdam News*. Notable shareholders included future New York City mayor David Dinkins, Malcolm X's widow Betty Shabazz, and Roberta Flack.

Inner City made a splash in New York City with WBLS, an R & B station led by Frankie Crocker (one of the iconic DJs Dr. Evans had had me study). During the late seventies and early eighties, the station became the number one black station in New York. Crocker was a true innovator, refusing to get boxed into the tradi-tional limitations of black radio. He'd play records by rock acts like the Clash and Blondie alongside new records from soul groups MSFB or Harold Melvin, giving zero fucks about what a black sta-tion was "supposed" to sound like. If a record had soul, he played it. That really resonated with me, because these were the same acts that my father used to play at Zebra Club back in Moncks Corner. Like I said, if some British white boys like Queen had a funky song, the club was going to play it right alongside James Brown and George Clinton. Good music doesn't have a race.

Unfortunately Crocker got caught up in a payola scandal and was forced off the station (leaving black radio a lot less interesting). But WBLS continued to dominate, thanks to a new wave of hip-hop DJs like the legendary Mr. Magic and Marley Marl.

By the mid-2000s one of the biggest personalities on WBLS (alongside Steve Harvey) was Wendy Williams. Wendy had risen to stardom at New York's Hot 97 before she was fired, according to the rumors, for either insinuating that Diddy was gay or getting in a physical fight with fellow jock Angie Martinez. Or maybe a combination of both. Regardless, after a successful stint at Power 99 in Philadelphia, Wendy made her triumphant return to NYC in 2001 after WBLS hired her to host afternoon drives. (If you're interested in hearing more about her story, I recommend her autobiography *Wendy's Got the Heat*.)

Since Inner City owned Hot 103.9, the company decided to syndicate her show in the afternoon in Columbia. It was a decision that didn't sit well with a lot of people locally. Our PD Chris Connors had been hosting a popular afternoon show that included the very popular "5 O'Clock Mega Mix." It felt like the suits in New York were shitting on us when he ended up getting bounced for Wendy. Wendy was a big star nationally, but the listeners in Columbia raised hell and kept calling in and writing letters to demand Hot bring Chris's show back. Finally Inner City gave in and put Chris back in his old slot, provided Hot would run Wendy's show at night from ten to two.

That compromise unwittingly changed the course of my life.

When Wendy's afternoon show got moved to nights, someone at Hot was supposed to make sure that that day's show was uploaded every evening at ten. Pretty simple, right? For whatever reason, that person was asleep at the wheel and Hot just ended up playing the same show over and over again each night.

When I heard the mistake, I decided to take it upon myself to call up Kevin Hunter, Wendy's husband and manager, who I'd previously met when he and Wendy had done a market visit in Columbia. I got Kevin on the phone and let him know what was going on with the audio. You might say this was another example of me snitching, but the truth is I just assumed the screw-up was coming from Wendy's end. I figured the big stars in New York simply forgot to send the station in Columbia the right audio and alerting them to it would just be a good way to get on their radar. Not to mention, as a fan I wanted to hear what Wendy was up to.

When Kevin found out about the situation, however, he was furious. Wendy's team had indeed been sending out the new audio every day and Kevin suspected that the mix-up hadn't been a simple mistake. Instead, he decided that Chris Connors must have still been salty about having his show bumped and had made sure someone was intentionally sabotaging Wendy's broadcast.

Kev was prepared to raise holy hell with Inner City (not that he ever needed much of an excuse) but decided first he needed to come to Columbia and check out the situation for himself.

When he told me he was headed down, I once again created my own opportunity by offering to pick Kev up at the airport. Then I made it my business to show him around town for the weekend. I got him some weed, took him out to the best clubs, and did everything I could to show him the best the city had to offer. By the end of the weekend, Kev and I had developed a real friendship. Of course Kev ended up screaming on the station after he was able to confirm they'd been running old shows, but he and I were good.

Spending that weekend with Kevin would prove to be a pivotal moment of my life. At that point, I had been at Hot 103.9 for a few years. I'd started off doing just weekends, and then they teamed me up with Bill Black, aka Big Sexy, to host the Hot Boyz show Monday through Friday, 6:00 p.m. to 10:00 p.m. We did the show for about a year until Bill got a job in Atlanta (today he's operations manager at Radio One Cleveland), after which I started hosting the show myself. Despite that success, here's the twist: the whole time I was at Hot, I was never a full-time employee. Even with a daily show, they were still paying me part-time money. So when Bill left and I was hosting the show myself, I figured Hot would finally make me a full-time employee. That meant a salary, benefits, vacations, and all that good shit.

I figured wrong.

Before I explain why, here's a second situation that also changed the course of my career. (I swear I'm going to tie all of this together—keep paying attention.) There was a popular club in Columbia that would advertise on the station. An urban legend spread around town that one of the managers was drugging women and taking advantage of them. Then a young lady came forward to say that, yes, she had been drugged at the club. The cops did some investigating and the manager ended up being arrested.

His arrest didn't get much publicity, but the girl's cousin sent me a link to the Columbia Police Department's website. Being the public servant that I am, I posted the report on my personal Myspace and wrote a little caption suggesting maybe we shouldn't patronize this spot anymore.

The club caught wind of my post and decided to sue both me

and the radio station. I don't know why they brought Hot into it, seeing that I posted the info on my personal MySpace, not the radio station's website. The suit also claimed I defamed the manager by making the arrest public. But I only knew about it from the police website. Didn't that *already* make it public? Their lawsuit was all BS.

Chris Connors, however, asked me to apologize to the club and the manager, which I flat out refused to do. I'm never going to apologize for speaking truth. Frankly, I was insulted that he'd even asked me. "Suppose it had been your daughter," I demanded to know. "Would you be upset at me posting his mug shot then?" Chris replied that if it was his daughter, he would have kicked the dude's ass in the streets, but he wouldn't have messed with the station's money by criticizing a sponsor. I understood where Chris was coming from, but I refused to budge. I wasn't apologizing.

The station ended up settling the suit with the manager of the club for what I heard was only a measly $2,000. I didn't get off so cheaply. My punishment for "criticizing" a sponsor was seeing my six-days-a-week schedule cut down to just Saturdays. Instead of getting put on full-time, I was barely holding on to my part-time status.

Not long after I was demoted, Kevin called to check in on me. When he heard how my shifts had been cut back, he figured it might have had something to do with how he had raised hell during his visit. In his mind, his tantrum had hurt my standing at the station.

I don't know if he was trying to make it up to me, but he told me to come to New York the following week for a party he and Wendy were hosting. A week later, I was up in NYC rubbing shoulders with one of my radio idols. Wendy had a couple of drinks in her and must have been feeling generous. "Charlamagne, why don't you sit in on my show tomorrow," she asked. Now, I'm the kind of guy you can't say stuff like that to unless you really mean it. Wendy might have just said that to be nice, but you can best believe that the next morning I was blowing up Kev's phone. "Kev, Wendy told me I could come on today. What time should I be there?" When I didn't get a response, I refused to let the opportunity slip through my fingers. "Hey, Kev, it's Charlamagne again. What's the address? Lemme know what's good!" Kev finally got back to me with the info and that afternoon I got on the air with Wendy.

Despite only being on the air with her for twenty-five minutes, I must have done pretty well, because that same night Kev took me out to dinner and made me an unexpected offer. "Wendy is looking for a cohost, but she doesn't want a comedian," he told me. "She wants someone funny, but they should be edgy, too, and preferably from the radio world. We think that person could be you." Then he added a caveat. "We can't pay you. But we can offer you a place to stay in Jersey for free while we figure things out to see if it works." The absence of a paycheck might have made a lot of people pause, but I didn't hesitate for a second. "I'm absolutely in," I replied. We shook on it and by the following week, I was unofficially cohosting one of the biggest radio shows in the country.

Landing the spot on Wendy's show is a perfect example of why you should never get caught up worrying about what people might perceive as a "loss." Before meeting Kev, I was a twenty-something-year-old former crack dealer and convicted felon who had already been fired from radio once and was barely holding on by a thread to his current job.

It might have looked like I was taking losses, but I refused to adopt a loser's mentality. A true winner values their integrity no matter what the fallout. If I had compromised my integrity and said sorry, maybe Chris Connors would have put me back on the air five days a week. Then maybe down the road he would have decided I was a good "company man" and given me a full-time position. I would have won security, but I would have lost so much more.

If I had gone the "safe" route, I would have completely screwed up the route God had planned for me. That path might not have looked like a straight line to success. But like I said, God's always got the latest GPS update.

I ended up cohosting Wendy's show from February 2006 to November 2008, a period I consider both the best and worst time of my life. On the plus side, I did learn a hell of a lot about radio from Wendy. She taught me how to properly prep for a show, instead of solely relying on my ability to come in off the street and wing it. That approach had helped me make my mark in South Carolina, but I needed to be better prepared if I wanted to be successful on the national stage. Wendy was meticulously prepared every day, and I saw the value in doing research and having questions ready for every guest, not just the big names or the people I was excited to talk to.

She also taught me the importance of sharing my own experiences on air. You can talk about all the magazines and blogs you've read, or discuss what rappers are dissing each other, but ultimately sharing your own life is what will take you to the next level. Honesty and intimacy is what forges a real connection with the audience. If I had understood that in South Carolina, I wouldn't have been upset when Corey Hill took my features away. I would have still had my greatest asset: my own experiences.

Wendy taught me so much, but sadly we don't speak today. A couple of years back when Elvis Duran (the man I call my radio godfather) brought me up during an interview with her, Wendy said, "Who?" The Internet took that as proof that we were beefing but ultimately, that isn't about anything that happened between us. It's about how Kev and I fell out over business. As for Wendy, she is the ultimate ride-or-die chick. I know she feels she has to have her husband's back and I have to respect that.

Even after I came onboard as Wendy's cohost, I was still doing my Saturday night shift at Hot in Columbia. For a while, that worked out great. I would be with Wendy from Monday to Friday and then fly down to South Carolina for the weekend. I'd do my show, host a couple of parties, make some bread, spend the night with Mook Mook, and then get back to New York by Monday morning. It was a great arrangement for me.

It wasn't meant to last. The first shoe to drop was when Hot 103.9 took issue with me co-hosting Wendy's show. To this day I've never quite understood that. If I was the program director of a station in South Carolina, I would be extremely excited about one of my weekend jocks cohosting a nationally syndicated show during the week. Especially if the jock was constantly shouting out the state and my station, like I had been doing. But the fatass, white devil, Boss Hogg look-alike Steve didn't see it that way. Chris Connors called me up one day and relayed that Steve had said, "Charlamagne can't have his cake and eat it too" (granted, Steve's fat ass would know about eating cake) and that the station needed to "move in another direction." Just like that, I'd been fired for a second time.

The other shoe was about to drop on Wendy's show. For the first year and a half, I was on a fantastic run. I was building up a fan base and advertisers had started requesting that I read their spots. When Wendy's contract got renewed in 2007, I was given a full-time salary of $70K a year. For someone whose sole income had been hosting parties in Columbia for $400 or $500 a pop, it felt like a windfall. Mook Mook had graduated from the University of South Carolina, so we settled into our own place in Jersey. In the summer of 2008 we welcomed our first daughter into the world. The future looked bright.

Then, in the fall of 2008, things got dark. The storm started when Nicole Spence, who was the show's talent booker, sued Wendy, Kev, and WBLS, claiming that Kev had sexually harassed her. In the suit, which made all the papers, Nicole also claimed that she'd seen Kev physically assault Wendy at the station. I was named in the lawsuit, with Nicole claiming that she'd heard Kevin tell me that he wanted me to "break" Nicole's spirit.

Wendy and Kev denied the charges and for a while it looked like both sides might settle. But ultimately the lawsuit tore the show apart. Not only was the publicity damaging, but Wendy was spending more and more time on the TV show she'd landed at FOX. Reeling from bad press and fearing that her heart wasn't in radio anymore, the word around town was that Inner City was looking for a way to get out of their contract with Wendy. So on November 3, Deon Levingston, the GM at WBLS at the time, called me into his office and told me, you guessed it, "We've decided to go in another direction."

I wasn't the only one who got let go from Wendy's show that day: they also fired Nicole, executive producer Tarin Donatien, and production director Trev Hollywood. When the bloodbath was over, the only people left were basically Wendy and a board op. It was clear that if Wendy wasn't going to leave on her own, they would try to starve her out. Still she took to the air the next day to say that things were still cool between the two of us. "[Charlamagne's] gone; he's not forgotten," she told her audience. "He is still part of la familia. That is still my boy. He still sleeps in the purple room when he comes to the house. We still drink our Patrón on Friday nights."

I appreciated Wendy's public love and support, but the stakes were higher after this firing. I wasn't just worried about the impact it would have on my career—this time I had a young daughter to think about.

The day after I was fired from Wendy's show, Barack Obama became the first African-American to be elected president of the United States. Any disappointment I felt over the Wendy situation was temporarily overshadowed by the pride of seeing a black man headed to the White House.

Once the excitement over President Obama's election had worn off, I had to confront the realities of being a father who could no longer provide for his family. Mook Mook and I had been living in Lyndhurst, New Jersey, where we'd put our daughter in day care. Without my check from Wendy, that wasn't affordable any longer. I could have signed up for unemployment in NYC, but my pride just wouldn't let me do it. I was an able-bodied young man. The idea of taking a handout from the government just didn't sit right with me. Plus, I could only imagine what people would say if a picture leaked of me standing in line at the unemployment office. The jokes would never end.

So I decided to keep my black ass home and watch our daughter while Mook Mook went to work every day for a blood lab in Manhattan. Now, for a lot of men, that situation would be the very definition of a loss. Going from a high-profile job to running a daddy day care while his woman goes out and brings home the turkey bacon. Not me. I consider those days to be one of the high-lights of my life. The reason is simple: it helped me build a lasting bond with my daughter.

I'll be honest, I hadn't been off to the best start in the daddy department. Literally the day after my daughter was born I caught a flight to Minnesota, where I was presented with an award for being one of the Top 30 under 30 in radio. It felt like a very big deal at the time—alongside my guy David "Tazz Daddy" Ander-son, I was one of only three black honorees that year—but in ret-rospect it paled in comparison to being there for Mook Mook and our daughter after the delivery. Plus, when I did come back from Minnesota, things were starting to get very hectic around Wendy's show. My professional life was becoming a blur and I wasn't home nearly as much as I should have been.

If I hadn't been fired, I might have never embraced being a father the way I was forced to through staying home with my daughter. To this day we're incredibly close and I attribute that largely to the time I spent with her in Lyndhurst. I fed her; I read to her; I changed her diapers, took her for walks, put her down for naps—for eight hours a day I did *everything* for my daughter.

This period in my life is a prime example of the principle that returning to your core doesn't always have to entail taking a physi-cal trip. Very few things will center you and recharge your spirit like caring for your child. The best thing that happened to me was that instead of rushing into another radio job, I was able to press reset through staying at home with my daughter and get my mind and spirit together. In retrospect, getting fired from Wendy's show was exactly the misdirection God wanted for my personal development.

Of course, providing for a child is tough when the funds aren't coming in, and we went through a period of what I would call "light" struggle. Even with me covering the childcare costs, it's still very difficult for a family to make it in metro New York City on just one income, especially a worker at a blood center's salary. After a few months we fell behind on rent and then the eviction notices started arriving. Since it was Mook Mook's name on the lease, she had to go to court and explain our situation to a judge. She's as prideful as I am, and it was very difficult for her to stand there and have to beg for a second chance. I hated seeing her in that position.

Even still, I didn't ask anyone for help. I could have probably hit up Wendy and Kevin for a loan, but I was determined to make my own way out of the situation. I was convinced that everything would work out for one simple reason: I had done what I was supposed to do on Wendy's show. I'd been blessed with an opportunity in a major market and I'd capitalized on it. I'd been funny, I'd been part of memorable interviews and I'd built relationships with listeners. Yes, I'd been fired, but only because I'd gotten caught up in something that was larger than me. I wasn't fired because listeners thought I was boring, or I was difficult to work with or even because I'd said something too controversial. I knew it wouldn't be a matter of *if* things worked out for me, but a matter of *when*. I was supremely confident, even in the face of unemployment, dirty diapers, and eviction notices that I was going to be able to write my own ticket again.

I just didn't know where it would take me.

Philadelphia Freedom?

The answer came in the spring of 2009, when I was approached by Elroy Smith, MoShay LaRen, and Johnny Glover about joining 100.3 The Beat in Philadelphia. The folks there liked what I'd done on Wendy's show (it turned out they didn't even know I'd had my own show in South Carolina) and wanted to give me a shot. So in May of 2009, I launched *Charlamagne Tha God and the Morning Beat*.

My show started off as stripped-down as it could get—no producer, no cohost, no sidekick. Just me and a board op. After a few weeks I was allowed to hire a producer, so I reached out to my homie Sasha Keady, who had been at WBLS with me. She was young, smart, and ambitious, and I was able to convince her to come work with me in Philly. I was still living in Lyndhurst at the time and Sasha lived in the north Jersey city of Elizabeth, so every day we would drive back and forth to Philly. It was about eighty minutes each way and we made that commute for several months. (For that reason, and that reason alone, I will always be grateful to Sasha and be there for her when she needs me. She'd later join me on *The Breakfast Club* as an associate producer, where she worked for five years before recently landing at Apple.)

The Beat might not have given me a lot of resources, but I connected almost immediately with the Philly audience. After a few months I was ranked number three with eighteen- to thirty-four-year-olds, which was the demographic the station was catering to.

It helped that I had a few interviews break nationally. These were the days when the Internet and social media were just coming into their own and people would jump all over an interview that had some action in it. One was with Cassie, a singer who didn't have much of a voice but had been given a recording contract largely on the strength of her looks and the fact that she was dating Diddy. Cassie was a sweet girl who happened to come on my show during a very bad week for her. Her nude pics had just leaked and she'd also delivered a terrible performance on BET's *106 & Park* when that was the show that everyone watched. Being a man of the people, it was my duty to point these issues out. I had to tell her she was living in a Rihanna/Beyoncé world and there would never be a spot in it for her. (Trust me, it was a very entertaining interview. It's on YouTube right now for your listening pleasure.)

Philly is also where the Donkey of the Day feature was born. I had been calling people donkeys since Wendy's show after I heard 50 Cent say, "Look at these donkeys! Bunch of fucking jackasses" on a G-Unit mixtape. There was something about how he said it that made me think it was the funniest thing I'd ever heard. I started using the phrase, too, and by the time I got to Philly I decided I needed to create a daily feature that gave folks the credit they deserve for being stupid. "Donkey of the Day" was born.

Not everything I did on the air was ratchet—I did some righteous work, too. One day I received a call from Rasheena Phinisee, the mother of a young girl named Assiah who needed a liver transplant. Rasheena felt she was getting the runaround from a hospital, so I let her come on and give the hospital's administration Donkey of the Day. It worked! Assiah got the transplant and today she is a happy, healthy little girl. Sure, I could have gotten sued by that hospital the same way I got sued by the nightclub back in Columbia, but I didn't care. I have no problem speaking up for what's right because I know that God will bless me for it in the long run.

Philly was good to me and I felt like I'd found a home. I was so confident Philly was going to be a long-term stop that Mook Mook and I decided the time was right to rent a town house in Cherry Hill, New Jersey, which is right across the Delaware River from Philly. The rent was more than we'd ever paid, but it would have cut my commute by more than half and allowed me to spend more time with the family, so it seemed like it would be money well spent.

Then, one morning in October 2009, I woke up to find Twitter buzzing about a new Beanie Sigel song that dissed his former mentor Jay Z. Being that Beanie was from Philly, it seemed only right that I get him on the radio to explain himself. So I reached out to a mutual friend and she arranged for Beanie to call into my show that very day.

When I got Beanie on the air, he was very forthright about why he was upset with Jay. He claimed Jay distanced himself from the Philly rappers he'd signed to Roc-A-Fella because they were Muslim and Jay's Jewish backers didn't like that affiliation. It was the type of conversation most radio hosts wouldn't touch without wearing surgical gloves, but being a man of the people, I felt I had no choice but to air the allegation if that's how Beanie felt.

The interview went viral and a reporter asked Jay Z about what Beanie had told me that weekend. Jay responded with the quote "Never has an artist done so much with so little," meaning that Beanie hadn't sold many albums in his career but Jay had still managed to set him up with a clothing line, sneaker deal, and his own record label. As Jay saw it, he'd set his protégé up to win, but Beanie (who'd had several run-ins with the law) just couldn't stay out of trouble long enough to take advantage of the opportunities.

The Beanie interview originally aired on a Thursday and I played it again during my shift on Friday. Thanks to Jay Z's comments it was also the top hip-hop story over that weekend, so of course we had to address it again during my show on Monday. I didn't anticipate any negative fallout, but after the shift was over, my program director Boogie D asked me to come into his office. I thought if anything he'd give me props for creating a national buzz, but instead he chastised me for running the Beanie interview in the first place. "Why would you want to make an enemy out of Jay?" he asked. "I'm not trying to make any enemy out of anyone," I explained. "I'm just trying to put good content on the air." Obviously there was no right answer for me to give, so he got to the point: "Sorry, but we're moving in another direction. We're going to have to let you go."

For those keeping score at home, that's Radio Industry: 4, Charlamagne: 0.

I can't lie, the Philly firing me caught me off guard. But as soon as those all-too-familiar words were out of Boogie's lips, I was already mentally moving on. I didn't argue the decision or beg for my job. Instead, I told Boogie, "Thank you for the opportunity," and walked with him to my office, where he had to make sure I didn't grab anything valuable on my way out. He had nothing to worry about. I just picked up my Wayne Dyer "Power of Intention" cards and headed toward the door. "You ain't got anything else in here?" Boogie asked. "Nope," I replied. "Because I'm always prepared for situations like this." That remains a tradition of mine—I don't keep any personal items in my office. Because you just never know.

As soon as I was out of the station, I jumped on Twitter to tell my audience what had gone down. *I just got fired from 100.3 The Beat in Philly,* I tweeted. *Salute to Philly. I hope you all enjoyed me the past 6 months.*

I made the announcement myself because I didn't have anything to be ashamed of. I truly did not give a shit about getting fired, because I knew I had done everything I was supposed to do while I was in Philly. I'd created great content. I'd used my platform to help people. And I'd conducted engaging interviews and asked the tough questions that it was my job to ask, no matter what the politics were. Whatever the reason they wanted to let me go, I knew it was only a temporary setback.

The Internet, however, wasn't ready to let things go so easily. Almost immediately rumors began flying that I'd been canned because my interview with Beanie had pissed off Jay Z. "Did Jay Z have Charlemagne* the God fired?" asked a headline from XXL.com; while TheYBF.com claimed, "Source Confirms Charlamagne Fired Over Beanie Sigel Interview." The story created so much buzz that I started trending on Twitter for the first time in my career. I might have been fired, but I was infamous.

To this day, I still don't know if Jay was behind the move. Recently *New York* magazine ran a profile on me that mentioned the rumor. Jay read the story and then texted me to ask, *Yo, did I really get you fired?* I don't think he was playing dumb. I've always found Jay to be one of the most down-to-earth and forthright dudes in the industry. If he had decided he wanted me fired, he would have let me know. I suspect it was a situation where Jay didn't push for it himself. Maybe someone on his label made a comment and the station ran with it. Or perhaps the station was moving proactively because they were worried about getting on Jay's bad side. No matter what really happened, I'm more than happy to have "the greatest rapper alive got me fired" on my résumé. Having people think, rightly or wrongly, that your interview made Jay Z pick up the phone is not a loss. Plus, since that moment I've always told people I knew it would read well in a book.

There is no better than adversity. Every defeat, every heartbreak, every loss, contains its own seed, its own lesson on how to improve your performance the next time.

—Malcolm X

---

*Yes, they misspelled my name, as most magazines seem to.

And just in case you think I'm looking back at the past through rose-colored glasses, consider this interview I did with my friend the culture vulture DJ Vlad literally the day after I got fired from Philly:

Vlad: Yesterday on Twitter, we got some shocking news. That you actually yourself broke.

Me: Yeah, I put out on Twitter that I got fired from The Beat in Philly. It wasn't nothing for me to break the news. My life is an open book. It's nothing for me to share something like that. . . . On to the next one. . . . I know what type of personality I have. I have politically incorrect views and potentially dangerous rhetoric. So when you're someone like me, there's always a chance you can get fired.

Vlad: What's the next move?

Me: Charlamagne's going to do what Charlamagne does. . . . You know, radio will be here in one hot second. There will be another station calling in one hot second. . . . They didn't cut my tongue out. I didn't lose my voice. I'm still good. You still going to hear from Charlamagne. . . . You gotta roll the dice. With great risk comes great reward. Wendy told me some real shit once. When Puffy allegedly got her fired from Hot 97 back in the day she told me that was the best thing that ever happened to her brand. So history has a strange way of repeating itself, doesn't it?"

The confidence I projected while talking to Vlad wasn't fake, but firing number four was still the toughest for me to handle. Not because I was concerned about how it would impact my career but again because of how it might affect my family. As I said, Mook Mook and I had signed a lease on a town house in Cherry Hill near Philadelphia. In anticipation of the move, she'd given her job two weeks' notice and sent our daughter down to Moncks Corner to stay with our parents while we packed up our stuff. The day I was fired, I literally had all our possessions in my Cadillac Escalade to take to Cherry Hill. Thankfully the owners of the town house gave us our deposit back and let us out of our lease, but that also meant we had nowhere to live.

Instead of moving into our new town house, we headed to Mook Mook's grandmother's apartment in the housing projects in Coney Island, Brooklyn. We crashed there for two weeks while I tried to figure out what I was going to do next. Half the time I was determined to ride it out in New York until the next opportunity presented itself. The other half I was telling myself, "I can't raise a child in New York. I'm not a city kid and I don't want my daughter to be one either." Every day I'd see the pros and cons of each path. My mind was all over the place.

Then one morning I woke up next to my girl and had a moment of clarity: I knew that I couldn't make any smart decisions where I was *at*; I need to make those decisions back where I was *from*. It was almost the inverse of those old Rakim lyrics. I needed to reconnect with my core before I could make the right decision about my future. And my core was Moncks Corner.

Still, the idea of moving my family back into my mother's house at thirty years old was a bit worrisome. Then I had a very powerful conversation with my close friend Kendra Gilliam, aka Kendra G, who was another jock on The Beat in Philly. It was truly one of the best pep talks I ever received. "Charlamagne, just enjoy your time in South Carolina," Kendra told me reassuringly. "Hit the reset button, because you've been going hard for years and you need this time with your family. And when the next opportunity comes, it's going to be a big one. And then family time is going to be hard to come by."

Encouraged by her words, I jumped into my Escalade with over 200K miles on it. My girl got in her 2003 Honda Civic, and together we made the thirteen-hour ride back to South Carolina. I hadn't lived in the state in almost four years, but it wouldn't be long before I'd be reminded that in the eyes of some, I'd fallen off. I remember not long after coming home I got into an argument with my little sister Ashley. "Look at you, you used to be with Wendy and had a radio show in Philly," she gloated. "Now you back living at home with Mama." It was intended to be a low blow, but what she failed to mention is that while I was moving *back* in with our mother, my sister at that time had never even *left*. "This is temporary for me," I reminded her. "But it's permanent for you." I know that's a harsh thing to say to your sister, but I like to think those words had a positive impact on her as well. Because after that she did move out of my mama's house and is currently living in Atlanta—with our sister. She's trying to better herself.

There were more than a few folk in Moncks Corner who probably took perverse pleasure in my less-than-triumphant return. Still, I wasn't going to walk around hanging my head. Instead, I savored and enjoyed every moment with my family, like Kendra told me to do. Unlike in New York, I had no problem walking into the Berkeley County unemployment office and picking up my checks. I hadn't collected anything the other times I'd been fired, so I ended up getting around $1,300 every two weeks. Not much to live off of in New York, but in Moncks Corner that's BALLING!

Without having to worry about rent or childcare, we were actually able to save up a little bit of money. I used that to take occasional trips back to New York to stay relevant. I would make appearances on Angela Yee's Sirius XM show *Lip Service*, or tape episodes of *Hood State of the Union*, a Web series I'd created with my good friend, the comedian Lil Duval.

Angela Yee played a major role in my life, even before *The Breakfast Club*. If Angela knew I had an issue with a certain artist and they were going to be on *Lip Service*, she'd give me the heads-up and let me call in. One time she let me go at the rapper Mims and I destroyed him. It was great radio. Another time Angela called me, a gay dude named Glitter Dick put out a video saying he was my boyfriend. We had fun going at each other and it turned into another great moment. Those moments kept me on the public's radar.

Angela, Lil Duval, and I also did a pilot for a hip-hop version of *First Take*. Terrence J was going to executive produce it, but BET never aired it. Terrence did tell me something I've always remembered, though. "Y'all three should do a radio show." It rang true to me, so I, in turn, told Angela, "One day you and I will do mornings on Power 105.1 in New York." I swear I said that verbatim. Angela was skeptical though. "How?" she asked. "You're not even on the radio and I've only done satellite. Plus, they'll never fire Ed Lover," she said, referring to the radio legend who was Power's morning show host at the time. "I don't know how it'll happen," I replied. "I just know it's going to happen." Today, I believe I spoke our current situation into fruition during that conversation with Angela.

I might not have been on the radio, but stations were still interested in me. Every few weeks I got offered a new gig, but the market or the situation never felt quite right. I could tell the program directors were shocked when I'd tell them "No, thanks." After all, I was living back in South Carolina and collecting unemployment.

Who was I to be choosy? But I was supremely confident that God was about to give me something greater than what those stations could offer.

The Hand That Feeds . . .

Before we get to the next stop God had planned for me, I want to take a look at one final situation that on the surface seemed to be a loss, but on deeper inspection actually helped set up one of my biggest wins.

When I became Wendy Williams's sidekick, I had two main goals: (1) Be the best I could be on her show, which I knew would set up the rest of my career, and (2) Put South Carolina's hip-hop scene on the map.

As much as I loved seeing the way the state had helped set up the careers of artists like T.I. and Jeezy, I also wanted to see local artists achieve the same level of success. To that end, in 2008 I hooked up with Lightyear/EMI to put out a compilation called *South Crack*, featuring artists from Charleston, Columbia, and, of course, Moncks Corner. The album didn't sell many copies, and since the deal called for me to pay for all the marketing, production, and publicity costs, I didn't make a dime off the project. But it did help create a buzz for several artists.

In 2009 I met Swizz Beatz at the video shoot for Maino's "Hi Hater." I was blown away when Swizz told me he loved what I was doing on Wendy's show—he had made the beats for so many songs that had been the soundtrack to my life. I couldn't really believe he appreciated what I was doing on the radio.

At the end of the conversation, Swizz told me, "Yo, if I can help with anything you got going on let me know." I didn't have to think hard about taking Swizz up on his offer. If someone offers me an opportunity, they're not going to have to tell me twice. "Well, I got this album I just put out and I'm really trying to get one of these guys signed to a major," I quickly told Swizz, while handing him one of the copies I always kept on me for situations just like that one.

God Jewel: When someone offers to help you, tell them exactly what you want. Don't beat around the bush. If you're not crystal clear about what your ask is, chances are you won't get anything.

When I followed up with Swizz a week or so later to see what he thought, he told me he hadn't had a chance to listen yet but added, "Just tell me the one artist you've got on there that's the most poppin'. And I'll take you to whatever label you want to."

It was an incredible offer. Having Swizz Beatz walk you into the label of your choice is like getting a hip-hop version of Willie Wonka's golden ticket. I wanted to make the right choice, so I hit up DJ Frosty to ask his opinion and without hesitation he said, "Lil' Ru." A lot of people thought Ru had an energy like Mystikal's, so it was a smart choice. "Yo, I like this kid's tone," Swizz replied after I sent him Ru's "Nasty Song." "Get him up here."

Ru flew up and spent a few days in the studio with Swizz, where they collaborated on four tracks. Swizz was one of the hottest producers in the game, but he still blocked off time in his schedule for Ru. After they recorded those four songs, it was time for us to decide on a label. I wanted to go with Asylum, since they were having tremendous success with Southern artists like Mike Jones,

Paul Wall, Boosie, Webbie, Gucci Mane, Waka Flocka, OJ Da Juiceman, and Shawty Lo. Swizz agreed with me, so he set up a meeting with Joey IE, the industry legend who was running the label at the time, and his right-hand man, J Grand.

The meeting included myself, Ru, Swizz, Jonathan Stevens, who was Ru's manager at the time, and Kevin Hunter, who was acting as my business partner. After we played them the tracks Swizz had produced, Asylum was all in. J Grand's idea was to release Ru's album under Shotty Records, an imprint he'd just set up, and everyone agreed that was a great look. The final deal was that 50 percent of the money would be split between my company, Stupid Dope Moves Inc., and Lil' Ru's company, Presidential, with the other 50 percent going to Shotty/Asylum. Swizz didn't even ask for a cut, even though he'd made the music and set up the meeting. He was just happy to give a new artist a shot.

On the way out of the meeting, Swizz pulled me aside and asked me a question I've always remembered. "Is Ru your man?" he asked. "Yeah, that's my guy," I replied. "Good," said Swizz. "But make sure all your business is straight anyway. I've done this a hundred times, and trust me, once money gets involved people tend to flip. Whether they're your man or not."

Before the paperwork was even done, we managed to get several important DJs to play "Nasty Song." Probably the most important was DJ Envy, who was one of the hottest DJs in the country on NYC's Hot 97. Envy agreed to meet Kevin and me for lunch, where we played him "Nasty Song." Envy recognized Ru's talent right away and promised to play the song, without asking for anything in return. I know we live in the payola age, but I promise you neither Envy nor any of the other respectable DJs we approached asked for a cent. It was a hot tune and they were happy to help out a new artist and an underrepresented region on the map.

Due to the hype we'd created around "Nasty Song," other labels began looking to sign Ru too. One day Jonathan and Ru called me out of the blue and said, "Charlamagne, we know we have a deal with Asylum, but we want to sign with Def Jam instead." "No, we already agreed to a deal with Asylum," I replied. "You don't want to mess with that! Trust me, it's the best look for you." Ru and Jonathan thought they could do better. Bless their hearts; those guys are country. I was country too, but they were on another level—like "match your car with your sneakers" or "get all your real teeth removed and replace them with gold" country. And they'd been overly impressed by Def Jam's star power.

"Go on Def Jam's website," Ru told me. "They got people like Jay Z, Rihanna, Kanye, Jeezy, and Rick Ross. That's where I finna be." "That's cool," I told Ru. "But now go on their site and look at the other sixty artists that they've signed that you've never heard of. That's what's going to happen to you if you sign with Def Jam." Ru still wasn't convinced, so I got him and Jonathan back on the phone with J Grand, who patiently went over the pros and cons of signing with Asylum. It seemed like he got through to them and I figured the matter was resolved.

The next week I was listening to Hot 97 and Envy played "Nasty Song." *My dog!* I texted Ru. *Envy's got "Nasty" on Hot 97 right now!!!*

Fuck You!!! You got me fucked up, Ru texted me right back. *It's on site when I see you. U got people thinking we in business together, ruining my life. Now I can't even do the deal with Def Jam because of you.*

When I saw that text, I was devastated. I literally had to sit down and collect myself. "Damn, all I did was help," I thought. "I gave this kid the shot of a lifetime and now it's 'fuck you!'?"

A few weeks later Ru signed with Def Jam and, as Swizz had warned me, the paperwork became a nightmare. Though he never mentioned it to us, it turned out Ru had already signed a deal with a production company in Atlanta. I became convinced Ru was a "contract whore," someone who would sign his name to anything without wanting to honor it down the road. Despite the complications, my attorney at the time, Jill Ramsey, negotiated a deal with Def Jam for $150K. Lil' Ru got $80K, then the company in Atlanta got $40K. That left $30K for myself, DJ Frosty, and Kevin Hunter to split. So when it was all said and done I only made $10K on the deal. Don't get me wrong, that was still the biggest check I'd ever received. Yet for some reason, to this day I hear Ru still tells people I stole $70K from him, which is complete bullshit.

More so than the accusations and the money, what hurt me the most was the missed opportunity. The Def Jam album bombed—only fourteen hundred people bought it its first week in stores, making it likely you've never heard of Ru until this book. I'm still convinced it would have been different if he'd kept his word and signed to Asylum. That misstep truly broke my heart. I used to get anxiety attacks just thinking about it, to the point where I had to go see a doctor. Putting South Carolina on the map meant that much to me and I knew (correctly, as it turned out) that it might be a long time before another opportunity that perfect came around again for another local artist. Oh, by the way, it still hasn't.

Still, as with all my so-called losses, I took several lessons from the situation. The greatest was that you can never—even if the situation blows up in your face—hurt yourself by helping others. Swizz showed me that no matter how big you are, you can always help the next person. If they don't capitalize on your assistance, that's on them. But never let it affect your willingness to give of yourself. As Swizz told me, he saw the situation between Ru and myself play out hundreds of times before. He probably pulled my coat because he saw what was coming down the road. But it still didn't stop him from setting up that meeting, or making those beats for Ru. That's just the type of individual Swizz is.

The same with Envy. You know how many people ask him to play their record every day? Today we're partners on the biggest hip-hop radio show in the country, *The Breakfast Club*, but Envy didn't know me from Adam back then. He didn't have to help me. But Envy is a giver. So when you go on Instagram and see his big mansion, fleet of fancy cars, and, most important, his beautiful family, know that's how he got to where he is today. Just like Swizz. They got all that through giving.

Good givers are great getters.

—Russell Simmons

In life there's no losses (even the ones that give you anxiety attacks), only lessons. That's because you live and you learn.

Put the Weed in the Bag!

Success is a process: there are no cheat codes, no life hacks, no shortcuts, and no half steps. Opportunity always comes before money, but sadly a lot of us don't recognize it unless there's a paycheck attached. Don't make that mistake. When you're just starting out, put yourself in the position to be a part of the process, and THEN get that money!!

Despite all the drama surrounding Ru signing with Def Jam, my relationship with J Grand and Joey IE remained strong. I stayed in touch with them throughout the rest of my run with Wendy, my time in Philly, and even after I went back to Moncks Corner. I wasn't on the radio then and couldn't "do anything" for them, but they would always reply to my e-mails and welcome me into the Asylum offices when I was in town.

I've never forgotten that. If you want to see a person's true character, watch how they treat people who seemingly can't help them. I've seen so many folks lose my number or stop returning my e-mails after I get fired. In the words of 50 Cent, "These industry niggas ain't friends, they know how to pretend."

Because Joey wasn't one of those fake industry guys, during one of my visits to New York he linked me up with Geespin, the legendary DJ who was then the music director at Power 105.1 as well as a DJ on Boston's JAM'N 94.5. A few weeks later, Kevin Hunter and I were able to get a meeting with him at Power to see if there would be any interest in me coming there. I thought the sit-down went well, but Power never followed up with anything firm. So I headed back to Moncks Corner and waited for the right opportunity to present itself.

I knew I had the talent to succeed in New York. But the longer the phone didn't ring with an offer from a New York station, the more I started questioning my value. Had I overestimated my worth? Should I take a job in the Carolinas so I could at least start providing for my family again? Get back to being on the air?

One night I decided to take a walk down the dirt road by my mom's house. As I breathed in the clean country air, I said a prayer, like I always do. Simply asking God for direction. After a few minutes, any worries or insecurities I had been experiencing faded from my thoughts. I felt completely at peace. And then out of nowhere a voice commanded: "Go to New York on Monday! Go!"

I didn't have a "reason" to go, but there was no disobeying this command. If Saul had had his epiphany on the road to Damascus, then I'd had mine on the dirt road in Moncks Corner. If New York was where I wanted to be, then I had to stop waiting on an invitation and take myself to the action.

God Jewel: Always follow your instincts, because your instincts are God's voice telling you what to do. And you better listen closely, because God doesn't repeat himself and God isn't loud. Whenever you hear that faint whisper in your head telling you what direction to move in, that's where you want to go.

That Monday I flew to New York and decided to pay a visit to Mike Kyser of Atlantic Records. Mike is one of my all-time favorite people in the game, one of those guys who will always treat you right, no matter what position you are in at a given moment. You might not have ever heard of Mike (you've probably seen him though—when Jay Z used to have courtside seats for the Nets, Mike was the tall dark-skinned guy who looks like John Salley always sitting next to Jay), but he's one of the most plugged-in people in the entire industry. He knows about almost every deal before it happens and has helped shape more of them than the world will probably ever know.

When I got to Mike's office, he quickly filled me in on some of the rumblings that were going on. "You know what Power is planning, right?" Mike asked me. "Nope, not really," I answered truthfully. Yes, I knew I was in the mix, but like I said, we'd been treading water for months. "They're talking about putting together a new morning show. And they've been kicking your name around," Mike said. "Word, that would be dope," I replied, knowing that if Mike was talking about it, it was probably more than just a rumor.

Sure enough, not more than a day after talking to Mike, Power's program director Cadillac Jack hit me up and asked if I wanted to grab lunch. We went out and ended up talking for several hours. It was an amazing conversation, as much about life as about radio. As we headed back to the station, we randomly bumped into a woman named Tia, who used to be an intern on Wendy's show. "Oh my god, Charlamagne, it's so great to see you!" she exclaimed upon seeing me. "When are you going to get back on the air? You were too good on Wendy's show. Radio needs you!" It couldn't have been scripted any better. When Tia left, Caddy turned to me and said, "That just doesn't happen. I walk the streets all the time with jocks who are on the air and nobody runs up to them with that sort of excitement."

I don't know if there had been any hesitation on Caddy's part before that lunch, but I left feeling like there was no doubt I was going to be working at Power in some capacity. Sure enough, a few weeks later my contract came through and I found myself part of the station's all-new morning show *The Breakfast Club*.

It had been thirteen years since I'd started as an unpaid intern at Jamz back in Charleston and now I was finally where I'd always wanted to be: cohosting my own show in New York City.

Spending a year in Moncks Corner waiting for the right opportunity had been hard, but in the end it had proven to be the right choice. If I had been able to draw up my own dream job, I couldn't have picked a better situation than *The Breakfast Club*. My cohosts on the show were going to be my friends DJ Envy and Angela Yee, who both had the perfect combination of experience and humility to succeed as cohosts. Envy had been Miss Jones's cohost on New York's Hot 97, and Angela had been Cipha Sounds' cohost on Shade 45. Add on that I was Wendy's cohost, and you end up with a team that knew how to play their positions. I knew that meant we wouldn't get sidetracked by the needless bickering that brings down a lot of shows. Plus, with iHeartMedia, we'd be working for the most powerful radio network in the country and have access to all their incredible talent and resources. It also meant I'd get to learn at the feet of two of the most influential people in radio: Doc Wynter, iHeart's longtime head of Urban Radio, and iHeart's CEO Bob Pittman.

Most important, the show would give me a whole new level of exposure. Despite my stint with Wendy, many folks across the country didn't have a real sense of who I was until I joined *The Breakfast Club*. It might have seemed like I was an overnight success, but you and I, faithful reader, know better. There were so many baby steps I had to take, so many setbacks I had to endure and obstacles I had to overcome until I finally made the leap into *The Breakfast Club*.

Too often we're given bad advice on what it takes to get from where we are to where we want to be. We're taught that the only accurate sign that we're moving toward success is making money. We get caught up sweating the results instead of embracing the process. Even though embracing the process is the *only* way you're ever going to get what you want out of life.

There are a lot of gems in the iconic hip-hop flick *Belly*, but perhaps my favorite one is when DMX's character "Tommy Buns" says:

"Learn how to put da weed in the bag first. . . . Then get money!"

Let me put that quote in context. DMX was speaking to a couple of young hustlers—Wise and LaKid—who hadn't even sold their first nickel bag of weed yet but were already talking about getting big-time coke money. Tommy Buns was telling them to slow down and focus on the work in front of them, no matter how small the job might seem, instead of immediately looking forward to the big scores. If they couldn't even put the weed in the bag first, how were they going to go out and become major players?

Belly might have been detailing the drug game, but "put the weed in the bag first" applies to every industry and profession. Whether you want to be a DJ, a lawyer, an engineer, a doctor, a musician, or an investment banker, there are no cheat codes, no life hacks or shortcuts to success. You have to embrace the process before you can reap the rewards. You're always going to have to put the weed in the bag first.

Working for Free

One of the first steps in embracing the process, especially when you're just starting out in your career, is accepting that you might have to work for damn near nothing. Maybe even for free. I realize that might sound like strange advice to find in a book from a hip-hop personality. After all, "Get money!" is pretty much the culture's mantra. From songs to videos to interviews, almost every rapper or hip-hop personality you hear from is going to tell you, "If it don't make dollars, it don't make sense."

Not me.

In fact, I'm here to tell you just the opposite. Often the smartest moves you make will be the ones that don't make you a pretty penny—at least at first.

I believe the first rule of the game should always be "Get your foot in the door by any means possible." If you demand a check, that door might only open a crack, if that. If you're willing to work for free, however, that door is going to open up, often wide enough for you to stride right in.

Working for free is usually seen as something only rich kids can afford to do. You know, those kids from fancy colleges who can take an unpaid internship at *Vice* or *Buzzfeed* because their parents are already paying the rent and giving them spending money. That might often be the case, but it doesn't mean that you need rich parents to work for free. Trust me, my pops didn't have any trust fund set up for me when I got my foot in the door with that unpaid internship at Jamz. Throughout the whole process of trying to establish myself as a radio personality, I was always hurting for money. Some times were better than others, but I never felt comfortable. Even then, I never let wanting to get paid get in the way of a good opportunity.

I was able to capitalize on the opportunity at Z93 Jamz by hustling my ass off at all sorts of menial jobs. I would take ANY job during the day as it meant being able to hang out at the station at night. Later, when Jamz was only paying me $19K a year, or when Hot in Columbia only put me on one day a week, I'd happily throw parties to make ends meet.

The most important time I didn't let money, or the lack thereof, get in the way of a golden opportunity is when I agreed to work for Wendy for free. Yes, I am making money hand over fist today, but that's only because I didn't have my hand out when Kev made me that offer over dinner.

When Kev casually threw in "but we can't pay you," that would have been the end of the conversation for a lot of folks. They would have said, "You guys are making millions? But I'm supposed to work for free? Get the fuck outta here." And according to conventional wisdom, I should have said the same thing. It's not like I was a novice at that point. I'd been on the air for several years and was hosting my own successful show in Columbia. How are you going to tell someone who already has a track record of getting paid, even if it's only ten dollars an hour, that they should start working for free?

Yet I ended up spending a year and a half working for Wendy for free. I didn't earn a dime from the show during that period. But I don't feel like I wasted a single second. In my mind I wasn't doing anything all those months but putting the weed in the bag. Without complaint. Every day I was bagging up my personality, my humor, and my POV and delivering it to the listeners. Over time the listeners (not to mention program directors) would smoke those proverbial bags and say, "Man, Charlamagne's got some good shit!" I knew once they said that, I was set. The radio game is no different from the crack game. Once the streets knew my bags had that boom, I was on my way.

What concerns me is how few kids nowadays seem to recognize opportunity if there isn't a paycheck attached to it. Not only do they want a check, but they often want ownership in what they're working on too. They'll hustle for a few months and immediately they want to start talking about "equity." I think they've all watched the *Facebook* movie too many times when they should have been watching *Belly*. Equity? Even though you're twenty-five years old and you didn't put up any money? Equity? Man, shut the hell up and put some more of that weed into a bag!

Can you imagine if after working Wendy's show for six months, I had come to Kev and told him I needed some "equity" in the show? "Well, you know, Kev, I've been putting a lot of time into this show. It's really become a big part of my life, there's a lot of other stuff I haven't been working on because I'm so tied up in this. So I think it'd be fair if you gave me sort of ownership stake. . . ." Man, Kev would have done me the way Uncle Phil used to do Jazzy Jeff on Fresh Prince: thrown me right out of the building! And rightfully so.

This is what many kids today fail to understand: you're *supposed* to be busting your ass for "nothing" when you're in your twenties. And sometimes even your thirties. That doesn't mean you're being exploited. It means you're building up the skills, connections, and reputation to eventually build a platform of your own.

Once you build your own platform, that's when you'll get the equity. Remember, Mark Zuckerberg didn't get all that equity in Facebook just because he worked hard. Half the world is working hard. He got it because he was a once-in-a-lifetime talent who came up with a completely unique idea. Unless you've got that same sort of talent, or have a truly unique idea, you don't own anything but your effort. Which is why I'll say it one more time: you better shut up and put the weed in the bag!

Take Advantage of Internships

Speaking of working for free, never forget that a lot of successful players in hip-hop culture started as interns. Puffy started as Andre Harrell's intern at Uptown Records. Kevin Liles was Lyor Cohen's intern at Def Jam. Angie Martinez started in radio as an intern at Hot 97 in New York City. Big Tigger got his first break as an intern at WPGC in DC.

It's no different outside of hip-hop: Xerox CEO Ursula Burns, the only female African-American CEO of a Fortune 500 company, got her start there as an intern. Steven Spielberg was an intern at Universal Studios. Steve Jobs got his first break as an intern at Hewlett-Packard. The list goes on and on. There's literally no limit on how far an internship can take you.

Second, radio is one of the most intern-friendly industries out there. Even the smallest stations have interns year-round. In the fifteen years I've been in radio, I've worked with hundreds of interns.

One of my all-time favorites was a Haitian girl named Sasha who used to intern with us at Power. Sasha's job was supposed to be helping us answer the phones, but she took it upon herself to start writing out questions for me whenever we had an interview. Not only did she come up with thoughtful and insightful questions, but she managed to write them in a voice that sounded exactly like my own. Once I told her how much she had my voice down and she just humbly replied, "Yeah, I guess I've been listening to you a long time." Even after her internship ended, she'd still send me questions. She wasn't getting paid to do that, or even getting school credit anymore, but she never stopped supporting me any way she could.

She showed love because she was a friend, but she also saw the value of putting in the work in order to keep our professional relationship strong. I never forgot her support and kept an eye out for opportunities for her. One finally presented itself after I got a deal to do a late-night talk show for MTV called *Charlamagne & Friends*. When it was time to hire writers, I immediately thought of Sasha. She didn't have experience writing for TV, but I knew she could capture my voice, plus her work ethic was unmatched. So I hired her over several people who, on paper, were more qualified. All thanks to the initiative and hustle she showed as an intern.

Another great intern we had at Power was a fat kid named Mack. He took his internship so seriously that he basically lived at the station. He'd start his day by prepping the morning show, go off to class for a couple of hours and then come back and look for ways to help out on the night shifts. A lot of times, he'd just crash on a dirty old futon in the jock lounge so he could already be at the studio when we got in the next day at 5:00 a.m. His work ethic was incredible, but we literally had to tell him to go home and bathe because he'd go for days on end without showering. We couldn't take him stinking up the studio anymore.

My favorite Mack moment came during Hurricane Sandy. Everyone knew the storm was going to shut down New York, so the station booked Envy, Angela, and me into a hotel in Manhattan so we wouldn't have to travel in to work. The streets were deserted. Nobody was on the roads, and the subways and buses were closed, as the mayor had banned all travel. But guess who popped up at the hotel anyway? Mack. "What the hell are you doing here?" we asked in disbelief when we saw him. "We'll, y'all are here," he replied. "So I figured you might need some help." We were blown away. The station had plenty of *paid* employees who didn't even think about showing up (who could blame them?) that day, but Mack the intern made sure he was there. That made a lasting impression on me.

As Mack's internship was winding down, Cadillac decided to take a job in Boston and started filling out his new staff. I wanted to help Mack out so I sent Caddy an e-mail saying, "You should give Mack a job up there, man. Nothing's going to be opening up for him at Power any time soon and the kid deserves a shot. He put in the work." Caddy had seen it with his own eyes, so he hired Mack as his associate morning show producer in Boston. Mack hadn't even finished college yet, but he still found himself in a major market making good money. Again, all thanks to the initiative and hustle he demonstrated as an intern.

I've also seen a lot of young people squander the opportunities that come with internships. If hard work is the best quality an intern can display, ambition is definitely one of the worst. That doesn't mean you can't be ambitious—Puffy, Kevin Liles, Steve Jobs, and Steven Spielberg were all incredibly motivated to win. But I guarantee their employers weren't too aware of that ambition when they were interning. They all knew how to keep that ambition in check until the time was right.

In order to be a great intern, you must have blinders on and stay focused on the work that's in front of you, instead of the work you want to be doing down the road. This is because program directors, managers, producers, and supervisors don't care about *your* dreams. They're focused on their own. So don't waste their time making noise about what you want or what your master plan is.

As Robert Greene says in *48 Laws of Power*, "Conceal your intentions." Your only value to them is the work you put in. If you've handled your internship correctly, when it's time to move on, your superior should come to you and say, "So, what are you trying to do with your career?" And when you tell them, it should be their first time hearing your plans.

We once had an intern at Power—let's call him Pedro—who never learned this. He worked hard, but instead of hustling on behalf of the team, he always tried to bring attention to himself. Pedro even went so far as to make up business cards that had his picture on one half and a picture of myself, Envy, and Angela on the other. When rappers came to the studio, he would hand them one of those cards and introduce himself as part of *The Breakfast Club*. Doing that in plain sight of the show's *actual* producers was a ballsy move, but it wasn't worth the risk. The guests could tell he wasn't really a part of the team—if he was, why wasn't he in the studio? Why hadn't he been on the e-mail thread that booked the interview? Why weren't any of the hosts talking to him? So it didn't get him anywhere with them. All it did was make us seriously question his judgment.

Not surprisingly, we had to fire Pedro. He was replaced by another crop of interns and we pretty much forgot about him. "Nice kid," we'd say if his name came up, "but too thirsty." Then recently I got into a car service and guess who was driving? That's right, Pedro. He immediately launched into this rap about how he was still "producing," but also selling a little coke on the side to make ends meet. "Man, this guy still does too much," I thought to myself as he yapped away in the front seat.

Granted, I had some of the same tendencies when I was younger. When I joined Hot in Columbia, my partner, DJ Frosty, and I started calling ourselves "the Future." The implication was that the older hosts on the station represented the past. Just in case anybody missed the point, we even put out a mixtape called *Disrespect Your Elders* where we dissed the older jocks on the station by name. At the time I thought I was being edgy, but in retrospect my ego and sense of entitlement were out of control. It's surprising the station took as long to fire me as it did. Nobody wants to deal with that sort of naked ambition from a kid who hasn't proven anything yet.

I also showed too much ambition the first time I met Wendy. She was in Columbia for a market visit and was recording her show in our studio. I'd just put out another mixtape, this one called *Hate Is Necessary*, which featured her on the cover. After the show I started pestering her to listen to some of the skits on the tape. At first she just politely declined, but I didn't know when to fall back. I kept bugging and bugging her until finally she turned to me and in an icy voice said, "Please get the fuck out of here with all that mixtape shit. I couldn't care less. Take that nonsense to my husband." As soon as she said it, I knew I'd been doing too much too soon. It was an embarrassing moment, but it taught me the value of being cool when you're trying to establish yourself in a situation. But I did take her advice and took the mixtape to Kev, which in retrospect was the genesis of our relationship.

Are there going to be people who will take advantage of your willingness to value opportunity over money? Who might appear to be getting over on you? Absolutely. Who gives a fuck? As long as they're giving you a real opportunity and cracking open a door— even if that crack is thinner than Wiz Khalifa's arm—then *you're* the one who is getting over.

I was recently talking about this with Joseph Kahn, the director of the movie *Bodied,* which I appear in. The film is set in the world of battle rappers, and there was one real-life rapper in particular whom Joseph really wanted in the film. He told me he offered the guy $70K to appear, but this rapper's mentality was "If they got seventy thousand, then they got one hundred grand. That's what I want." Joseph explained that $70K was all he had in his budget, but the rapper wouldn't move until he got that extra thirty. Eventually the movie studio got tired of trying to convince him and went with another rapper, who was willing to do it for fifty. It's too bad, because the first guy lost an opportunity to show a movie audience just how great a battle rapper he is. If he had done it for $70K and killed it—like he undoubtedly would have—he'd probably get $100K for his next movie. Maybe more. But because this guy was so adamant about getting that extra $30K he was sure they were holding out on him—and they probably were—he ended up blocking his own blessings.

Look, I've done plenty of TV deals in the past few years where I could have adapted a harder line and gotten more cash. But TV is a relatively new medium to me at this stage in my career, so I'd rather take less money now if it helps set me up to get more in the long run. I'm focused on creating opportunity for myself, not wringing every last penny out of a deal. This is why whenever I'm working on a deal, my mentality is "Just let me get whatever is fair. I don't need to 'win' this thing. I'll stick them up later."

By not turning every negotiation into a dragged-out battle, I've increased my overall value by building strong relationships. It's paid off for me, especially in TV. I still have much more to accomplish, but even as I'm writing this, I have my own office in the Viacom building. But do you know how much my first contract with Viacom was for?

$55K.

That's right, I signed a TV production deal that didn't even come close to landing me $100K. And I was fine with it. Frankly, I didn't even know why they were offering me that much. I was just excited to get my feet wet in TV.

But supposed I had said, "Fifty-five thousand, what the hell is that?" when I got the offer. "I'm one of the most popular person-alities on the radio. MTV had better come off some real money!" The process would have stalled before it ever really got started. Why should MTV have offered me a bundle of cash? I'd proven myself in radio by that point, but I hadn't done anything signifi-cant in TV. I needed to build my reputation in the industry, and the contract reflected that.

Whether it's radio, TV, movies, books, podcasts, or whatever, I never enter into a situation with a "get money" attitude. Again, I'm in this for the long haul, not the short money. And trust me, the money's much longer now.

Represent Yourself

The first time I learned the value in not demanding too much money is when I was negotiating the deal to come to 100.3 The Beat in Philly. And in many ways, that situation is at the root of why me and Kev—and by extension, Wendy—don't fuck with each other anymore.

Kev has always had an attitude similar to that battle rapper's: if someone offers you ten bucks, that means they really should be offering you fifteen. But instead of just saying "No, thanks" to the deal, it felt like Kev was going try to shake you upside down until that other five bucks fell out of your pocket. He was always extremely aggressive in trying to get more money out of situa-tions. He'd yell at and often threaten people till he got what he wanted. I can't lie: it's worked for him with Wendy. But it wasn't how I wanted to do business.

The issue came to a head for the first time when I was approached about the job in Philly. Even though I'd been fired from Wendy's show, Kev was still my guy. He had still given me that initial opportunity and I'll forever be grateful for that. At the time, Kev was looking to expand his client base beyond Wendy, so of course he wanted to represent me in my negotiations. That put me in a bit of a bind. On one hand I wanted to go with Kev—I owed him, after all. On the other, I also knew how he got when it was time to talk money.

When Philly had first hit me up, they'd thrown out an initial offer of $70K a year. To me, it was a fair number, right around what I'd been making with Wendy. Plus the economy was absolutely terrible at that moment. This was just after the financial crash of 2008, when a lot of the big banks, auto, and insurance companies needed to be bailed out. Every industry was suffering and cutting back. I was excited to have a job when so many other people were losing theirs.

Kev didn't see it that way. "We gonna go in there and get three hundred and fifty thousand out of them," he told me. "Trust me, nigga, we got this." He was confident, but it felt like a suicide mission to me. "Kev, this is not the nineties, and I'm not Wendy," I explained. "There ain't three hundred and fifty thousand a year for me in Philly."

Kev didn't want to budge off $350K though. So finally I said, "Fuck that, I'm going up to that station to talk to these people myself." I just couldn't demand an unrealistic number. It was a hard conversation to have, but ultimately I had to tell Kev I was going in there solo. He didn't like that, but I stuck to my guns and accepted for $75K. Could I have held out for a little more? Sure.

Maybe $80K. Or even $100K. But never $350K. I'm happy Kev thought I was worth that much, but that was Wendy Williams money at the time. Not Charlamagne money.

The money wasn't my priority anyway. I wanted a chance to do what I love. To compete in the biggest markets. Not to mention have my own morning show. *That's* what I was focused on. The opportunity. Because I knew that if I did what I was supposed to do in Philly, that $350K would be waiting for me down the road (and then some, it turned out). But I needed to put the weed in the bag first.

The Philly situation created a fracture in my relationship with Kev that never fully healed. One day out of the blue I got a text from him that read, *I'm not fucking with you any more. You did some foul shit. Lose my #.* I immediately hit him back and asked, *What are you talking about?* No reply. When I called him, he didn't pick up.

I always take a man at his word, so after that I deleted his number. I didn't call Wendy to ask what was wrong, or ask any of our mutual friends to mediate the situation. I just took that number out of my phone and didn't look back.

I quickly realized it was the right decision. When I went back to Power to talk to Cadillac, one of the first things he asked me is, "Is Kevin Hunter still your manager?"

"Nope," I replied.

"Why did you make that move?"

"Because when I pray to God to take negativity out of my life, he's not swinging at spirits. He's swinging at people who are the living embodiment of negativity in my life."

Caddy just stared at me, then finally smiled.

"That guy does have a lot of weird energy, doesn't he?" Caddy said. He then went on to tell me that he was glad I'd made the switch, because as long as Kev was my manager, it would have been hard to make a deal. Apparently some of the sales folks at Power had worked with Kev before and weren't looking forward to doing it again. That's why I hadn't heard back from them after our first meeting.

God Jewel: There might be thousands of radio stations in the country, but the radio industry is small. As are most industries.

That means the people you piss off at one stop are probably going to pop up at another one sooner or later. So treat people with respect where you are, or you might pay for it later.

Thankfully, I was already flying solo at that point. I'd come to realize that a good manager is a great ambassador for their client. A good manager has the connections and has built up enough trust with companies that they can both ask for and get what they deserve. My impression was Kev didn't have those kinds of relationships. Instead of trust, he'd built up too much ill will with executives and program directors. To this day, I don't know why he sent that text. Until he explains it to me, I'll never know. Whatever his motivation, breaking with Kev removed the biggest obstacle between me and where I wanted to go.

For a long time after that incident with Kev, I didn't have a manager in the traditional sense. One day I was hanging out in Los Angeles with my OG Paul Ricci, the famed TV executive who is one of the smartest guys I've met and is responsible for my first TV deal. We were just shooting the shit about different TV personalities, breaking down their careers or lack thereof. At one point I asked Paul, "Tell me how people who've achieved fame manage to fall off?" "Their attitudes and managers," he replied. "Bad attitude speaks for itself. But you know, you get these managers that speak for you and they take a bunch of your money and they create drama where there is no need for it," he told me. "The most dangerous thing they do is gas up the talent. They make you feel like you're bigger than the company, which you never are. I don't care how famous you are, or how much press you get, you're never bigger than the company. And if a manager makes you feel like you are, they're doing you a great disservice." Paul told me that as the deals get bigger and bigger I'd need an agent, but for the time being not necessarily a manager.

I've always kept that conversation in mind, and for a while did handle those situations myself. Finally I got to the spot where I really did need one, and I hired a triple OG named Karen Kinney, who I trust and value. If I was going to hire a manager, I had to make sure they were a good person with great character. Karen more than fits that description. (Not to mention she's Geespin's cousin. See how the universe works?)

Manager or not, no matter how well a show I'm on does, or no matter how much I'm getting paid, I always remind myself I'm not bigger than the company.

That doesn't mean I don't have confidence in myself, I do—supreme confidence in fact—or that I don't expect my checks to get bigger. Again, there's no question on that count.

But it does mean that I won't become so full of myself that I shut myself off to new opportunities. No matter how far you get in the game, there's always another level to reach. That's true for radio jocks, but it's also true for chefs, lawyers, rappers, accountants, and teachers. Measure your success by the opportunities you're presented with and the opportunities you're creating for others. Not the amount of zeros in your paycheck. When that's your sole measurement, you're going to come up short in the end.

Put Yourself On

A few years ago Lil Duval and I were walking out of the Viacom building in Times Square when some random dude ran up on us. "Yo, I keep seeing you guys on TV," he said, almost out of breath. "I wanna get down too. So what I gotta do to become famous?"

Duval and I just started laughing, but this guy wasn't joking. He really thought there was some sort of cheat sheet he could read and *bam!*—the next time we walked out of the Viacom building, he'd be right there with us.

I've said it before, but I've got to say it one more time for the people in the back: there is no book, no cheat sheet or secret formula that's going to allow you to skip over any rung on the success ladder without putting in the work first.

There was no shortcut Duval and I could have taken on our road to MTV that didn't involve years and years of grindin'. Years of me working on the radio for free or damn near it. Years of Duval playing little comedy clubs in the Dirty South for little to no money. Not to mention years of us, collectively and individually, pitching shows and concepts that never got picked up. Pitches that often never even earned us an e-mail or phone call back to say, "No, thanks."

We didn't let any of that discourage us. If TV networks didn't seem interested in what we were pitching, we would just put out our own content. We paid for *Hood State of the Union*—a web series where we talked about current events and pop culture— out of our own pocket. The cameraman, the editors, the green screen—we scraped the money together for all of that ourselves. The production value might not have been great—it sounded like it was recorded in a bathroom and looked like it was edited by someone taking a class in Final Cut Pro in community college—but the product was still good enough. People fucked with it and the episodes began to rack up respectable numbers on YouTube. (Thank you to my man Scenario, who helped put that whole thing together.)

Tiffany Williams from MTV eventually saw it and was impressed enough to invite us into the building for a meeting. Once we were inside, the rest was history. But we created that initial traction ourselves. No one put us on, or gave us a break. Of course, years later, when MTV2 started promoting my show *Uncommon Sense*, that didn't stop people from tweeting, "Man, MTV is just handing out shows now." Every time I saw a tweet like that, I just had to laugh.

Everything I've gotten my hands on, I've grabbed. Nothing was served up to me on a platter. That's why if you're reading this and want to make a name for yourself in the entertainment world—TV, radio, video, podcasting—please take this very simple advice: put yourself on. By that I mean don't wait for someone to give you a deal. If you do, you'll be waiting for a very long time. Maybe forever. There is no one reading this book right now who couldn't do what Duval and I did with *Hood State of the Union*. Those videos literally didn't cost more than a few hundred dollars to shoot and produce. If you can afford a cell phone plan, you can afford to make your own video.

It's true of any lane you want to be in. If you want to be a writer, start fucking writing! Again, it doesn't cost anything to post your thoughts on a blog, Facebook, Tumblr, or any social media site. If what you're writing is good, eventually someone with a larger platform will notice and give you an opportunity.

It's no different with podcasting. So many people hit me on Twitter, or see me in the streets and say, "Yo Charlamagne, I love *The Brilliant Idiots*. How do I get my own podcast?" You get it by buying a couple of mics, sticking them into your computer, hitting record, and starting a conversation that people are going to be interested in. That's it. If you're consistent with it, eventually it will take you where you want to go. But no one is going to "give" you a podcast. Or anything else of value.

I'm not trying to be a dream killer here, but I can't tell you how many people come up to me looking to get on at iHeartRadio, or Viacom, or the Loud Speakers Network without having put the weed in the bag first. It's so easy to build a digital résumé today, but so few people do it. You're telling me you want a talk show but you haven't even recorded yourself talking about pop culture topics on YouTube? You're telling me you want a podcast but you haven't even recorded yourself on your computer and uploaded it to SoundCloud? If you haven't even taken those small baby steps, then I know you're just looking for a shortcut. Sorry, but once again, there aren't any out there.

I believe one reason people are looking for shortcuts, instead of opportunities to do the work and be productive, is because social media has given them a false sense of value. They really believe that if they tweet something, or even just retweet it, and it gets a couple of likes, the next step is radio or television. So let me say this very clearly: being active on social media can amplify the work you're already doing, but it is not work unto itself.

If you're reposting a link to your podcast, a story you wrote, or even something creative you did, that's one thing. You're using those platforms to alert people to your talent. But only retweeting other people's stuff, or even just making a few funny comments? Sorry, but that's not enough to get put on.

I say that as someone who is actively involved in doing just that—putting people on. I am literally *always* looking for new talent. I don't demand a ton of experience, but I do want to see someone using all these incredible, yet inexpensive tools at your disposal to create. I want to see short videos; I want to listen to podcasts; I want to read blogs. The platforms change—when I started, I was posting content to Myspace, or my man IllSeed was posting it on his rumor page on AllHipHop. Then I got onto Facebook, then Twitter. As I'm writing this book, it's Snapchat and Instagram; by the time the book comes out I will probably be onto something else. But the passion to create, to be part of the conversation, never changes. That passion has to be evident for someone in a position of power to give you a look.

While we're debunking some myths about what it takes to "get on," let's kill the dream once and for all that reality shows create a path to anything meaningful. I know the Kardashians are getting three trillion dollars a year plus Ryan Seacrest's firstborn from E!, but I'm not talking about them. I'm specifically talking to all you people who think being on a show like *Love & Hip Hop* is going to make you successful. Trust me, the vast majority of stars on shows like that get very little money for their efforts.

How little? Let's say you're on a bigger network, you might get $1,500 an episode over the course of a fifteen-show season. So that's around twenty-three grand. Not really that much money, right?

Let's say everything breaks in your favor: you end up being one of the stars of the show and you're brought back for season two. You might even get a slight raise. You are still only making forty grand a year. Thanks to the show, you can also host fifteen to twenty parties in little clubs around the country at $2,500 a pop. You're still barely making over $75K a year.

"But, Charlamagne," you might be thinking, "didn't you just finish saying that it's important not to get hung up on the money? That you should work for free if you have to?" You're right; I did say that! But you left out an important part: I said you should be willing to work for free if it leads to a greater opportunity. Unfortunately, for most people on reality shows, that greater opportunity most likely isn't out there.

For every Bethenny Frankel who gets her own daytime talk show or multimillion-dollar margarita mix, there are hundreds (maybe even thousands by this point) of other reality stars who get nada except for the occasional club appearance. And even those dry up after a year or two.

The worst part about being a reality star is that the experience ruins you for most other careers. Once you've been on TV, you'll probably think that you're too good to work in a bank, or as a trainer at a gym. Plus there are a lot of places that won't hire you because they only know you as that wild woman who throws drinks at people, or who slapped her best friend. So even if you were willing to take a traditional nine-to-five, a lot of those opportunities will be off the table. Ultimately, trying to "make it" as a reality star just leaves you in a state of limbo. You can't move forward in the entertainment business, but you feel like you can't go back to a "regular" life either. So if being in entertainment is really your passion, look for another route other than reality TV.

The Passion of Pitbull

One of the best things about working in radio is that I get to meet a lot of unknown artists before they blow up nationally. One guy who really stood out for how he pulled himself up from the gutter to the pinnacle of the music game was Pitbull.

I first met Pitbull in Miami around 2000, while helping Never So Deep master an album for Infinity. It took about twelve hours to drive from South Carolina to Miami, but every couple of weeks DJ Bless, Dr. Evans, and I would make the trip. We did a lot of work at Abebe Lewis's legendary Circle House, one of the best studios in the country.

I can still remember hanging out there one night and telling Abebe that I did radio back in South Carolina. "Oh man, then you should check out this guy who's on air part-time on Friday and Saturday nights. He's dope," Abebe told me. "He's going to blow up one of these days."

"What's his name?" I replied. "DJ Khaled," said Abebe. So if you only know Khaled because of his Snapchat or his songs with Drake, understand he's another example of a guy who's been out here putting the weed in the bag for years and years.

One of the young rappers hanging around Circle House was Pitbull. He wasn't signed to a major label yet, but he was doing everything he could to put himself on. You know how DJs and radio personalities often have a rapper put together an intro or promo song at the top of their shifts? It seemed to me like Pitbull was doing one for almost every jock in Miami. I knew from being a radio personality that those are very coveted looks for local rappers, so I was impressed that Pitbull had convinced multiple radio personalities and DJs to let him do theirs.

Pitbull had a great ear and he immediately identified Bless as a special producer. Whenever he saw us, he would always ask if he could get on one of Bless's beats. "Come on, Bless, let me rock that 'Awww man,'" Pitbull would say, referring to the chorus of his favorite track that Bless had produced. But Bless wasn't with it. For whatever reason, he didn't like Pit as a rapper. He thought his style wasn't hardcore or aggressive enough. I'd even say, "You've got hundreds of beats, just give him one. Dude is nice." But Bless wouldn't budge.

Finally, one day Pit asked him straight up, "Bless, why won't you ever let me get on one of your beats?" To his credit, Bless told him straight up in return, "Because I think you're a corny rapper."

When Pit heard that, he got very serious. "Man, you know where you at? You in Miami, baby, this the 305. . . . One day you'll regret talking like that." "Whatchu mean?" countered Bless, thinking that Pit was threatening him. "Don't you know I'm DJ Bless?"

It might have sounded like Pit was trying to punk Bless, but Pit later told me that wasn't the case. He explained what he was trying to say was, "One day I'm going to help put Miami back in the spotlight and you're going to regret passing up on the opportunity to have been part of it." And you know what? He was right. He is a superstar today, and I'm sure Bless wishes he'd given him that beat.

Bless might not have seen Pit's talent, but it shone through with me. I still remember watching Pit drive off from the studio one afternoon in a raggedy-ass car, maybe an old Saturn or something, and thinking to myself, "This dude's at the bottom right now, but he's gonna be something someday." He just had that combination of charisma and work ethic that made him stand out despite his surroundings. The same way I saw a young T.I. take over a room while wearing a dirty sweatshirt, Pit had a similar aura that just made you believe in him.

Seeing folks like Pitbull and T.I. put in the work is why I get frustrated when people speculate on the shortcuts artists allegedly take to become famous. If you let Twitter tell it, every successful artist is the beneficiary of a conspiracy theory. "Oh, you gotta sell your soul and perform gay acts to get on now," someone will say. Or you'll see tweets like, "You can't get a deal nowadays unless you in the Illuminati." It would be comical, except a lot of people take it as fact.

Trust me, no one gave Pitbull a break he didn't create for himself. Pitbull pulled himself up to the top of the game. Just like I watched T.I., Jeezy, 2Chainz, and so many other rappers put the weed in the bag (probably literally and figuratively). I watched them beg to get their records played, perform in front of crowds of ten to twenty people, and get turned down by record label after record label. Yet they never stopped grindin', never said, "Let me take a break and chill out until someone puts me on." No, they kept at it until someone was forced to give them the exposure they deserved.

My experience was no different. I can't even begin to tell you how many air checks I sent out over the years that I never even heard back about. I didn't consider quitting for a second; I always knew I was going to find my way. On my own. I didn't partake in any secret Illuminati initiation ceremony where I had to sacrifice a hamster in front of Jay Z, Beyoncé, Kanye, and Rihanna. Nor was I sworn into a secret cabal of gay music executives. If you believe in that sort of shit, ladies and gentlemen, I don't know what else to tell you. But just know that while you're making excuses about your favorite artists' success, someone else is out there putting the weed in the bag and creating opportunities for themselves.

Get In Where You Fit In

A final word on interns: a crucial mistake a lot of them make is worrying about the specific branch or department of an organization their internship is in. I saw this recently when an intern named Saige came to me for advice as her time at Power was winding down. She'd worked hard, was reliable, and had managed to build strong relationships with the staff. People wanted to help her. There was a job opening up in Power's promotions department, and several staffers said they would recommend her. Perfect setup, right? But Saige told me she was apprehensive about the gig. "Promotions isn't what I really want to do," she explained. "I'm really more interested in being an on-air jock or a producer."

"You're going about this entirely the wrong way," I told her. "You should have one goal: *get in the building.* Or in your case, *stay* in the building. If that means taking a job in promotions, take the job in promotions. If that means taking a job in sales, take the job in sales. If it means being the receptionist, be the receptionist. Who cares if those aren't your dream jobs? Fuck your dreams. Your reality is you need to be in this building. Once you're here, you can use that access to start hanging around the studios. You can build relationships with the jocks and producers. You can find ways of making yourself useful even if it's not part of your job description. Eventually, that hustle will pay off."

Saige understood the value in what I was saying and took the job. It only paid her ten or eleven bucks an hour, but once she was in the building, she made a point of stopping by and visiting her old friends at *The Breakfast Club* every day. A few months later Envy decided he needed an assistant, saw Saige, and gave her the job. Then when he decided to start The Casey Crew podcast with his wife, Gia, he needed a producer and gave that job to Saige too. So even though she isn't officially producing and working with talent, just by keeping her foothold in the building, she ended up with the experience she was looking for.

Saige's situation is a great example of the value of just getting your foot in the door, but I still see narrow-minded attitudes in interns time and time again: if a position isn't *exactly* what they want, then they're not interested. So please, if you're up for an internship, or really any entry-level position in a company, do not get hung up on what department your opportunity comes in. If you're willing to put in that hard work I've been talking about, then *every* job in an organization you want to be in should be viewed as a golden opportunity.

168 Hours

One indicator I use to tell whether someone is built for success is their attitude toward time management. Time is something that you can't fight or try to escape. If it takes an hour to get somewhere, stop trying to get there in forty-five minutes.

It pisses me off when I hear people say they don't have enough time. I was once tweeting about the value of internships and this young woman hit me back to say, *I work 40 hours a week; how am I supposed to have time for an unpaid internship on top of that?* I know a lot of young people feel that way, so I had to break it down for her mathematically.

There are 168 hours in a week total. Let's say you work forty hours a week at a job and then you're in school for another forty hours. That still leaves you with another eighty-plus hours. Those additional hours are more than enough time to deal with your reality, pursue your passions, *and* get the most important thing, which is some damn sleep.

Sleep is the one area you simply can't cut corners. I got gassed up too back in the day when I heard Nas rap, "I never sleep, 'cause sleep is the cousin of death." I spent too much of my twenties thinking, "Damn, if I'm sleeping, I must be slacking," but now I know better. If anything, a *lack* of sleep is what's going to kill you.

The truth is, unless you're an artist in a creative groove that you just don't want to break, there's not a lot of legit business being conducted at 4:00 a.m. Sorry. For everyone working nine-to-five hours, you need rest to be effective. I was always told when you sleep God does maintenance on your soul, and when you get a good night's rest, it damn sure feels that way. You feel refreshed physically and spiritually.

Another great thing about getting a good night's sleep is it helps you retain information. One of my favorite things to do before bed is to read something uplifting in a book. Maybe some Bible scriptures, passages in the Quran, Don Miguel Ruiz's books on Toltec wisdom, or Jennifer Lopez's Instagram. I try to end my day with positive information that can settle in my mind as I sleep and then really stick in my brain.

So let's say you sleep at least six hours a night, or forty-two hours a week. That still leaves you another forty-plus hours that could be spent pursuing your passion. I can hear some of you now, "Well, what about my social life? What about time with my friends?" Fuck your social life, fuck your friends, and while I'm at it, fuck your feelings, too. If that's what's important to you, then spend time with your friends. But don't expect to be successful, because if you're truly passionate about your career, then that's where you need to dedicate those extra hours. If the folks you want to hang out with are really your friends, they will understand and support you.

I remember when I was trying to juggle night school, working a day job, and putting in time in the streets (I might have been misguided, but at least I took the streets seriously), I *always* made sure I never skipped school. At the time I was hanging with my homie Joe, who was deep in the drug game and would go on to become a *huge* kingpin before being busted on federal charges. One time Joe told me, "Man, I fuck with you because you're focused. No matter what we doing out here you still take your ass to school. That's some real shit." See, like I said: real friends, even those who sell crack, will understand.

After I finally gave up the street life, I still needed to make money while I was interning at Jamz. I was determined to do it legally, so I started working odd jobs around Moncks Corner. First I worked in a warehouse called Industrial Acoustics Company, loading and unloading trucks. Then I worked at a telemarketing company called Paragon Solutions, where we hustled CDs for BMG music group. Their tagline was "Ten CDs for the price of half," which basically meant that after shipping, you'd get ten discs for twenty-seven bucks. Not a bad deal.

The toughest gig I had during that period was at the Carolina Nursery, aka the Flower Garden, which was a Moncks Corner institution for years before it shut down. The Flower Garden housed over six hundred acres of plants and garden supplies and they would hire anyone to lug bags of soil and potted plants around the premises. Flower Garden was a place where you went when you couldn't get a job anywhere else. When I worked there, it was nothing but Mexican guys and a couple of older black dudes.

I didn't last long. One day they assigned me to move soil to a part of the facility that was right next to a bus stop. I was out there sweating in the sun, covered in dirt, when a school bus pulled up with a bunch of kids I knew on it. They all started pointing at me and cracking up. I couldn't take the public ridicule, so I moved on to other jobs.

At one point my sister Teresa got me a job at the Taco Bell she was the manager at. I thought I could mess around because of her position, but my sister wasn't having it. After watching me BS for a couple of weeks, she fired me. I also worked in the local mall at an urban clothing store called DEMO, where I tried to sell the latest in cheaply produced garments from companies like Enyce, FUBU, Phat Farm, and Rocawear.

It wasn't easy dragging soil around or stacking boxes all day and then heading to the radio till the middle of the night. But I was more than happy to do it. If I could make legal money and pursue my radio dreams at the same time, then I was going to pack as much into those 168 hours as possible.

For everyone who thinks that what I'm suggesting might sound extreme, it's still the life I live every day. Here's what my schedule looks like: Every weekday I wake up at 3:45 a.m. and give God a little prayer of thanks for blessing me with another day. After I take a shower, my longtime friend (more like my brother) Wax picks me up in Jersey.* After about a half-hour drive, we make it to Power's studio in Manhattan by 5:00 a.m. to prep for the show. Every day we're live on air till 10:00 a.m., after which we'll tape

*A word about Wax, who is already familiar to fans of *The Brilliant Idiots* and *Uncommon Sense*: I've known Wax since 2002, when he was playing football for Allen University in Columbia. I had a side hustle selling mixtapes of East Coast artists like Dipset and G-Unit. Wax was from Jersey, so of course he became a steady customer. After that we just clicked, and whether I was on the radio or out at a club, Wax and our boy Dre would roll with me everywhere. It's been like that for the past fifteen years, which is why it's funny when people say, "Charlamagne be with security." I wouldn't call Wax security, he's my family who just happens to be six four and 240 pounds of solid muscle and will knock your head clear off your shoulders.

additional interviews till about noon for the following day's show. For those of you keeping score, that's already a seven-hour work-day right there.

Depending on which day of the week it is, after wrapping up at Power, I'll either head over to MTV to tape one of my shows with them, or to another studio to tape my podcast *The Brilliant Idiots*. After I'm done taping those, I'll take meetings with the agents, producers, and writers who are working on the various projects I've got cooking.

On a good day I'll be able to leave the city by three or four so I can spend some time with my daughters and catch up with my wife. Then I go to the gym to get a workout in, since physical fitness is nonnegotiable. I'm back in the crib by eight, grab another shower, and then spend some more time with the kids before they go to bed. Once they're tucked in, I'll jump on social media and see if there's any good content for the next day's show (which there always is). After that it's time for some positive reading and then in bed by eleven.

That means at least four times a week I'll put in a fifteen-to-seventeen-hour workday. And I cherish every single second of those hours. I know all too well what it feels like to be unemployed or shut out from what you want to be doing. I worked at Taco Bell and a flower garden. I sold crack! What I'm doing now isn't work to me. What's that saying, "If you love what you do, you will never work a day in your life"? I can vouch that the saying is 100 percent the truth.

Notice that I didn't allocate any time in my schedule for socializing, or just hanging out. I'd say out of my week, 95 percent of my waking hours are spent either working on my career or with my wife and kids. I wouldn't have it any other way. The question is, are you willing to put in those kinds of fifteen-hour days if it means getting closer to your dreams? Are you willing to get up at 3:45 a.m. and go to bed at 11:00 p.m. five days a week?

If you're in school, are you prepared to study from 4:00 a.m. to 8:00 a.m. every day and *then* go to work? And *then* head to your internship at 3:00 p.m.? Or do you need more time "for yourself"? Do you need more time to play video games? To text with your friends? To mess around on social media? Choose to do what you want with your time, but just understand you have to live with the consequences of those actions. No matter how you spend the next ten years of your life, you do not get a redo.

If it makes your decision easier, I can tell you that socializing and "me time" is not what the other successful people I know choose. They always choose a lifestyle that allows them to get in the most work possible. I'm talking about people like Ryan Seacrest, Steve Harvey, and Bobby Bones. Folks who put in more work by 10:00 a.m. than many people do all day. Who are squeezing everything they can out of those 168 hours. Radio shows, TV shows, podcasts, books, movies—they're not passing up any opportunities.

Those are the examples that inspire me when I feel like I'm running out of gas a bit. I'll tell myself, "Ryan Seacrest is out there in a meeting somewhere right now getting more paper. I can make it to my meeting, too." Or, "I know Steve is probably taping his second TV show of the day right now. I can hang out on this set for another hour until we nail this final take." Bobby Bones is like my radio brother, a great friend, and we talk all the time about how we are next in line for the thrones Steve and Ryan currently sit in. So I know Bobby is working his ass off, whether it's his syndicated radio show *The Bobby Bones Show*; touring with his band, the Raging Idiots; editing his latest book; or producing a TV show. I know he's not wasting a minute, and unlike me, he doesn't have a wife and kids. It's just him and his dog. So right there he's got an advantage and I've got to work even harder if I'm going to keep up.

Of course, just *saying* you're going to make the most of your week isn't enough. To *do it*, you're going to have to develop some real discipline in your day-to-day schedule. First you have to say good-bye to the smoking and drinking if that's part of your lifestyle. That's right, the kid who used to smoke weed like Red and Meth's little brother hasn't had a puff in God knows how long. Sure, if I'm down in Anguilla, my favorite vacation spot, I might take a few drags off a joint. When I do, I always hear Jay Z's verse in my head:

> OK, I'm getting weeded now
> I know I'm contradicting myself
> Look, I don't need that now
> It's just once in a blue when there's nothin' to do

The key words in that verse are, "ONCE IN A BLUE WHEN THERE'S NOTHIN' TO DO." If you're smoking more than every once in a blue moon, you're smoking too much. You have to view weed as a treat. Not an everyday thing. I used to smoke every day and it wasn't getting me where I wanted to go. The only place it got me was being around a bunch of dudes who were more interested in getting high than making moves. Sure, we had some funny moments that I'll always remember, but like Jay said, "I don't need that now."

I have a similar relationship with alcohol. Yes, I'll still sip a little Rémy Martin when I'm back in Moncks Corner on vacation or during a special occasion in New York. But drinking on a normal weeknight? Out of the question. I'm not straight edge—I got a full bar in the crib—but I'm never tempted by it because I'm buzzed off the work I'm putting in. Not to mention, drinking takes too much of a toll on you physically, especially when you've got to be up at 3:45 every morning. I'd be out of gas and ready to go home by noon every day if I'd been drinking the night before. That would mean literally half my career would be off the table.

I learned that the hard way. Back in 2011, I went on a two-week run of being out in the clubs every night. I was drinking, smoking, not watching what I ate and not getting enough sleep. One morning I was in *The Breakfast Club* studios and I didn't feel right. I tried to lie down between breaks, but I could tell it was more than just being tired or hungover. A voice in my head told me to go to the hospital, so I checked myself into the emergency room. Come to find out I was seriously dehydrated.

I used to read about celebrities getting sent to the hospital for "dehydration" and assume it was code for something else, most likely drugs. Nope. Trust me, dehydration is real and it's no joke. I felt like I was going to die. Ludacris wasn't lying in his song "Catch Up": "All this drinking gon catch up / And all this smoking gon' catch up / But some niggas just really don't give a fuck." It definitely caught up with me, but that was one situation where I *did* give a fuck. So much so that I vowed to wean smoking and drinking out of my lifestyle after that.

Another big adjustment I had to make was eating better. For most of my life I was on a diet of Chick-fil-A, Bojangles', Pizza Hut, McDonald's, and sodas. The garbage that tasted good when you're a teenager ruins us in the long term. I didn't think it was affecting me that much, but boy was I wrong. It got me to a point where I literally had to fix my face.

A few years ago I was at a party in Manhattan when a woman approached me and said, "I can do something about that, you know," in a British accent. "What are you talking about?" I asked. "Those dark spots on your face," she replied. "I can help you get rid of them."

I don't know if you've seen any pictures of me from earlier in my career, but I absolutely used to have crazy dark patches on my face, especially below my eyes. I remember the comedian Marlon Wayans once said I looked like a bruised eggplant and I can't say he was wrong. I developed them as a teenager and my pops figured they were from smoking crack. "Look at your face! You got them black spots under your eyes," he yelled. "You must be on that shit!" I wasn't smoking crack, but I didn't know what was causing the discoloration. Nor did I bother to find out. The spots weren't stopping me from getting girls, which is all that matters to a teenage boy.

Still, when the woman said she could get rid of them, I said, "Hey, why not give it a shot?" It turns out she was a dermatologist named Dr. Natasha Sandy and she suggested I come in for a consultation. I was game and went to her office, where I told her from the jump, "I don't know how you plan to get rid of these, but I'm not doing no bleaching." I only mention that because once Dr. Sandy did get those spots off, the Internet decided that I had pulled a Sammy Sosa and bleached my skin. It was hilarious to me; the one thing everybody accuses me of doing is the one thing I was adamant I *wasn't* going to do. That's the Internet for you.

It turned out it wasn't even an option, as Dr. Sandy explained that the dark patches weren't a skin condition unto themselves, but rather a symptom of my shitty diet. She promised that if I started eating cleaner—no fried food, sodas, white breads, and other heavily processed foods—the patches would start to clear up. She prescribed pills to get the inflammation out of my face, gave me chemical peels, acne pads, and complexion-correction pads.

God Jewel: If you're trying to lose weight, it all comes down to diet. I've worked out for years, but no amount of bench press will offset working out and then going to Chick-fil-A after the gym. So now I eat vegetables or something green with every meal, whether it's spinach with an omelet, salad at lunch, or asparagus at dinner. I also snack in between meals. Protein bars, peanuts, and fruit. Finally, I don't eat after nine if I can help it. It's all about discipline. That's the biggest part of any process—patience and discipline. Nothing happens overnight.

It all added up to a major transformation. In addition to cutting out processed foods, Dr. Sandy also had me start eating four to five times a day to speed up my metabolism. I ended up losing close to thirty pounds. When I first saw Dr. Sandy I was 202; today I float around in the 170- to 175-pound range. For the first time in my life, I have abs.

I'm glad I came to the realization that I didn't want to be one of those people who treat their material possessions better than they treat their own bodies. I know plenty of folks who will refuse to put anything other than premium gas in their car but are more than happy to put any old type of fast food down their throats. Who will clean their Jordans by hand with a toothbrush but won't put nearly the same amount of care into their health.

Do I miss some of the foods I used to enjoy, like chicken wings and burgers? Of course. But when you start eating healthy, after just a few weeks you don't want the garbage anymore. You realize that eating trash foods makes you feel like trash. Are there a couple of times a month that I'll "cheat" and wolf down some barbeque or a pizza? Sure. But then I get right back on my healthy shit. Because I know if I ever go back to eating trash full-time, I'm going to start looking and feeling like trash again too. And then I'll never have the energy and the focus to get to everything I want to accomplish.

That sort of sacrifice is why I get a little insulted when people say I bleached my skin. I had to work hard to transform myself from a potentially pudgy dude with dark patches under his eyes to a healthy-looking guy with abs. How dare you say I achieved that by taking a couple of pills? Nope, it's not that easy.

Just like I find it insulting when people say I must have joined the Illuminati, or be gay, to achieve my success. Trust me, if all you had to do to be Will Smith was give an old movie exec a blow job, there would be a lot of Will Smiths running around out here (unless of course Will's head is just that fire). But there aren't. Because success like the kind Will has enjoyed only comes through putting in thousands and thousands of hours' worth of work and sacrifice.

Whether it's becoming a movie star, transforming into a healthier lifestyle, or simply getting the most out of an internship, no matter what you're trying to accomplish in life, it always comes down to this:

You must put the weed in the bag.

Live Your Truth

Always live your truth. That way no one can use your truth against you. When you are completely honest about yourself and with yourself, you give zero fucks about anything anyone has to say about you. People can slander you all day, but no judgment or opinion formed against you shall prosper when you Live Your Truth.

I've never been comfortable with those who are loose with the truth, or even worse are straight-up liars. When I was a kid, my father would tell me, "When you tell one lie, you're always going to have to tell another one to keep it up," over and over again, until it was beat into my head. "Better to tell the truth and deal with the consequences right away."

Truth is like the sun. You can shut it out for a time, but it ain't going away.
—Elvis Presley (Though, to quote the great Chuck D, "Motherfuck him and John Wayne.")

No matter how stupid something I have said is, no matter how asinine I've acted, and no matter what sort of stunt I've pulled, I'm going to own it. I won't run from it. Trying to moonwalk past the truth doesn't change reality.

There was one time I lost sight of this truth and it cost me dearly. When the cops first pulled us in for the shooting incident, I panicked and decided to try to lie my way out of the situation. As if a sixteen-year-old kid could outsmart a police department. The cops asked me to write down a statement about what had happened and I proceeded to compose my greatest work of fiction to date. It started with me hitchhiking and getting picked up by a bunch of strangers in a red car. I claimed they drove me around for a couple of hours, smoking weed and drinking beer, then without warning opened fire on the kids in the Jeep. After the shooting, I said I asked to be let out of the car, and they dropped me off on a highway not far from Moncks Corner. Before letting me go, they promised they'd come back and kill me if I told the police what I'd seen. Which is why I hadn't reported anything.

The story didn't even remotely begin to add up, but the cops still did their due diligence and explored the phony "leads" I'd given them. A few hours later they came back to the station supremely pissed off. "You know what? We were going to let you go today for talking with us," one of the cops told me. "We were going to tell the judge to give you a bond, but since you sent us on a wild-goose chase and wasted our time, now you're going to sit." So I sat. And sat. And sat. I ended up having a few months to reflect on why my father was right: honesty is always the best policy.

When you are completely honest about yourself, there is very little people can say about you that's going to have a negative impact. It's hard for a person to slander you about something you've already revealed to the world. As I like to say, "No judgment or opinion formed against you shall prosper when you live your truth."

Remember, there's no moment or situation you're ever going to encounter where honesty *isn't* the best policy. Just got pulled in by the cops? Tell them the truth because they're going to figure it out anyway. Busted stepping out on your wife (and when I say "busted," I don't mean she *thinks* you're sleeping with someone. I mean busted like you're caught butt-naked in the pussy)? Tell her why you did it—because you have a dick—and salvage the relationship (if you want to). Own what you did and let the chips fall where they may. You might be surprised that they actually fall in your favor.

Honesty is such a rare commodity these days that when you do tell someone the truth when they were expecting a lie, you'll catch them off guard. They might even be willing to look past transgressions that might have otherwise seemed unforgivable. People are thirsty for the truth. Sate that thirst, and they should always appreciate you.

But before you can reap the benefits of being honest with other people, you have to learn to be honest with yourself first.

The Big-Nosed Idiot

Word is I'm ugly. Maybe I am, but the truth is, I've never felt that way about myself. I've always overachieved in the pussy department. So any so-called lack of looks never got under my discolored skin. Still, I've been hearing it long enough that there must be something about the way I look that offends some of y'all.

The first time people started making fun of my looks was back in middle school when they began calling me "Boonky Nose." Now, for those of you uninitiated in Southern slang, a "boonky" is a butt. So a "boonky nose" is a nose that looks like a big ass. Evidently mine did, because that's what girls would say when I walked down the hallways at school. "Hey, there go Boonky Nose," they'd shout. "What up, Boonky Nose?"

Even then, that sort of teasing normally wouldn't have bothered me too bad. But it happened to trigger a very shitty experience from back in elementary school that had left me wondering whether in fact there *was* something wrong with my nose.

I was molested by my cousin's ex-wife when I was around eight years old. I should call her out by name, but I won't. So let's call her Linda. She was probably in her late twenties or early thirties at the time and was supposed to be watching me after school when my grandmother wasn't around. All Linda needed to do was feed me snacks and make sure I didn't get into any trouble, but for whatever twisted reasons, she added making me suck her titties and giving me head to our activity list.

I can't say I was traumatized by the sex, because the truth is I liked it. When she told me, "If you tell a soul about this, I'll never let you do it again," I damn sure kept my mouth shut. But clearly this wasn't a healthy situation.

The abuse (even if I liked it, it was still abuse) went on for close to a year, and probably would have lasted longer, but one afternoon Linda showed up at my Grandma's place with a brand-new Jheri curl.* The smell from the chemical relaxer almost made me gag. I tried to get past it, but it was too much. Suddenly I wasn't interested in her titties anymore. I guess smell is a stronger sense than sex for young boys.

I did everything I could to keep her away from me. Remember

---

*A Jheri curl's gotta be one of the top three stupidest hairstyles of all time. I don't know whose culture black people were appropriating back then, but not only did those Jheri curls look stupid and smell terrible, they were also a fire hazard. You would think after Michael Jackson's curl went up in flames, people would learn their lessons, but nope, niggas had to have that drip! Kids, if you still don't know what a Jheri curl is, see Eazy-E's character in *Straight Outta Compton*.

those little poppers you got from the fireworks stand? That looked like sperm and made a bang when you threw them on the sidewalk? I hated the smell of that Jheri curl activator so much that I'd throw those poppers at her when she'd try to molest me.

After a while Linda got tired of me fighting her off and accepted our inappropriate affair was over. But instead of handling it like an adult—surprise—this grown-ass lady became vindictive. I guess she felt rejected by my eight-year-old self, so she went out of her way to make me feel bad about myself, too. She started saying things like, "Damn 'Nard, you got a big-ass nose." Or, "'Nard, why your nose so big? Your cousins' noses ain't big like that." Again, this was a grown-ass woman talking to an eight-year-old boy. Of course it got into my head.

I wasn't sure what to do, so I went to my grandmother and begged her, "You have to help me do something about my nose." Like all grandmothers, she wanted to help, so she started rubbing cream on my nose every day, claiming it would shrink it. It could have been Preparation H for all I know, but whatever it was, of course it didn't work. How could it have? There was nothing wrong with my nose in the first place. I was just a kid growing into my body who happened to have a big nose.

Once all the girls started calling me Boonky Nose, it was fair game for the guys to clown me too. First I was Toucan Sam. Then they started calling me B.A.N. or Big-Ass Nose. It got so common that I remember I got stuck in a remedial math class with this slow kid everyone called Peter Pan.* One day I was really mess-

---

*I have no idea what the kid's real name was. We called him Peter Pan because he was obsessed with, you guessed it, Peter Pan. Kids would go up to him and say, "Hey, Peter Pan is dead." Then he would go crazy and chase them around yelling, "Peter Pan is not dead! He's alive!" As I've said, there's not much to do in Moncks Corner.

ing with him and he made an outburst in class. "Who is bothering you?" the teacher asked. Peter Pan pointed to me and said, "Larry McKelvey—the big-nose idiot!" When he said that, I thought to myself, "Damn, even the special kids are calling me 'big nose.' This is outta control. . . ."

Between my abusive babysitter and those taunts, I probably should have developed a serious hang-up about my nose as an adult. But I didn't. Sure, the comments stung, but I can't say they gave me a real complex. I credit that to a couple of factors.

The first is that, as I grew older, I realized there's nothing you can really do about a big nose. You can wear a hat if you have a funny head, or grow a beard if your chin's weak. Short of plastic surgery, which isn't an option when you live in a trailer on a dirt road and eat free lunches at school, you're pretty much stuck with the nose God gave you. So at a young age, I learned the power of acceptance. I had to accept that I had a big nose and just keep it moving.

Plus, there were some big-nose rappers poppin' at the time. Like KRS-One, who should have called himself "Nostrils Reign Supreme Over Everyone." Or Humpty Hump, who spit the classic bars, "I get laid by the ladies, ya know I'm in charge / Both how I'm living and my nose is large."

It also helped that, growing up around my cousins and friends in Moncks Corner, I was forced to develop a pretty thick skin and learn how to laugh at myself. As brutal as we could be toward other kids, we were even crueler toward each other. Nothing— and I mean *nothing*—was off-limits. If your mother was having an affair, that was fair game. Father strung out on crack? Fair game. Your uncle is living out of a van 'cause he lost his job? Fair game. Your sister's baby has Down syndrome? We had jokes for that, too.

There were a million examples of how hard we went at each

other, but two still stand out vividly to me. One was the morning my cousin Kwame's dog got hit by a car. We were all hanging out at the school bus stop when it happened. Kwame ran out to the highway, dropped to his knees, and did everything he could to comfort his best friend.

When we saw Kwame weeping over his dying dog, did we go over and console him? At least tell him we were sorry his dog had just gotten run over in front of his eyes? Of course not. Instead, we started laughing our asses off. "Yo, did you see how that nigga ran out there? Like that shit was in slow motion!" someone screamed. Another yelled, "Yo, that nigga acting like someone fucked his girl. What is wrooong with him?" As Kwame walked off with his dead dog in his arms, we were still rolling around on the ground, laughing and holding our sides. There was never a moment when someone said, "Yo, chill, that's not cool." We literally had no chill.

Another time I was watching TV with my pops and cousins, and the news came on that the actor John Ritter had died. *Three's Company* was a popular show in our house, so did my dad have a good word for the man? Hell no. "He needed to die," offered my pops. "Living in that house with those two women and ain't never fuck nothing? What was wrong with him?" That's just how it went growing up. Nothing was off-limits. Nothing was sacred or inappropriate. *Everything* could be turned into a joke.

Black and Ugly as Ever

As I grew older, one person who inspired me to stay positive and ignore the haters was the late, great Notorious B.I.G. Especially his line in the remix for "One More Chance," where he spit:

Heartthrob, never
Black and ugly as ever
However . . .
I stay Coogi down to the socks . . .

It was only a couple of bars, but for a black kid getting used to hearing he was ugly, those lines were empowering. The greatest MC in the game admitting to being ugly while refusing to admit that it mattered gave me true confidence. When Jay Z started popping, he became another role model for the cosmetically challenged. Like Biggie, Jay knew he wasn't the best-looking individual, yet his charisma and confidence overshadowed what he lacked in looks. You can say he looks like a camel, but he's got the "hottest chick in the game wearing [his] chain." So don't tell me God isn't real!

Guys like Biggie and Jay taught me that as long as you focused on the "however" instead of the "ugly as ever," you could still be attractive to people. I couldn't control my height, the color of my skin, or how big my nose was growing, but I could control my aura. I could control walking into a room with confidence no matter what was being said about me.

I'm always motivated by people who own being Black and Ugly as Ever. Take Eric Williams, the former NBA player who was on *Basketball Wives* for a few seasons. Who's more cosmetically challenged than him? Not only is he ugly, but he's a got a huge keloid on his forehead that makes him look like a black unicorn. When he came on *The Breakfast Club* I had to fire off some jokes on him. First I put up a poll on our website asking listeners to vote on which of us was better-looking (for the record: I won). After teasing him about the poll results, I told him, "Man, you look like Hellboy!" "That's fine with me, Hellboy making money," Eric shot back. "Who else you want me to look like? Someone gotta play that ugly position. I'll take it."

I asked him why he'd never gotten the keloid shaved off. I wondered because I'd grown a very similar bump on my forehead after Darnell beat me up in high school. I'd told the doctor to shave mine off—I wasn't trying to be Boonky Nose *and* Boonky Head. Eric explained that he'd gotten his back when he was a teenager selling drugs in Newark. Someone stabbed him in his head while trying to rob his stash. The bump grew out of that wound, and he could have had it taken off, especially after he made millions in the NBA, but he never did. "It's a constant reminder for me of how I grew up . . . when I was young and dumb."

Even though you can't control your height, your skin color, or sometimes even your weight, you can *always* control how you come off to other people. Someone might meet you and think, "Ugly as ever," but you can make that impression fade after a few minutes. Someone who wrote you off initially can leave a conversation with you thinking, "That dude is cool," or "That girl is funny," or "That dude is smart." Not "That dude is ugly," "That girl is fat," or "That dude has a small mountain on his head."

That's why if you're feeling ugly—and most of us do sometimes—always ask yourself, "What's my 'however'?" If you don't feel like it's your personality, it's gotta be something else. Maybe you're a great musician. Then let the world hear your music. You might be a great artist. Then let the world see your art. You might be a great cook. Then let the world eat your food. Maybe you enjoy working out in the gym and staying in shape. Then let the world be impressed by how ripped you are. Whoever you are, you can have a "however."

If it's already there, then let it shine. If it's not, get to work on developing it. Remember, Biggie didn't sit there in his mom's crib feeling sorry for himself because he was a fat dark-skinned kid with a lazy eye and an AWOL father. He hit those Brooklyn streets and developed a bunch of "howevers." Chances are, you don't have it any worse than Biggie did, so get to work on your "howevers," too.

The *8 Mile* Theory

Another rapper who helped me understand the power in living my truth was Eminem. His whole career has been built on raw honesty, but one moment in his semi-biopic *8 Mile* in particular has always stuck with me:

Em's character, Rabbit, is about to go onstage and battle Anthony Mackie's character, "Poppa Doc." Rabbit knows that Poppa Doc will likely try to diss him on several fronts: Rabbit is white trash, his friends are losers, and Poppa Doc's crew has already beat him up and had sex with his girl. Exactly the type of revelations that would normally get you crushed in a rap battle.

So what does Rabbit do? Instead of letting Poppa Doc use those facts to take him down, when it's Rabbit's turn to rap, he gets out in front of the situation and disses himself *first*:

> I know everything he's going to say against me
> I *am* white, I am a fuckin' bum
> I *do* live in a trailer with my mom
> My boy Future *is* an Uncle Tom

As soon as Rabbit dissed himself first, he'd won the battle. He'd taken all of Poppa Doc's ammunition before he even had an opportunity to let off a shot.

Similar to Rabbit's strategy in that scene, I believe you should put your flaws and insecurities out there for the world to see *before* anyone can even try to hold them against you.

It takes courage to proactively reveal your flaws to the world, but if you can find that confidence, you'll always be one step ahead of your opponent. You can never be embarrassed or discredited about something if you share it with the world first.

If you would not be laughed at, be the first to laugh at yourself.

—Benjamin Franklin

That's why before you can get a joke off on me, I'm always going to clown myself first. I've known I look like a Teenage Mutant Ninja Turtle since the first movie came out. I've even dubbed myself, the rappers Jadakiss and Jeezy, and the singer Ne-Yo the "Teenage Mutant Nigga Turtles" because the four of us really do look so much like Leonardo, Donatello, Michelangelo, and Raphael. (We need our own movie on BET.) So no one is going to be able to use that diss against me.

There's very little that someone can "reveal" about me that's going to make me lose my cool or get me off my game. For instance, what's the worst thing you can say about a guy? He's got a small dick? Guess what? I've already talked about the fact I don't have the biggest penis in the world on air. So what sort of "damage" is that diss really going to inflict on me?

Now, for the record, my penis isn't that small. I once got a little concerned about some of my competition, so I took out the tape measure (like all men have, whether they want to admit it or not) and checked out how I measured up. The verdict was that I'm seven and three-quarters inches in the winter and eight inches in the summer. Plus two and a half very respectable inches of girth no matter what the season. So while I had been concerned I was on the small side, now I would argue that, in fact, my penis is decent sized. Or as I recently tweeted, *Not too big, Not too small. It's like the baby bear's porridge JUST RIGHT.*

God Jewel: Fellas, always put it out there that you have a smaller penis than you actually do. If you tell a woman about how your dick ain't that big, how you're just average, she'll like that you're humble and comfortable in your own skin. She might let you get her in bed because she thinks she's doing you a favor, but then when you finally pull it out, you're going to surprise her in a good way for once.

Women are so used to having dudes brag about how big they are, but then fail to measure up in the moment of truth. When you do the opposite, you'll be a breath of fresh air. . . .

And if you have had the misfortune of being born with a pint-size penis, might as well be honest and let her know ahead of time. If she still lets you hit, then you can be comfortable and know she really likes you.

Still, just by even *suggesting* that I didn't have the biggest dick in the world, I'd given myself so much power. The majority of black men in America would be ashamed to walk up to the counter of a drugstore holding anything other than a pack of Magnums (they happen to fit me very well). Especially someone in hip-hop. So to even joke about having an average-size penis makes me seem confident and secure.

Not long ago, the comedian Katt Williams tried to take me down during one of his shows by calling me "Charlamagne Tha Dog." Man, I almost felt sorry for him. I've been seeing that one since they invented social media. Whenever someone wants to diss me, they'll always try to flip the "Tha God" part of my name. If it's not "Charlamagne Tha Dog," it's "Charlamagne Tha Broad." Or "Tha Fraud."

Some of the best Twitter slander directed at me:

"Charlamagne's cheeks look like dried-up eye black."

"Charlamagne looks like a seahorse with diabetes."

"Charlamagne looks like he just got out of a chimney."

"Draymond Green's penis looks like Charlamagne's before and after pictures."

"I got a dark-skinned friend that looks like Charlamagne. / I got a light-skinned friend that looks like Charlamagne."

"That nigga really looks like Jerome wearing Morris Day's make up."

Penis size, bleaching, being ugly—no matter how much someone slanders me, I'm going to laugh. I'd be a hypocrite otherwise. Lord knows how many jokes I've made about other people's shortcomings: I said Drake looked like "a thumb with eyebrows." I told Natalie Nunn from the *Bad Girls Club* reality show she looked like the McDonalds character Mac Tonight. I told Lil Mama if her face was the Bible it would be the Old Testament. I said Adele is shaped like a Twitter egg. I told Ed Sheeran he looks like Jar Jar Binks. I even slandered the living legend Stevie Wonder, saying he looked like Jeezy from the front and 2Chainz walking away.

How the hell could I possibly get upset that a comedian called me "Tha Dog?" Or said I look like a bruised eggplant?

It's all jokes. And I'm going to laugh at them whether they're coming at me or from me. I don't respect anybody who can't poke fun at themselves if they also go at other people. To me, that's a sign of weakness. I pride myself on being strong.

One of the reasons I respect Bobby Bones so much is because he fully embraces the *8 Mile* Theory. Despite being from Arkansas, Bobby is kind of an outsider in the country music world. He didn't really grow up in the culture and a lot of people resent him for that. But instead of getting uptight about it, he's completely open about not being fully accepted. People will tweet about him being a fraud or a poser and he'll read their comments on air. He doesn't hide from that perception—he addresses it head-on.

A couple of years ago he played a clip of the emergency broadcast signal during a bit, which accidently triggered the real thing. It was a huge deal in the radio industry and iHeart ended up having to pay a million-dollar fine. Most people would have tried to throw their producer or an underling under the bus, but Bobby fully owned the situation. He got props from me for that.

The dude isn't trying to be anyone but himself. He's blind in one eye, so when it was time to name his production company he called it Right Side Blind. I love that.

Laugh loudly, laugh often, and most important, laugh at yourself.

—Chelsea Handler

Another person who employs the *8 Mile* Theory is the comedian Andrew Schulz, my friend and cohost on *The Brilliant Idiots*. Though he's never 'fessed up to it, Andrew clearly has a stomach condition. (If you know Andrew, then I know what you're thinking right now: he's full of shit.) Well, I'm no doctor, but he has to have irritable bowel syndrome. I've literally never been anywhere with this guy when he *hasn't* had to take a shit. Middle of a podcast? He's dipping out to take a shit. At a fancy restaurant for my birthday dinner? He's taking a shit. Six-hour flight from New York to LA? He's definitely taking a shit. Maybe two.

This guy's bowels aren't irritable. They're downright cantankerous.

Now here's the thing: most people would be extremely embarrassed and uptight about having a condition like that. Whenever it was time to take a dump in public, they'd be sneakier than Bill Cosby serving you a drink. Personally, I *hate* it when people know I'm about to shit. If I get that feeling, I'll try to hold it until I get home.

Andrew is the exact opposite. We can be in a room full of people and he'll calmly (and loudly) announce, "Okay, I'm gonna go take a shit. I'll be back in a few." Then he'll look around for a newspaper or book and proudly waltz to the bathroom.

Taking a stinky shit in public is probably near the top of the list of things people will make fun of you for, but by embracing the *8 Mile* Theory, Andrew has made himself immune to slander. It's amazing. Nobody can laugh about him or make snarky comments about him because there's zero shame in his shitting game. Think about how much stress and negative energy he's avoiding because he's honest about his nonstop need to number two.

Irritable bowels. Boonky noses. Big-ass bumps. Blind eyes. Cosmetic challenges.

We've all got that one thing, or even a few things, that the world might perceive to be flaws. It's inevitable. The key, as DJ Khaled would say, is not wasting your energy trying to cover them up. If you're uptight about something, the *best* thing you can do is be completely candid about what's bothering you.

Try it. Pick something that you've always been self-conscious or guarded about and start sharing it with the world. If it's physical, show it. If it's emotional, share it. I'm confident you'll see that, far from making jokes at your expense, people will be sympathetic, even supportive. And most important, you're taking all the power out of it. At the end of the day, everyone respects honesty. When you free yourself of all the insecurity and anxiety that's been weighing you down, you'll be shocked at how high you can soar.

Can I Get a Drop?

If you search on the Internet, besides folks accusing me of bleaching, I get clowned the most about the time I got punched in the head on camera outside of Power's studios. It's another great example of why you should always live your truth, no matter the situation.

For many years, the dominant hip-hop station in New York City was Hot 97, led by radio personalities and DJs like Angie Martinez, Funkmaster Flex, and Ed Lover. Then Power 105 and *The Breakfast Club* came along, and suddenly Hot's grip on the city wasn't so tight anymore. The personalities at Hot felt threatened, especially Funkmaster Flex, who had been at the station since it switched to hip-hop in the early nineties.

Around the same time *The Breakfast Club* started dominating the morning drive, Hot's longtime DJ—and Flex's good friend—Mister Cee was revealed to be a serial purchaser of penis. By that I mean Cee was arrested three times for soliciting transgender prostitutes. Before I go any further, I want to be clear, rival or not, Mister Cee is a hip-hop legend. From starting as Big Daddy Kane's DJ to helping Biggie get his first record deal to his work at Hot, Cee is absolutely a part of hip-hop history. Nothing, or no one, can ever take that away from him.

Unfortunately, instead of owning his actions, Cee tried to deny it. Every time he got busted, he tried to say it was just a misunderstanding. When that didn't work, he tried to insinuate that *The Breakfast Club* was creating the rumors (as if we could make up police reports) in an effort to defame him. Flex picked up on that theme and delivered a very aggressive rant toward me over the air.

"You are soft," Flex said in a theatrical voice. "You are baby-bottom, doo-doo soft, man." In addition to questioning my toughness, Flex also called me out for not spending enough time outside of Manhattan. "You don't go to the boroughs; you sneak in and out like a baboon when you're washing Carmelo Anthony and La La's underwear. You run out to the Laundromat, go back inside, shut up, man. Out-of-town, fried-chicken-eating—I bet you know all types of chicken, right? Lemon chicken. Soy chicken.* One of

---

*I guess Flex was referring to a time I appeared on La La's reality show. For the record I've never washed Carmelo and La La's underwear. I'm sure they have maids who do that. And while I do enjoy lemon chicken, I'm not really a fan of soy. . . .

those types of dudes, right? You're soft. You're cakes, man. I heard that little shot you threw this morning. Is that what you want? Is that what you want?"

That's exactly what I wanted.

Now if *I'm* being honest, I'd been hoping that Flex would come at me like that for a long time. I simply couldn't wait to catch that body. Like Cee, Flex is an undisputed hip-hop legend. But over the years, he'd developed the habit of talking way too much trash about other people without being honest about his own situations. Which meant he was fair game. So I let Flex have it. I gave him Donkey of the Day and then blessed him with the nickname (which has stuck to this day) "Flex Hogan," since he sounded like Hulk Hogan when he would go on his rants.

Then I added a little extra fuel to the fire by releasing a video called *What If Funkmaster Flex Told the Truth?* In the animated clip I pondered whether Flex would ever talk about his domestic violence charges, or the time he got beat up by DJ SNS for talking smack, or the time some thugs allegedly stuck a pistol in his mouth for dissing Tupac almost fifteen years after Pac had been killed. I'm sure he didn't appreciate the video one bit. But everything in it was true as far as I knew it.

I don't know if there's a connection, but the Monday after that video aired, I was walking into work around 5:00 a.m. when I was approached by a dude with a camera. He asked if he could "get a drop" from me.*

I gave those guys their drop, but something about the exchange

---

*For those of you who don't know, "drop" is shorthand for a "name-drop." Back when DVDs were still a thing, drops were a way for struggling rappers to look like they were hanging out with popular personalities. An artist or DJ would look into someone's camera and say, "Yo, this is Charlamagne Tha God, and you are now watching us sneak up on niggas and hit them on camera dotcom" . . . or something like that.

didn't feel right to me. Who the hell is hustling at 5:00 a.m. for a street DVD? I smelled a setup. I was so suspicious that later that morning on *The Breakfast Club* I talked about the situation. For our daily feature Question of the Day, I even asked, "If you get attacked on camera, do you fight or run?"

Fast-forward to the next morning: once again, I'm walking to the station—solo—at 5:00 a.m. and once again, a guy approaches me with a camera.

What happened next has been viewed over a million times on Worldstar.

First the guy asks, "What's good, my G? Can I get a drop?" In the video, you'll see that as soon as he says that, I could tell the bullshit was brewing. "What's up with y'all and these drops, man?" I ask, my spider senses tingling. The cameraman doesn't answer me, but repeats, this time with a little more force in his voice, "I need a drop, son . . ." While he was saying it, another geriatric goon that was with him snuck up behind me and landed a sucker punch to the side of my head.

God Jewel: Always be wary when someone over forty calls you "son" unless it's your own father.

Now when you get punched in the back of the head unexpect-edly, your fight-or-flight instinct immediately kicks in. In this case I chose: "Flight!"

I listened to my brain's command and started to remove myself from the situation. I backpedaled into the street and started to jog away, but had to sidestep a car that was headed straight at me. Once I got around the car, I saw the dude that hit me, the cameraman, and two other senior sluggers headed toward me. I kept moving backward, Madden agility on 99, and did a half jog, half run until I was safely inside the Power building.

As a tax-paying, law-abiding citizen with a child, I handled that situation *exactly* the right way. How you should do, too, if you find yourself in a similar situation. I have zero shame saying that. Why would I stand my ground and try to fight four complete strangers? I didn't know what those guys had planned for me if they'd caught me, and I wasn't about to find out. *

Since I always own my truth, as soon as I escaped into the building, I went on *The Breakfast Club* and shared *exactly* what happened with our listeners. That's a key point. When someone jumps you and you run, it's tempting to retell the story in a way that's sympathetic to your cause. To exaggerate how tough those goons were, or to skip over the part where you almost got hit by a car. I didn't do any of that. I told my listeners the undiluted truth. Four old-ass goons, looking like they could have been extras in a Spike Lee joint, had punched me in the head and tried to jump me on camera. And I'd hauled ass.

Period.

A couple of days later, the goons (or more likely, whoever sent them) finally released the video on Worldstar, complete with a produced intro and subtitles. The Internet pored over it like a Kardashian sex tape, looking for inaccuracies in my account. Ulti-

---

*A little while after this incident I got tried again when I went to get some money out of the ATM in a Manhattan pharmacy. Some guy who was about six three and 250 attacked me the moment I walked through the door. I don't know who sent this person, and maybe I was supposed to be intimidated by his size, but to be frank I beat the shit out of this guy with a pair of brass knuckles I had on me, just like my pops had back in Moncks Corner. I left him laid out on the floor, then I called the police and filed a report to have him arrested. Because that's what you do when you're a law-abiding, tax-paying citizen of America and someone attacks you for no reason.

mately they had no choice but to say, "Damn, it went down exactly the way Charlamagne said it did." The incident had been set up to clown me, but I'd flipped it in my favor. Because I'd owned my truth.

Don't get it twisted; it could have been bad for me. If I hadn't gone on air and told people *exactly* what happened, Flex could have buried me with that video. If I'd gone on air and embellished how I reacted, he'd have caught me in a lie. Even worse, if I'd never spoken on the situation, and tried to front like it hadn't happened at all, that would have hurt me. It would have looked like I was embarrassed about what happened. My credibility would have been shot.

Instead, by owning my truth, I turned a potentially negative situation into one of my greatest moments. First off, over a million people have laughed at that video. Why shouldn't they? Some old dude smacked me in the head and I backpedaled like a NFL cornerback dropping into coverage against Tom Brady. It *was* funny. I would have laughed at that too. Whether people were laughing with me or at me doesn't matter to me. I just appreciate them sending energy my way.

Second, I truly believe there was an educational aspect to that video. Hopefully it helped folks see that you don't have to "win" every situation you find yourself in. Sometimes you got to give people *today* so you can have *tomorrow*. Imagine if I had stood my ground and fought. Maybe I would have caught one or two of them in the face. But then what?

What if they'd broke my jaw and left me unable to do my job? Why even risk escalating the energy to that level? I'd much rather escape than find out. I'll always let goons win the moment if it means protecting my future. My future is so much brighter than anything a bunch of hired goons have to look forward to.

God Jewel: "For those that fly may fight again / Which he can never do that's slain." That's the British poet Samuel Butler explaining in the nineteenth century what's still true today: running away when outnumbered is always your best tactical choice. . . .

While that incident ended up having a positive effect on my career, sadly it didn't turn out as positive for everyone involved. A couple of years ago, I got word that the dude who hit me was shot and killed in Delaware. I don't know his name, don't know where he was from or anything about him. I was just told how it ended for him. I can't say that it surprised me—if a guy will get up at five in the morning to punch somebody in the head on camera, then imagine what else he would do. He probably was into all kinds of dirt, and that energy finally caught up to him. Like my father said, when you live that life, you're going to wind up one of three ways.

Of the Industry? Or of the People?

Growing up in Moncks Corner, I used to listen to the jocks conduct interviews on the radio and wonder why they didn't really seem to have an opinion. Why didn't they ever ask the obvious question when they had the chance? Which is why from the moment I got on the air at Jamz in Charleston, whether it was music, celebrities, movies, sports, sex, or politics, I called it like I saw it. Even if that honesty cost me a job, I refused to cut back on my candor. As my career progressed, I kept hearing the same refrain: "Man, Charlamagne's so honest. The dude is so real." I appreciated the compliment, but I couldn't help but think, "Why am I being applauded for telling the truth? Shouldn't everyone do that?"

I came to understand that honesty is a rare commodity in the music industry. Part of that is the artists' fault. They've created a very toxic environment for the truth to flourish. As far as I can tell, hip-hop is the only culture where saying you don't like an album, or didn't enjoy a performance, are literal fighting words. Siskel and Ebert might have given a movie two thumbs down, but no one was threatening to shoot up their cars. Simon Cowell could tell a guy he was a lousy singer, but the dude and his team weren't trying to see him in the street afterward. When the Rolling Stones get embroiled in a lawsuit over royalties—which they have—I'm sure Mick Jagger doesn't go on a radio station with his goons and tell the label heads they're beefing with they're going to drop a refrigerator on their heads off a twelve-story building—shout out to my guy Jadakiss! The consequences for talking about a story—or simply having an opinion—in hip-hop culture become too real.

Think about it. When Birdman infamously rolled into *The Breakfast Club* with a bunch of goons and warned Envy, Angela, and me to "put some respek" on his name, what exactly had been our crime? Only that we'd talked about how he has a long history of allegedly not paying his artists, including Lil Wayne. A man who we saw him kiss on the mouth (which we talked about too). It's not like we'd revealed some dark industry secret. Birdman's label, Cash Money Records, has literally been sued more than ten times by artists claiming they hadn't been paid properly. *Of course* we were going to talk about it. That's our *job*. Or at least it should be. Which is why I told Birdman, "Don't act tough with the radio guy." At the end of the day, we're only there to give our opinion. If you don't like that, then address the issues we're talking about. Not us.

When artists and their teams try to intimidate personalities for having opinions, all it does is shut down open discussion and make for boring radio. Personally, I'm always going to state my opinion no matter the perceived consequences. Most on-air personalities won't though. They'd rather play it safe than deal with some goons for saying they didn't like a song.

Having said that, I can't place the blame solely on the artists. Another reason too many radio jocks and writers don't share their true opinions is because they're more concerned with making friends in the industry than being advocates for their audiences. Wendy was the first person who broke down this phenomenon to me. "Every time you get on this microphone, you have a fundamental choice," she once told me. "You're either going to be 'of the industry,' or you're going to be 'of the people.'" She went on to explain that if you are representing the people, then you will give your honest opinions on situations, instead of the politically correct stance. When you're of the people, you will ask the questions that the fans want to hear, instead of the talking points the publicists would prefer you stick to.

If you choose to be "of the industry," you'll always support the narrative that the record label is trying to push. When you're "of the industry," you'll hype every album like it's a masterpiece, even if you couldn't make it past the first track.

Most jocks end up choosing "the industry." They want to be invited to the listening sessions, the album-release parties, or the label exec's birthday party in the back rooms of fancy restaurants.

They can't be "of the people" because they think if they ask too many uncomfortable questions, then the publicists won't bring them A-list artists anymore. So they play it safe.

Wendy gave zero fucks about being safe, which I loved. Wendy and I are both Cancers, and we share an instinctual need to speak our minds. I always understood why she was so fearless about asking tough questions and didn't spend a second fretting about the consequences. She couldn't do it any other way. Nor can I.

Wendy didn't care about being on the scene. You never saw pictures of her popping bottles in the clubs with rappers, or dining downtown with executives. Her idea of a good time was smoking with Kev and chilling out at home. I know because whenever I'd hang out with them, we'd just knock back a couple of bottles of champagne in their crib and I'd pass out in their purple-painted guest bedroom. That was it.

Wendy's attitude didn't discriminate. I even felt it when I first started cohosting her show. When I say her audience hated me at first, man, they REALLY hated me. They didn't like my accent, they didn't like my looks, and they especially didn't like that I had the audacity to walk off a dirt road in Moncks Corner and stroll into the Big Apple freely stating strong opinions.

Did Wendy try to cover up their outrage? Did she try to protect her young protégé from the slander being slung his way? Hell no. She threw me in the deep end and then stepped back and watched to see if I could swim. If someone wanted to slander me, she'd put them on the air and let them go off on me live. She even put a poll up on her website asking whether she should keep me on or send me back down South. Something like seventy percent of the people said, "Naw, send the lisping motherfucker back home."

The attacks were unrelenting. If you want a contemporary example, imagine Beyoncé's Beehive swarming against someone on social media. That's how Wendy's fans were coming for me.

I wasn't sure I was going to survive the slander.

Still, I couldn't stop being me. What's the saying? "I'd rather be hated for who I am than loved for who I'm not"? That became the mantra I'd repeat in my head every weekday between two and seven as Wendy would unleash her army of haters on me.

The turning point came one weekend when I was down in South Carolina trying to make some extra bread hosting parties. I was hanging out with an old man I befriended named Ronald Ferguson. He was a talented artist who I met after I commissioned him to paint a big-ass portrait of my girl.

Ronald reminded me of Rafiki from *The Lion King*—from the outside he seemed batshit crazy, but he was actually a wise dude. Ronald used to listen to me on Wendy, and when we'd hang out, I'd talk to him about what was happening on the show. That one weekend I was sitting in his yard as he painted and I was being unusually silent. I was preoccupied with how much hate I was getting from Wendy's listeners. I'd thought New Yorkers, out of everyone, would appreciate my honesty. If New Yorkers, who prided themselves on keeping it real, weren't going to support me, would anyone? Was I already at the end of the road?

Ronald must have been reading my mind because out of nowhere he said to me, "You know you going to win up there, right?"

"Huh?" I replied.

"In New York," he said. "They don't like you now, but that's only because they don't know you yet. Just keep being honest, keep being yourself, and you're going to be all right."

It wasn't a long speech—I don't think Ronald even looked up from his canvas as he spoke—but that simple advice was exactly what I needed to hear. I took his words back to New York with me that Monday and doubled down on being myself.

I couldn't just tell the truth about how I felt about the industry.

I had to start telling the truth more about *myself* too. So I told the listeners about how I was having a hard time making the transition to New York. How lonely it was to be up here without friends or a place of my own. How I felt like a fish out of water, struggling to figure out how to catch a bus or ride the subway. How discouraging it was to go on Wendy's site and read that most of them wanted to send me packing.

Opening up was the turning point. Instead of dissing me, they began to root for me. They wanted to walk my journey with me. As an added bonus, after hearing how lost and lonely I was, a lot of women felt like it was their duty to take care of me because I was a long way from home. I can't even begin to tell you how much sympathy pussy and free meals I got during this time. I learned the esophagus of a woman with empathy for your situation is a perfect place for your penis.

Slowly but surely, the tide started to change. The barriers started to be broken down. The "I hate Charlamagne" comments started to turn into "I hate Charlamagne, but that was some real shit he said. . . ." And from that point, I was good. But only because I listened to Ronald and didn't try to be anything but my true authentic self.

Standing by Your Words

Birdman wasn't the only artist whose feathers got ruffled by my refusal to pander to the industry. Since landing on *The Breakfast Club* I've dubbed myself the "Prime Minister of Pissing People Off, the Architect of Aggravation and the Ruler of Rubbing People the Wrong Way" for my penchant for getting under artists' skin.

Over the years, there have been dozens of rappers, singers, actors, and even moguls who've been pissed off by my unfiltered opinions.

One time P. Diddy didn't appreciate my assessment of *Last Train to Paris*, the album he made with his female group Dirty Money. In addition to calling it garbage, I described it as "shake-weight music" and said it was made for men to rub each other's calf muscles to. Remember when everyone thought the NBA star Chris Bosh was gay? I joked that Bosh probably liked listening to *Last Train* in his headphones while he warmed up for games. Sure enough, that night—ring, ring!—Diddy on line one.

Ever the salesman, Diddy tried to get me to change my opinion on the album. It wasn't hip-hop, it was dance music, he explained. I should appreciate it as such. Finally Diddy told me, "You are going to get on this train," one way or another. It was a good line, but I still wasn't buying a ticket. So I had to tell Diddy my original review still stood: trash.

(To be fair, I was far from the only one with that opinion. *Last Train* ended up derailing not long after leaving the station and we haven't heard anything from Dirty Money aka "the New Total" since.)

Sometimes the complaints don't arrive in the form of a civilized phone conversation like I had with Diddy. Often they come during uncomfortable face-to-face encounters when I see an artist at an event, awards show, or party.

I feel like these kind of encounters happen to me more than most. One reason is because I don't roll out with a lot of security, just Wax (though that's really more than enough). Maybe people feel like I'm an easy target, especially after watching *Can I Get a Drop*.

The second reason is that when artists see me, I somehow become the manifestation of everything negative that's been said about them. Not just a comment I might have said on the radio, but what other jocks have said about them, too. Or slander they've read about themselves on social media. All that negativity rises to the surface when I enter the room. They work themselves into a frenzy and want to take action.

I embrace that energy because I take pride in standing behind whatever I might have said on *The Breakfast Club*, *The Brilliant Idiots*, social media, or *Uncommon Sense*. If I don't stand by my words in person, then it's cowardly for me to talk tough on the radio. It's an important policy to have, but it admittedly leads to some tense situations.

A prime example is when the former Bad Boy star Mase tried to roll on me at the Revolt Music Conference in Miami a few years back. He was upset because I had been very vocal in my opinion that he was a hypocrite. Here's why: Just a few years after being one of the hottest rappers in the country, Mase "retired" from rap to dedicate himself to serving God. He wrote a book about his new life and started preaching at a church in Atlanta. He must have gotten bored with that life, because a few years after that, he started hanging around rappers again and divorced his wife. Most of his congregation got fed up and he left the church. So Mase said "fuck it" and became a rapper again. Not a Christian rapper either: he signed with the gangsta rap god 50 Cent.

Look, everybody is entitled to change their mind, but I couldn't understand how you go overnight from being a man of the cloth to a G-Unit soldier. I expressed this opinion on several occasions but hadn't been in the same room with him until the conference. I was waiting to be seated at a restaurant at the Fontainebleau Hotel when, out of nowhere, Mase walked up on me and said, "What's up?" in a way that insinuated the next thing coming from him was going to be a punch. "What's up," I replied back to him in the same tone, which he didn't appreciate. He started to aggressively move forward, but he clearly didn't see my brother from another, Wax, standing right behind me. Before I could even respond, Wax was already manhandling Mase and threw him clean out the restaurant.

It's situations like that where I have to be smart. When you have a weapon of mass destruction like Wax at your disposal, you can't misuse it. As much as I would have liked to teach Mase a lesson for rolling up on me like that, it wasn't worth it. There was absolutely no reason to demolish a way-past-his-prime rapper-turned-preacher-turned rapper-again at the Revolt Music Conference. It would be pointless. So I told Wax to fall back from Mase, who of course had changed his tune. "I just want to talk; I just want to talk," he kept saying, while keeping one eye on Wax.*

Eventually things cooled down a bit, and Mase and I went to a corner of the restaurant to talk. He told me while he didn't like being called a hypocrite, he was really upset because he felt I was behind a conspiracy to blackball him from New York radio. Huh? I told him straight up that that was nonsense and the reason he wasn't getting played on the radio anymore was A) it wasn't the 90s anymore, and B) people had lost respect for him. "You can't go from rap to the church, back to rap, back to church like that," I told him. "It's not believable." The exact same thing I had been saying on the radio.

All he could do was give me dap and say, "I respect that." If I had backpedaled, or tried to distance myself from what I'd said

---

*Just in case you think I'm exaggerating, ESPN commentator Bomani Jones happened to be eating in the restaurant at the time and witnessed the whole thing between Wax and Mase. This is how Bomani, who didn't have a dog in the fight, described it on his podcast: *Mase walks in and he just gets a couple steps in* [toward Charlamagne] *and next thing I know Mase is on the retreat. And some big dude in a white T-shirt and tight camouflage-type pants and Timberlands is coming back the other way. The gentleman wearing Timberlands at the Fontainebleau has Mase on the retreat. Now obviously this was a music-industry event, but I also feel like if you're in a tropical environ and you got a dude walking around in boots, he's ready.*

on the radio, Mase wouldn't have respected me and I wouldn't have respected myself. You have to stand by your words—that's the only way they can hold weight. Mase and I still don't like each other, but at least we know where the other person stands.

Busta Rhymes is another artist who decided to take out his frustrations on me in public. I forget the year, but the day was definitely June 29, which is my born day. I was in LA, drunk as hell at Melanie Fiona's birthday party (she's a Cancer too). I was celebrating with Angela Yee, our homegirl Lore'l, and, of course, Wax. At one point we were chopping it up with my dude Bu (Akon's brother) when Busta Rhymes walked into our section. I could feel him looking at me, but it was my birthday, and I was in a good mood, so I didn't sweat it. Then Busta approached and said he needed to have a few words with yours truly.

"Do you know me?" he asked.

"What?" I replied.

"Do you know me?" Busta said again.

I was pretty drunk, so my tolerance for BS was running on empty. Of course I knew him—Busta was one of the greatest live performers in the history of hip-hop. A living legend. So that clearly wasn't what he was really asking. He was trying to punk me. Probably because I had spoken several times on the radio about how I felt Busta had fallen off musically. I'd even wrote on Twitter *You put the TV on mute while Busta is performing the closed captions would probably read, "!!!!!!&*&*&*&*&*#########&*&*&*&*&*!!!!!!!???????????"*

"Yeah, I know you. You're a rapper I used to like," I told him. "But your shit is wack now."

That set him off. Busta started ranting about how I'd tried to sabotage his situation with his baby mama when she was on Wendy's show. How I'd tried to turn her against him. He was passionate about what he was saying, but there was one slight problem: the interview happened three years *before* I was on Wendy's show. "Busta, I have no idea what you're talking about," I told him in all honesty. He thought I was trying to play dumb.

"You Charlamagne, right?" he shot back.

I was getting tired of this game. "I was not on Wendy's show when your baby mama was there," I said, adding, "Plus, if you don't know who I am, then why are you complaining about something I allegedly said?"

That must not have been the answer he was looking for, because then he turned into the "rah rah, like a dungeon dragon" he used to rap about. "You better stop all this tough-guy shit!" he roared.

"*You* better stop this tough-guy shit. We can get it on in this restaurant," I told him, perhaps foolishly.

Busta's security guard stepped up like he was going to do something. But Wax appeared out of nowhere and sternly announced, "I'll fuck you up!" That stopped Busta's guy dead in his tracks.

Just as things seemed like they were going to get physical, Bu and my man Dennis Ortiz (Joell Ortiz's brother) stepped between us and calmed things down. I'm glad they did, because truthfully, testosterone, ego, and liquor were fueling that situation, and there was no need for us to fight.

And for the record, I got no issues with Busta now. We give each other a mutual "peace" when we see each other. Truthfully, I don't know if I could beat Busta Rhymes in a fight if things had gotten to that point (if you look at pictures of the confrontation, I look like a lapdog barking at a pitbull). But I also didn't care. I've had my ass kicked a few times. I'm not afraid to lose a fight. To me, it was about the principle of standing next to my words. I could take a stand for saying he's become a wack-ass rapper, but I couldn't stand by the baby-mama beef because I'd had nothing to do with it. You have to be able to stand by *your* words at all times. If you don't, then they don't mean anything.

The Danger of Yes-Men

Another reason honesty is so hard to find in hip-hop comes down to the bedbugs of the industry: the yes-men. It feels like you never see one, but these guys (and girls) are everywhere. The reason it seems like you never see them is because no one wants to own up to the job. You won't find anyone whose job description is being a rapper's "yes-man," but trust me, the vast majority of the rappers I know have one, if not several.

I believe one of the reasons Kanye has been so emotional about his career is because he feels like he doesn't have anyone keeping it real with him. When I hear Kanye rant, I hear someone searching for truth. Someone hoping at least one person will give him an honest opinion.

Instead of honesty, I suspect Kanye only gets validation. When he taped his "Kanye Kardashian" interview at *The Breakfast Club*, he had the usual horde of handlers: label publicists, management company people, and security. He also had two dudes with him who were dressed fresh to death. At least by Kanye's standards, because I don't know what the hell they were wearing. Maybe they were his stylists.

Someone who was there later told me that while we were interviewing Kanye in the studio, those two dudes were in the lobby, which also serves as our greenroom. The studio has big glass windows so you can watch the interview from the lobby. Throughout the interview those two guys stood there watching. Every time

Kanye made a point, they'd get animated. Maybe give him a fist pump or cheer him on. He kept looking at them throughout the interview and seemed to feed off their energy. Nothing wrong with that, right? They were just being supportive.

Now here's the thing: the audio from the interview *isn't piped into the lobby*. That means they literally couldn't hear what he was saying. They were just giving him positive affirmation because they saw that as their job. He could have been crashing and burning during that interview and they'd still be cheering him on like he'd just dropped the greatest gem in the world. The people who were in the lobby with them later told me it was surreal. The very epitome of yes-men.

After the interview and we walked out together, the first thing he told those guys was, "Charlamagne told me ain't none of y'all keep it real with me!" Kanye knew that I'd at least told him the truth. I heard after he left our studio, he went over to tape with my buddy Elvis Duran at Z100 and kept shaking his head and zoning out during the preinterview. When Garrett, one of the producers, asked him if everything was okay, he said, "Yo, my bad. I just got finished talking with Charlamagne. . . ."

When all you've been getting is preapproved validation, hearing the hard truth can mess your head up. I'm sure that's how Kanye felt. All the more reason he needed to hear it. If the people closest to you won't be real with you, how else can you improve? How else can you push yourself? How else will you know when you're playing yourself?

I practice what I preach in this department. If you listen to me on any of my platforms, you know that not only am I honest with my cohosts and the people around me, but I also demand the same honesty in return. A lot of folks are shocked when they listen to *The Brilliant Idiots* because of how hard Andrew Schulz and I go at each other when we get into a heated debate. I'll see comments like, "I can't believe Charlamagne doesn't punch Schulz in the mouth. Son is mad disrespectful!" or "Charlamagne needs to let that white boy go. Always disagreeing with him!" Why would I get rid of Andrew for disagreeing with me? That's what I want—and what the listeners should want—from a cohost. It's so much healthier than a cohost just saying, "Yep," or "No doubt," every time I make a point.

It's no different with Wax. If he is doing something foolish—which admittedly is often—I'll let him know in no uncertain terms. I've gotten on his case both on and off air many times. But if I respect something he's working on—like opening a chicken farm in South Carolina—I'll publically give him props as well as supporting him behind the scenes. All my friendships are built on a similar foundation of honesty.

I don't want any yes-men around me. I want everybody to tell me the truth even if it costs them their job.
—Samuel Goldwyn

Here's the thing: Everyone *says* they don't want yes-men around. Everyone *says* they want their people to keep it real with them. In reality, however, very few people do. For all their talk about "my team always gives it to me straight," they don't actually want that at all. They're much more comfortable dodging the truth than facing it head-on.

Are you one of those people? When one of your close friends, family members, or crew give you a little constructive criticism, how do you react? Do you get defensive? Are you dismissive? Or even worse, do you lash out at that person?

If the answer to any of those questions is yes, then your actions are *discouraging* honesty. And *encouraging* yes-men. When you dismiss, or lash out at a person who keeps it real with you, what do you think eventually happens? They stop keeping it real. They might not lie to you, but they'll probably just keep their mouth shut when they see you screwing up. They'll sit there and watch as you self-destruct. Can you really blame them? They tried to help, but you weren't receptive.

This is why it's so important to empower your inner circle. Get your ego in check and listen when they slander you. Instead of pushing an honest friend away, bring him or her even closer into your decision-making process. Sure, it hurts to be criticized at first, especially by people close to you. But you'll get over that little sting.

Remember, yes-men aren't only unproductive—they can get you killed. Figuratively and literally. You know what happens when you have nothing but yes-men in your corner? You eventually get knocked the fuck out.

Honesty in Your Relationship

Sure, you want your team—your squad, your people, your folk, your crew, your clan, your niggas, whatever you want to call them—to be honest with you and vice versa. But the person you really need to be brutally honest with is your significant other. Your boo. Your old lady. Your old man. The person you are sharing bodily fluids with on a consistent basis. The person you go to sleep with at night. Whatever the hell you call him or her, you'd better be all the way honest with them if you want your relationship to truly flourish.

Again, I have largely practiced what I preach on this subject, to a degree that might shock you. I'm convinced the only reason Mook Mook and I are happily married today is because of raw, brutal, and ultimately beautiful honesty we've shared with each other over the years. We've been together off and on since we were sixteen years old. We literally grew up together. We've gone through so much it would be pointless for us to lie to each other. No matter what bullshit we have done, honesty has been the *glue* that's kept us together.

I've done a lot of dirt over the years, but perhaps my lowest moment took place at Mook Mook's senior prom. In Moncks Corner the tradition was that after the prom all the kids would head down to Myrtle Beach and hang out for the weekend. That year Mook Mook went with her crew, her cousin Trica, and her best friend Uquinta, while I brought along my cousin Anthony.

We were all at the hotel getting wasted—I'm talking that kind of dangerous "rockstar" wasted. The girls were having a great time listening to music and cracking jokes, but Anthony and I were thinking like savages. Back then our mind-set was "HAVE SEX WITH EVERYTHING!!!" Yep, I'd come with my girl, but we wanted to fuck the whole crew.

It's not a good excuse, but back in those days we didn't have much else going on in our lives. The more fly chicks you could smash in Moncks Corner, the more badges of honor you could strut around town with. That's all that mattered to us.

So even though Anthony had his girlfriend with him and I had mine, we hatched a scumbag scheme to get with Trica and Uquinta. Somehow we convinced our girlfriends to go back to their room, then we crept off to the room Trica and Uquinta were sharing. One thing led to another, and I started having sex with Trica.

If that wasn't bad enough, after a while Anthony and I switched up and I ended up getting with Uquinta too. No need to tell me I was a complete piece of shit. I already know. . . .

After my dirty deed(s), I went back to Mook Mook's hotel room and acted like everything was good. The next day, we all headed back to Moncks Corner and it seemed like she was none the wiser for what had happened. Then a couple of days later Trica and Uquinta showed up at Mook Mook's house. Uquinta, with her fake, God-fearing ass, declared she needed to get something off her chest.

"God wants me to let you know something," she told Mook Mook dramatically, before turning to Trica. "Go ahead, tell her, Trica." Then Trica tearfully confessed, "I had sex with Larry over the weekend in Myrtle Beach."

Mook Mook immediately called me and said, "Larry, is there something you want to tell me?"

"Like what?" I asked.

"Like you and Trica having sex after the prom. Because that's what Uquinta just told me!"

I didn't freak out or start weaving a bunch of lies together. Actually, I was pissed off because if you're going to tell the truth in God's name, then you'd better tell the whole truth. Which Uquinta evidently had neglected to do. "Word, that's what Uquinta told you?" I calmly replied. "You know what, she's right. I did fuck Trica. But I fucked Uquinta too. Did she tell you that?"

Mook Mook was still furious with me, but I believe she was more pissed that Uquinta had come over there with a holier-than-thou attitude and tried to palm the whole thing off on Trica. I guess God didn't tell her to own up to *her* own dirt. Even after I told my girl the truth, Uquinta still denied it. But, as I pointed out, why in the hell would I confess to more crimes if I didn't have to?

Yes, I was a scumbag. But I was an honest scumbag. That doesn't absolve me, but I do think it's better that somebody be with me knowing exactly what I am than be with me for what they *think* I am. I believe I was only able to salvage our relationship and build it into the place it is today by being honest. It's easier to forgive somebody when they tell the truth about a situation, especially in a relationship. Mook Mook might not have trusted me when it comes to other women, but she could trust me as a person.

Now, I'm not telling y'all to cheat and then tell your significant other the truth and expect everything will be okay. If you cheat, chances are your relationship isn't going to work out too well. But I am telling you your odds improve if you are honest. Not only about what you did, but why you did it too. And just to be clear, the primary reason Mook Mook even gave me a second chance was because we were both young and still relatively stupid. No way she would put up with that sort of shit now.

And to be fair, I wasn't the only one who has done dirt in this relationship. Most women go through their hoe phase in college (as I believe they should), and Mook Mook definitely cheated on me when she attended the University of South Carolina.* Since honesty has always been at the root of our relationship, she told me all about it, too.

When a woman drops that atomic bomb, almost all men turn into a complete shell of themselves. I was no exception. Like an idiot, I didn't just accept that information and keep it moving. No,

---

*Calling it cheating might be a little harsh, because, as I said, the truth is we were on and off for many years until we finally got engaged.

like so many other clueless men before and since, I started to ask questions. Especially about one dude that she seemed to have had a thing for.

"Was he better than me in bed?" I queried.

"He wasn't necessarily *better*," she said.

I took the bait.

"Was he bigger than me?"

Silence.

"What, he was bigger?" I yelled. "How much?"

"Yo, I ain't ever seen no shit like that before," she confessed.

My mouth went dry. I got light-headed. I had an anxiety attack. I felt like one of those guys who passes out in a courtroom after getting hit with a long-ass prison sentence.

"I really didn't know dicks that big existed," she continued. "The way it was just hanging there, I couldn't believe it."

The conversation was getting too real. The kind of moment when being in a relationship with your best friend backfires. I wasn't even thinking straight at that point, so another dumb-ass question spilled out of my gaping mouth.

"Well, were you at least taking it?" I asked. I did not want to imagine her screaming and making faces while she's getting dicked down by this freak of nature. "I hope you weren't flinchin' or nothing."

"Hell no," she replied. "Not at all. I handled it."

"Good," I reassured myself. At least she took that dick like a champ and he didn't make her scream.

That conversation left me a little uptight about my penis size for a time. Previously I'd always assumed I had a big dick by the reactions I'd gotten, but after what Mook Mook told me about her college homeboy, I wasn't so sure anymore.

I started looking at all the penis-enhancement products on the back pages of *The Source* and *XXL*. I ended up ordering something called Magna RX pills, which promised it would enlarge my dick in sixty days. In addition to the pills, they also had me do a daily exercise where you grabbed the tip of your penis and basically tried to stretch it out. I took the pills and faithfully did my penis-pulls, but nothing really happened. For better or worse, I was stuck on 7¾ inches in the fall/winter months and eight inches during warm seasons.

Now, before I move on, I can still hear some of you out there sucking your teeth about that prom story. "The hell with that, there's no way I'm taking any man back after he sleeps with my best friend and my cousin." Some of you fellas might be saying, "Forget that, I'm not taking my girl back after she she cheats on me with a dude with a Shaq-size dick." And in theory, I agree: nobody should feel like they have to put up with infidelity.

I would argue, however, that a lot of us have hurt people we love, especially when we were young. A lot of us have done some incredibly stupid and selfish things as part of our growing pains. (Or in the case of wild sexual escapades, growing pleasures.)

I was one of those young men, but Mook Mook and I were friends. Or more like family, to tell you the truth. And you don't just cut your family off. Yeah, we did a lot of stupid stuff. But clearly there was something else there too, which was deeper than whatever I did prom weekend, or whatever she did in college.

I can't promise being brutally honest after you mess up will work for you. I can only tell you what worked for me. Mook Mook and I are happily married with two kids, and I love her more now than I did back then. I treat her like a queen because I still feel bad for all the drama I put her through.

The only acceptable apology I can give her is truly changed behavior and I am a completely different individual now than I was fifteen years ago. I don't want to hurt my wife the way I saw my dad hurt my mom. It's really that simple. In a romantic relationship, it's always better to deal with reality than fantasy. I'm not going to sell a dream to my wife—I would rather live the dream with her, and that only happens when the relationship is rooted in honesty.

Give People the Credit They Deserve for Being Stupid

Knowledge is infinite. That means there's no limit to what you can learn. So if you THINK you're the smartest person in the room, then you clearly have been in that room—and around the same people—for far too long. You must always stay open and receptive to new information via friends, family, coaches, elders, and experiences.

You must give people the credit they deserve for being stupid.

Starting with yourself.

Lord knows I do.

I'm happy to tell you that I don't know shit. I got kicked out of two high schools. I barely graduated from night school. My "higher education" consisted of half a day at a technical institute.

I can't quote the US Constitution, name the capitals of more than a handful of states, tell you who the US presidents were, recite Shakespeare, or explain the laws of physics. There's a reason I named my podcast *The Brilliant Idiots*.

But here's the thing: I'm *extremely* comfortable with my lack of formal education. It's my secret weapon. Waking up every morning knowing that I'm ignorant is what motivates me to keep learning.

Do you know what *does* make someone stupid? Being *unwilling* to learn. Being closed off to absorbing new information.

That's why I'm never going to be uptight about not knowing something. Here's an example: When the Dominican-American actress Dascha Polanco of *Orange Is the New Black* came on *The Breakfast Club*, she mentioned she identified as an "Afro-Latino." "What's that?" I asked her in all sincerity. Dascha explained that it referred to a Latino with African roots, but man, you would have thought I just said I didn't know who America fought in the Revolutionary War. Folks jumped all over me for supposedly being ignorant and uninformed. Latina.com ran a story with the headline "Dascha Polanco Schools Charlamagne on What it Means to Be Afro-Latina," while *Jezebel*'s headline announced, "Dascha Polanco Is Forced to Explain the Existence of Afro-Latinas to Charlamagne."

The implication was I should have been embarrassed by not being familiar with the term, but why? I'm from South Carolina, where not too many people go around identifying themselves as "Afro-Latinas," simply because there aren't that many Dominicans or Puerto Ricans down there. Does that make me an idiot for not knowing the term? I don't think so.

To put it in context, could Dascha make the distinction between being a "Freshwater Geechee" or a "Saltwater Geechee"?* Probably not, since there aren't many Geechees in Brooklyn. Does that make her an idiot? Of course not. It just shows that the two of us have had different experiences and been around different kinds

---

*It's actually pretty self-explanatory: Freshwater Geechee live inland and Saltwater Geechee live closer to the coast.

of people. I wasn't familiar with her kind of background and by asking the question, I got educated. I'll never feel bad about doing that.

One of the many things I love about my eight-year-old daughter is that she reminds me why it's so important to keep asking questions. Yes, it can get a tad annoying after the five hundredth question of the day, but you still don't ever want kids to lose their inquisitive instinct. Asking questions is what helps them evolve. It's what teaches them how to avoid danger. It's what helps them make sense of their place in the world. It's what inspires them to dream.

Unfortunately, as we grow older we tend to lose that childlike curiosity. Instead of asking questions when we don't know something (which still happens every day), we keep our mouths shut. Instead of pestering our elders to explain the many things we don't understand, we try to act like we know as much as they do, if not more.

As a result, our evolution slows down to a crawl. We get set in our ways. We think we have all the answers and stop asking questions. Then one day we look up and can't understand why we haven't progressed as far as we wanted to in life. Why we seem stuck in a rut while other people continue to get further and further ahead.

The answer is simple: if you're not evolving, then you're regressing.

There's no middle ground.

This is why it's no coincidence that every succesful adult I know has a thirst for knowledge that rivals my eight-year-old daughter's. They might not ask as many questions verbally, but they share the same energy. They are constantly trying to soak up new information, new ideas, and new approaches. It's like they're in a constant state of evolution. No matter how many records they've sold, how much money they've made or houses they've bought, truly successful people are always looking to find out more.

You are getting better or you are getting worse. You never stay the same.

Banner at the San Francisco 49ers practice facility

I just heard about how Bob Pittman, the CEO of iHeartRadio and one of the most important people in media, went to Burning Man festival out in the Nevada desert. That means it's likely he didn't shower for a week and was so covered in dust he looked like an extra from *Mad Max*.

He's also sixty years old and a multimillionaire. Maybe even a billionaire? There are more luxurious ways he could be spending a long weekend. So why was he out there living like a twenty-something-year-old raver? Because he knows there are a lot of unique people at Burning Man. He knows the festival is where interesting minds congregate. He knows that if he walks around for a week talking to eclectic people, he's going to come home with some new ideas. Different kinds of inspiration than he would get spending a weekend with rich white people on a yacht. Bob understands that despite running iHeart, despite cofounding MTV and being its most successful president, it's critical that he still stay open to new ideas. That childlike inquisitiveness is exactly what has allowed him to remain a player all these years.

It's important to remain open in your relationship with the world. They say that closed mouths don't get fed. Well, the same is true for minds. This is why you must stay open to making new friends. Open to who you work with. Open to criticism. Open to changing your mind. And open to changing your relationships.

Because when you close off your mind to those opportunities, you are also closing the door on your ability to get the most out of life.

Yes New Friends

No new friends, no new friends, no new friends, no, no new
    Still here with my day one niggas . . .
        "No New Friends," DJ Khaled and Drake

You remember that song? Did you like it? Well, I absolutely hated it when it dropped. Don't get me wrong, Drake, Rick Ross, and Lil Wayne all got busy. What I couldn't stand was the song's message: *avoid making new friends at all costs.*

Listen, I know what Drake and Khaled were *trying* to say: the more money and fame you get, the more opportunistic people will try to infiltrate your inner circle. There's certainly a lot of truth to that. But I still don't think a fear of fake people should color how you see the world. That's why I'd get bummed when #nonewfriends was trending on Twitter. Every time I saw that, I knew someone was unwittingly blocking themselves from so many potential blessings. Plus, the only day one friend you truly have is your goddamn mama (and your pops if he's not a deadbeat).

I've done pretty well for myself over the years and I'm certainly not afraid of making new friends. If anything, I can say that 95 percent of what I've achieved in my career is due to the new friends I've made along the way.

There's my homegirl Devi Dev, who I became friends with while I was Wendy's sidekick. Back then Devi was working at KDAY in Los Angeles, where she became my literal angel in the City of Angels. There were several times when I landed an audition or had a meeting with an agent and Dev helped out by letting me crash at her pad. Once, she had a bunch of roommates who clearly didn't appreciate me sleeping on their couch, but Dev still insisted on putting me up. Not to mention Dev had several beautiful interns over the years who I had the pleasure of having sex with (yes, I'm a creep). Dev has done so much to support me over the years. I can't imagine I would have made it this far without her help.

But suppose I had a "no new friends" policy when I'd first met Dev. Remember, I was broadcasting with Wendy at the time. I was being syndicated around the country, including on KDAY, the heritage station in LA. I was probably being heard by more people in Dev's market than she was. I could have easily said to myself, "Who is this chick? She's just sweating me 'cause I'm hot right now. I'm not messing with her." Think of the friendship I would have missed out on (a friendship that remains to this day, I'll add) if I'd thought that way. Think of the positive affirmation I wouldn't have gotten when I needed it most. And, most important, think of all the beautiful young interns I wouldn't have gone to bed with if I'd told myself "no new friends," when it came to Dev. (For the record, Dev had no idea I was fucking her interns, so don't blame her.)

Bobby Bones is another great example. I met Bobby about four years ago at the iHeartRadio Music Festival. On the surface, we didn't seem to have much in common. I'm a black guy doing hip-hop radio—he's a white guy doing country. It would have been very easy for us to have shook hands, made some small talk, and then kept it moving. Yet even in just a few minutes of conversation, on a human level I could tell Bobby and I had a lot in common. I came to find out that, like me, Bobby had grown up Southern and poor. Like me, he was considered a bit of a bad boy in radio. And like me, he'd even been physically attacked outside of a radio station and had to run for his life.

We became "new friends," and let me tell you, the relationship has paid off for me. Literally. Bobby has been incredibly helpful in helping me navigate the world of syndicated radio. Once *The Breakfast Club* got put on in dozens of markets, I had to start asking questions like, "How do I renegotiate a syndicated contract? How much do I deserve to get paid?"

Only a handful of jocks ever get syndicated in their careers, so it's not like I'm constantly bumping into peers who can share that information with me. Luckily my new friend Bobby knew the terrain. So when it was time for me to renegotiate my first really big contract, Bobby was happy to walk me through the process. He told me which questions to ask. What clauses were worth fighting for and which weren't. He even connected me with a great agent, Paul Anderson. Far from costing me, my new friend Bobby probably helped me get more money than I would have on my own.

I'm not suggesting you get rid of all your Day Ones, or shouldn't go to them when you need someone to talk to. It's great to keep the connection with the people you grew up with, who you share memories with, and who understand where you come from. But in order for them to remain relevant in your life *today*, they need to be evolving at the same pace as you are. If not faster. Because if a person is stuck in the same place mentally where they were when you were kids, then that's not someone you should still look to for meaningful advice.

That might sound harsh, but I've seen too many people who have failed to reach their potential because they've been too loyal to their Day Ones. Look, if you see those Day Ones when you're around the way, by all means give them a pound. Ask them about their folks, or how their sister is doing. Grab a drink with them and spend an hour laughing about all the BS y'all used to do. Then keep it moving. Unless they've demonstrated that they're evolving, do not rely on them for inspiration. Do not use them as a sounding board when you're trying to make an important decision. If they're still stuck in the same place where they were ten or fifteen years ago, they'll never point you in the right direction.

You can tell if your friends are evolving at the proper pace by the type of conversation you have. For instance, when you and your boys get together, what sort of heated discussions do you get into? Debating who are the Top 5 MCs of all time?* Arguing whether Jordan would have been better than LeBron if he played today? Whether *Shottas* was better than *Belly*? If you find yourself having those same old, tired conversations again and again with your Day Ones, it's time to make some new friends.

Don't get me wrong, I enjoy a good sports or rap debate as much as the next person. In fact, I love them. But I don't want those conversations to be the outer limits of what I discuss with my friends. I want friends who can talk about those subjects but who can also recommend new books about spirituality, history, or

---

*For the record, I don't have a Top 5. I do, however, have a Top 7. In no particular order: Killer Mike, Ghostface Killah, Jay Z, Scarface, Nas, Jeezy, and T.I.

success. Who can put me on to new restaurants that I should try, or send me links to interesting articles. Who can talk to me about what's happening in politics just as easily as they can what's happening in hip-hop.

When you are constantly around the same old people who are experiencing the same old things and having the same old discussions about it, you will stagnate. They say insanity is doing the same thing over and over again while expecting different results. So don't you think it's insane to expect to be further along in life if you're still acting and thinking the same way that you always have? Change is the basis of growth. And growth is the basis of life. So if you stay immobile in your ways and refuse to grow, you're going to get left behind. It's that simple.

Instead of smoking a blunt with your grown-ass friends and arguing who won the Jay Z and Nas battle, for the five hundredth time, have a more challenging conversation. If you need inspiration, take a look at how Jay and Nas themselves are moving in middle age. I'm sure they're aware of who beat who in the latest rap battle, but they're more focused on investing in companies and expanding their business portfolios. They want to create financial legacies that are going to support their children and their children's children.

That's another reason why I still love sitting in my old room and leafing through those *XXLs* and *The Source* magazines from back in the day. I get inspired reading about what Dr. Dre was doing in 2001, or revisiting a feature on Jay Z from 2003. As hot as those guys were in that era, they'd still barely scratched the surface of what they'd eventually become. And almost twenty years later, we still don't know what heights they're ultimately going to reach. That's because they keep evolving. Those guys were never satisfied staying in the same spot, even a coveted one. They have always been committed to pushing themselves and reaching even greater heights.

Muhammad Ali once said, "The man who views the world at fifty the same as he did at twenty has wasted thirty years of his life." Well, unfortunately I can pull up to any proverbial tree in Moncks Corner, park bench in New York City, or corner in any Hood, USA, and find too many people who have pissed those years away. It truly saddens me to see people in their forties and even fifties trying to live the same way they did in their twenties and thirties. They're still bitching over who put in how much for the weed, or who drank more than their fair share of the Henny. They're still wearing jeans and T-shirts when they hit the clubs. They swear they've still got it, but to everyone else it's plain to see they're washed.

I am not the same man I was thirty-five years ago. And I hope that five years and ten years from now, I'll be a better man, a more mature man, a wiser man, a more humble man, and a more spirited man to serve the good of my people and the good of humanity.

—Louis Farrakhan

I'm not saying you have to stop hanging out with your friends in middle age, but have age-appropriate fun. If the person I just described sounds like you, please leave the clubs alone, that's for kids. Remember when you used to be out in your twenties and you'd see those old men lurking near the bar? How you and your boys used to laugh at them? Well, that's likely many of you now.

You all have become the old men in the club. Which is never a good look.

When you're in your forties and fifties, your job isn't to be out with the twenty- and thirty-year-olds all night. Your job is to be dropping gems on them during business hours. Your job is to be sharing your experiences—both good and bad—with them so that hopefully they can avoid some of the pitfalls that tripped you up. Your job is to show it's possible to evolve without losing touch with your roots.

If you are in your teens, twenties, or even thirties, understand that *your job* is to shut the hell up and to listen when an OG tries to share some gems with you. Don't make the mistake of thinking just because you're cooler than them that you're also wiser, that you somehow know everything already. We get it—you're wearing the right clothes, listening to the right music, using the right apps for this era. All that good stuff. But you're still in the infancy of your evolution.

Instead of rolling your eyes at an OG because he's wearing dad sneakers, or he's a little chubby around the middle, listen to what he's got to say. Never forget that every fifty-year-old was twenty once. Every. Single. One. No one was born old (except for maybe Morgan Freeman and Betty White). They were young and fly once too, probably flyer than you are right now. They've been through so many things you haven't experienced yet. Let them guide you if they're willing.

I've heard it said, "Smart people learn from their own mistakes. Wise people learn from the mistakes of others." It's easier than you think to be wise. Just listen to the elders when they want to share with you. Don't squander it by thinking you already know it all. Give yourself the credit you deserve for being stupid and then soak up every last drop of game that's being shared with you.

Stay Open to Who You Work With

One area I constantly see people fail to demonstrate the necessary evolution is in the workplace. I can't tell you how many times I've seen folks bring in their small-minded attitudes they've grown up with to their jobs and then be surprised when their careers fail to take off.

Sorry, but in this day and age there aren't *any* industries or careers where you can get ahead if you're afraid of or uncomfortable around people who you think are different from you. Specifically, I'm talking about attitudes toward people of the opposite sex, other races, and different sexual orientations than you.

I say that as someone who was once guilty of having many of the close-minded attitudes I'm going to warn you about. You can't come from a more unenlightened background than I did. Nineties hip-hop was great, but one of its failings was promoting a lot of casual misogyny and homophobia. I grew up nodding my head when Snoop said, "Bitches ain't shit but hoes and tricks," or "It ain't no fun if the homies can't have none." Just as I rapped along when Sadat X rhymed, "I can freak, fly, flow, fuck up a faggot / Don't understand their ways / I ain't down with gays . . ." It's not an excuse, but growing up I thought those attitudes were normal.

Especially the homophobia. I lived under the impression that I didn't know any gay people. In retrospect I knew plenty, but the environment in Moncks Corner was oppressive enough that the gay folk there didn't feel comfortable coming out.

The first openly gay person I met was a dude I'll call HJ, who gave me a job in the promotions department at Z93 Jamz. Initially I was a little concerned about what people would think if they saw me around him. The job, however, required us to spend hours together setting up tents for promotional events and, in a short time, we developed a friendship. As soon as we started having real conversations, one of the first things I asked was how he found men to have sex with. (Remember, in my naive mind he was the only gay guy in South Carolina.) "Oh, that's easy. I just pay for it," he told me. "You'd be surprised who will have sex with me for money. I'll offer $150 for head and $250 for penetration. And there are *always* takers."

Even after befriending HJ, I was still a little concerned about the perception of being around gay guys when I joined Wendy's show in 2006. Which was an issue, because Wendy was a magnet for gays. When I showed up on the scene, a lot of those dudes started hitting on me hard. Instead of having fun with it, I'd get uptight and try to act tough. I'd always pull out that Chris Tucker line in *Friday* on them: "I ain't with that gay shit."

Even though a lot of straight guys spend their lives making uninvited advances toward women, getting hit on by a gay dude is somehow a traumatic experience for them. I remember one day I was walking down the street past a bunch of gay dudes when one of them called out, "Ohhhh, Charlamagne's got a fat ass!" I didn't know how to reply, so I just kept walking. That really pissed them off, and one of the dudes started moving toward me while shouting, "Uh-uh, you're not going to just walk past us like that. Don't act like you don't see us!" I can't lie: I was a little shook. So I stopped, turned around. and said, "OK, thank you. I appreciate the compliment." After that they left me alone.

As I walked away I had to remind myself, "That's *every day* for women. That's what women have to put up with from men since they were teenagers. So why do we as men get so bent out of shape when the shoe is on the other foot?" I actually feel homophobic men aren't afraid of gay men, they're actually afraid of their own karma. They're worried that a man is going to treat them the way they've treated women all these years.

In the end, being around so many gay people, both men and women, was one of the best parts of working with Wendy. Outside of the friendships I made, it also helped me shed that casual homophobia that I'd grown up with. If I hadn't been exposed to so many gay folks through her show, I'd probably still be uptight around gay dudes, or saying "pause" every other sentence.*

Some people have a very hard time accepting this. The other day I was talking to an up-and-coming comedian backstage at a TV show and out of nowhere he told me, "Damn, there's a lot of gay people working here. I ain't with all this faggot shit." And this guy is from New York, too, just to show that it's not a small-town problem. I decided to have a convo with him.

"So you mean to tell me, if a gay man saw something in you and wanted to invest in a business you may have, you wouldn't want to do business with him because he's gay?" I asked.

"Well, I might take the money," the guy conceded. "But I still wouldn't really mess with him like that."

"I don't get it," I replied. "Someone believes in you to the point that they're willing to put money behind you, but you wouldn't want to 'mess' with them because of who they sleep with?"

"It's not just gay men," he protested. "It's also liars, thieves, murderers—I don't kick it with anyone that the Bible says is sinning, I won't get too close to them."

---

*For those unfamiliar, "pause" and "no homo" are basically the homophobic version of "That's what she said." You're supposed to declare, "pause" or "no homo" after anything that could remotely be considered "gay." And I mean anything. If a guy says, "Let's play ball," he has to say "pause" after it. I can't lie: I've cracked up at a few "pause"es in my time, I even wrote "pause" under a picture where Dr. Oz was trying to kiss me on Instagram. But after a while it just gets childish. Guys don't know when to quit.

"How does two people being attracted to each other even remotely equal murder?" I asked, before adding, "And to be clear, *we've all* sinned according to the Bible. I've had premarital sex. Eaten pork. Wore blended fabrics.* Ate shellfish. But you're ready to overlook *those* sins, aren't you?"

The guy didn't really have an answer for that. How could he? I had to tell him "peace" and then get on my way because I've got very little time for people like that—those who only like to cite the Bible when it's convenient to their argument. Folks like that are a joke to me.

I especially get a kick out of dudes who are chronic cheaters and who have five kids by five different women, but still think that they have some sort of moral authority over gay people. *You're* going to judge two men who are raising a child together and showering him/her with love and affection every single day? When you can't even be bothered with taking care of your own kids? It's insane.

Whether it's the comedian I was just describing, or so many other people I know, a lot of folks out here are unwittingly holding themselves back by being biased toward people they perceive as being different from them. You may think you "know the Bible," or "know what God wants," but the truth is you don't know nada. It's not up to you to give the universe ultimatums like, "I only mess with *this* sort of person." Or "I won't have anything to do with *that* sort of person." When you start making declarations like that, you're setting yourself up to fail.

All you can do in this life is hope that the universe brings positive people into your life. Whether they're gay or straight is irrelevant. And if you're closed off to those blessings, best believe

---

*In case you thought you were going to heaven in a polyester suit, according to Leviticus 19:19: "Keep my decrees . . . Do not wear clothing woven of two kinds of material."

they're going to make their way to someone else who's operating with an open heart *and* an open mind—and open butthole (hey, a little gay humor never hurt anyone).

Working with Women

Another way I see a lot of men block potential blessings is by having trouble accepting women in positions of authority. They can meet a woman in a professional setting but still view her as a sexual object first and foremost. Doesn't matter how old the woman is, or how senior her position, the first thing that crosses their mind is "Would I fuck her?" That might sound crude, but it's the truth, as most men will tell you if they're being honest. For a lot of dudes, the only women they treat with the proper respect are their grandmothers, mothers, and daughters. Everyone else is judged on their fuckability. Even Oprah and Michelle Obama.

Not too long ago I was on the red carpet with some of my friends at MTV's Video Music Awards in Los Angeles. Every time we saw a major male star, we'd salute them with respect. "Oh my god, there's Will Smith. You know how many times he's topped the box office?" or, "Look, it's Justin Timberlake! He's still killing it!" But when we saw Katy Perry, the respect went out the window. All the comments became, "Yo, that bitch Katy Perry is fine as a motherfucker!" Or "Yo, her breasts are big as shit!" Katy Perry is a *mega* star, someone who has sold millions of albums worldwide. But all anyone wanted to talk about was her body.

I try not to fall into that trap. I don't see female coworkers as sexual objects, I just see them as colleagues, because that's what they are. Now, I won't lie, if they happen to have a fat ass that will be duly noted. But only after I've evaluated what I think of them as a person and a coworker first.

For a lot of guys, however, working under a strong woman feels like an injustice. I remember one of my mentors—we'll call him Richie—who gave me so much good advice, used to get upset when I worked for Wendy. Especially when I would tell him how Wendy would put me in my place sometimes during shows. "Stop working with that bitch," he'd tell me. "Why are you working for a goddamn woman?" "I'm working for her because she's giving me an incredible opportunity," I had to tell him. "She's teaching me how to be a better on-air personality!" Yes, she was being tough on me. But if a man had treated me the same way, it would have just been seen as him giving me good training. Hell, Richie was tough on me himself. It wasn't a problem when he would get me in line, or push me to do better. So why should it be a problem when Wendy would challenge me in the same way? I could never understand that.

Personally, I love working with and *for* women. I like to call them "the Original CEOs," since they've been getting men together since the beginning of time. Thea Mitchem (or "Coach" as I call her) is my current boss at Power 105.1 and she's an incredibly smart, savvy, and strong African-American woman. Getting to work under her has been such a boost to my career. I remember one time I was in the studio and Thea brought in Kris Kelley (RIP), who was the program director at WGCI in Chicago, and Bailey Coleman, who was the program director at V100.7 in Milwaukee. It was three female African-American women holding down important positions in major markets. It was dope to see. I just wish we could see that sort of representation in more industries.

Supporting women is important to me because of how hard my mother worked without getting the advancement she deserved. My mother was an English teacher for thirty-five-plus years, yet she recently told me she never made more than thirty grand a year. How can that be? All the kids she worked with, all the young minds she helped mold over three decades, and she still never made more than thirty grand? I can't imagine that a male teacher would have had to work that long for that little.

Collectively we've got to do more to support all women, not just our immediate family members. I've got two daughters, and I don't want them entering a workforce where they're going to have to do more just to earn less. My eldest isn't even nine years old yet and already she's very articulate about what she wants to accomplish in her life. To think that she'd have to overcome extra barriers to reach those goals is unacceptable to me. We don't accept that possibility for our sons. So why is it acceptable for our daughters?

Working with the White Man

One of the things I didn't like about the Five Percenters back when I used to study their lessons is they believed that all white people are the devil. I can't believe that any entire race or nation of people is inherently evil. Now I can accept that a good 60 to 70 percent (okay, maybe 80 percent) of white people might actually fit that description. But to put ALL of them under that banner is a bit of a stretch.

Despite growing up in a country controlled by some of those "white devils," I don't have a prejudiced bone in my body. I deal with people on the basis of good and evil. Period. If you're a good person, then I rock with you. If you're an evil person, then fuck you.

Yet despite my straightforward way of evaluating people, I still find myself slipping into the "us versus them" mentality. It's hard not to. When you work with a lot of white people, no matter how friendly they act, no matter how nice they seem, no matter how many times they ask you what you thought of the last episode of *Empire*, I often can't help but feel there's just a touch—even just a light touch that barely leaves a fingerprint—of prejudice in their decision-making process. In light of the racial history of this country, it's hard to see it any other way.

For example, let's look at the battle I had to wage over the title of this very book. For years, my plan had been to call it *I Don't Give a Fuck and Neither Should You*. That was the title of the proposal when I was shopping for a deal. And when the publisher bought the project, they seemed to love the title. But the closer we got to the press date, suddenly my publisher, my editor, and my book agents (all white folks) didn't want "fuck" in the title anymore. Why? "Well, the book won't be carried in a lot of stores with that title" was their argument.

Meanwhile a quick Google search on my part revealed books have already been published with that word in the title. Books like *"Fuck, Yes!" A Guide to the Happy Acceptance of Everything*, *Fuck the Navy . . . Fuck the System: The Unpleasant Truth About a Lot of Things*, or *The Subtle Art of Not Giving a F*ck*. Evidently there's a fairly rich tradition of books dropping the f-bomb on their covers. I couldn't help but assume the reason it was an issue for me lay in my skin tone. When someone with my melanin count uses that word, it's immediately seen as offensive.

In the end, they showed me their true issue was that books with "fuck" in the title don't get great placement in the stores and most don't sell well. I felt that was a legitimate concern and decided to let go of the battle in order to win the larger war. And to be fair, it ended up being a great note from the publisher and helped me refocus on the core of the book, which is the concept of Black Privilege.

Still, that one little fight, that one minor entanglement, offers a window into the larger struggle black folks have to endure every day often within their own minds.

I've done well for myself, but I still can't get out of my head when it comes to race. I'll give another example. I was standing in line with my family for the *Despicable Me* ride at Disney World. One of the ways they entertain you while you wait (and man, you've got to wait at Disney World) is with a big-screen TV that shows the crowd. Every once in a while they'll have the camera zoom in on one section and then the Minions will pop up and say, "Ewww, what's that smell? This section stinks." The type of joke that's designed to get a laugh from a five-year-old. Well, they did that to our section, and I got bent out of shape. "They're only stopping on us because we're black," I hissed to my wife. "This is bullshit." "You do realize we're not the only people on that screen right now," she shot back. "They're like twenty other families with us. Relax, baby." She was right, of course. But it was still troubling just how quickly my mind went there.

Another example: I recently pulled up to the airport in Charleston with my wife and kids after spending the holiday visiting my peoples. We were driving in a black Denali. Just as we started to unload at departures, another identical Denali (this one white) pulled up in front of us and parked. A white guy jumped out and started unloading his bags while his family got out.

A black security guard walked over, passed the white family, and zeroed in on me. "Hey, you can't park here, buddy," he told me. "Gotta move." I couldn't believe it. "Why you ain't tell that to the white family?" I asked. "He's doing the same thing as me. Same truck too. But you just walked right past him." The security guy thought for a second, then looked at me and said, "You're right. My bad." I was happy that guy was honest enough with himself that he could see how he had been conditioned to just give the white guy a pass. But most folks can't be that honest. When I see situations like that all the time, how can race not always be in the back of my mind?

While I accept the reality of prejudice, I won't surrender to it. As soon as I start thinking about prejudice, I immediately tell myself to get over it. It's not that I'm in denial about racial realities. Just the opposite. I know that if I give them too much credence, they will become a crutch for me to lean on when times get tough. I might slip up and let myself think, "Man, these white devils are at it again. No matter how I get, they're always going to be ready to take me down." Once I start thinking like that, I have an excuse not to win. But as the great Hov once said, "I will not lose."

Instead of getting frustrated with white devils waiting for me at every level, I try to stay focused on the 20 percent of the non-devilish white folks who I not only work with but consider my friends as well. Yes, despite my misgivings, I'm a big believer in diversity. I'm not going to blindly buy into the worst stereotypes about white people, because I hate it when they blindly buy into the worst stereotypes about black people. My manager, Karen Kinney, is white, as is my assistant, Paige O'Donnell. They do great work for me every day, and I trust them implicitly, no matter what their white devil cousins are up to.

Having said that, when it comes to lending a helping hand, I will always try to look out for my own first. Who are my own? Anyone from South Carolina—including white folk. If you're a white person from South Carolina, I'm going to show a positive bias toward you. I'm not saying I'm just going to hand you a job, but I will give you first dibs to prove that you're the right person for it.

Now, if you're from South Carolina and you're black? Man, forget about it. That trumps everything. Not only are you going to the front of the line, but I'm going to do everything in my power to make sure you get what you need once you're there. That's Black *and* South Carolina Privilege.

If you think I'm conducting prejudicial hiring practices, guess what? You're right! That's exactly what I'm doing. I feel completely justified in doing it, because, as African-Americans, we've historically been placed at a disadvantage by white people doing the same thing on a much larger scale. Every time a white boss interviews someone for a job, they're moving (either consciously or subconsciously) someone with a background similar to theirs to the top of the list. Maybe someone who went to the same college as them, or worshipped at a similar church, or whose parents came from the same region in Ireland. Or someone who just knows a friend of a friend. I can't even be mad at those situations, because it's human nature for us to gravitate toward people who share similar backgrounds and experiences. Still, the end result is an informal, but colossal, network of friends and family that white people can tap into, but that everyone else is largely excluded from.

As one of the relatively rare African-Americans from South Carolina who has enjoyed success on a national level, I am absolutely going to go out of my way to show some bias toward people with a similar background. And I'd encourage every African-American reading this book to do the same if they find themselves in a position of power. Don't get in the door and then just congratulate yourself for having made it. When you are able to wield a little bit of influence, do what you can to help a brother or a sister out. Bring in a guy from your old hood for an interview. Reach out to a sister from your college, or a guy you used to play ball with, or the granddaughter of the old lady next door. Even if you don't end up hiring them, help bring them into the system. Give them the experience of going on an interview and learning how to make a case for themselves. Let them get a taste of the corporate experience. At the very least, they'll have a better shot on the next job they go out for.

God Jewel: Get in the habit of going out on interviews for jobs you don't necessarily want. It will keep your skills sharpened and your confidence up. When a job that you do want does open up, your interview game will be on point. Interviews are like dates; the more you go on, the more comfortable and confident you'll come across. When you only go once every few years, you'll probably come off as nervous and thirsty.

Now, let me switch gears slightly. If you're a white person reading this section, hopefully it's been a bit of a wake-up call. Yes, a lot of the minorities and oppressed people you're working with do consider you to be the devil. Maybe you already sensed that, or maybe it's coming as a complete shock. Either way, it's reality.

The question is, what are you going to do with this information? My suggestion is be proactive in making it clear that you're part of the good 20 percent, not the evil 80 percent. The first time you meet an African-American, a Mexican, or an Asian, or really any nonwhite coworker, just walk up to them and say, "Hi, I'm

Tanner, and I'm not a white devil." Trust me, that will ease a lot of the racial tension in the workplace. The fact that you're white and woke enough to even acknowledge the concept of "white devils" will let your coworkers know you're one of the good guys. I know some white people are reading this right now and saying, "Hell no! Isn't there anything else we can do?" Now that I've got your attention, the answer is yes: just treat people the way you'd like to be treated.

Yes, I just got finished calling 80 percent of white people devils, but that doesn't change a fundamental fact about me: I'm incredibly polite. When I was a kid, my grandmother Rosa Lee Ford would always tell me, "Manners will take you where money won't." For a poor kid raised on a dirt road, that was an incredibly valuable lesson to have drilled into my head.

Thanks to her teaching, I've always made a point to be polite and respectful to *everyone* I meet. When I walk into a room, I go around and look each person in the eye, introducing myself and then shaking their hand. I don't just shake the "star"'s hand if I'm walking into a studio; I say hello to the assistants, the cameramen, the weed carriers, whoever. If you're in the same room as me, I'm going to introduce myself. I'm going to show you the respect you deserve as a human being.

Energy is contagious. If you walk into a room acting grumpy and mean mugging, the room is going to get uptight. If you walk in with a hello and a smile, you automatically make the energy positive. I'm not saying you have to kiss everyone's ass. Just a hello and a smile will suffice. That's all it takes. Trust me, when people begin to associate you with smiles, positive energy, and respect, it will open up so many doors.

Not long ago I found myself having the privilege of sitting in a room with Jay Z when Beyoncé happened to come in. I noticed she made a point of walking up to everyone and saying hello. Even me. Can you imagine Beyoncé walking up to you and saying, "Hi, I'm Beyoncé." In that moment, I understood why she's been so successful. Forget about her singing and dancing ability or her great beauty: I saw that she had tremendous manners and understood the importance of showing respect toward everyone she met. That moment cemented my commitment to introduce myself properly and showing respect toward every single person I encounter. Because if Beyoncé can do it, I damn sure can too.

I'm a firm believer in treating people the way you'd like to be treated. If someone walks into a room and says hello to a bunch of people but overlooks me, I'm going to feel left out. Even if they didn't know me, I would still take that as a sign of disrespect. I don't ever want to make someone feel that way.

My grandmother might have "only" been a lunch lady in Moncks Corner, but she really did understand a fundamental rule of getting ahead. When you meet someone, not only do you not know who they are, just as important, you don't know *who they're going to be*. That guy sitting in the corner not saying much might not be a big name today, but he could wind up being a very big deal five years from now.

Imagine you were a young rapper walking into a studio for a meeting with Jay back in 1999. Of course you would have made a point of giving Jay a pound and saying what's up to Dame Dash, but would you have made sure to say what's up to the quiet young guys hanging in the background? It would be easy to overlook them, but if you did, you would have cost yourself a chance to make a connection with a young Kanye West, or a young Just Blaze.

But let's say you *had* taken the time to show them respect and introduce yourself. "Great to meet you, Kanye. Where are you from? What do you do around here?" Who knows where those conversations could have led.

Maybe to a friendship. So when they were popping, when they were the hottest producer in town, they would have given you a beat, or produced a song for you when everyone else was begging to work with them. Simply because you took the time to show them that respect way back when.

I hope I've made it clear how many positive lessons I learned from Wendy Williams. On the other hand, one thing I learned *not to do* from watching her was to treat the people who work for you poorly. Wendy and Kev could be very cruel to the people who worked under them. There were plenty of examples, but one that still stands out to me is how they treated Zoey, Wendy's former assistant. Zoey was polite, well-spoken, and just generally a sweet individual. Everyone, it seemed, liked her.

So I was shocked one day when Kev and I were heading to the station and he called to check in with Wendy. Zoey answered and Kevin just started going off on her, for no reason. "Yo, if you can't handle this shit, you need to quit!" he yelled before hanging up. "What was that all about?" I asked. "Nothing really, I just like messing with Zoey," he said with a laugh. "Man, she just lets me talk to her any kind of way."

When we got to the station, I found Zoey alone in an office crying. After I gave her a big hug, Zoey looked at me and said, "I can't take it anymore." I guess it wasn't the first time Kevin had screamed on her, because she ended up quitting that day. I figured Wendy would have tried to talk her into staying because she respected Zoey's work, but she just let her go. When I asked her why she hadn't tried to stop her, Wendy just said, "Well, she was no good anyway." "Now she's no good?" I thought to myself. "That was your girl yesterday."

But Wendy was right. Zoey wasn't good—she was *great*. She was a beautiful person who worked hard at her job and didn't deserve to be belittled and disrespected, *especially* for no reason.

It was demoralizing to see my bosses treat another coworker that way. I promised myself that once I made it to the level Wendy and Kevin had, I'd treat the people under me differently. Instead of messing with people just because I could, I'd show them support just *because I could*.

I like to think I do that with the staff behind *The Breakfast Club*, *Uncommon Sense, The Brilliant Idiots*, or anywhere I work. Yes, I definitely tease and mess with people a lot, but it's always done with love. And it's always delivered peer to peer, instead of from boss to subordinate.

I expect the same from other people in positions of power. If you're a producer, an agent, a manager, or a writer working with me, I'm not judging you off how you treat *me*. I'm the talent in those situations, so of course you're going to treat me well. I'm judging you off how you treat everyone else whose working on the project. If I notice a director constantly screaming on a camera-man for no good reason, or an agent habitually being rude to their assistant, then I'll make a note that that's someone I don't want to work with again in the future.

Some have said, "If you believe in treating people with respect, then why do you attack people so much in your interviews on the radio?" My response is always that I don't feel I'm attacking people. If I give my take on a story, or say that I don't like an artist's song, that's just giving my honest opinion. I'll tell an artist exactly how I feel to their face and then give them a chance to respond. And truly listen to that response, too.

I don't think there's anything disrespectful about being honest. If anything, I believe what's disrespectful is sitting down with an artist and acting like you really appreciate them in person, but then trashing them once they leave the studio. So many personalities do that. I won't. I'm going to tell you how I feel and what I think to your face and then have an honest and open conversation about it with you. People might not be used to that sort of direct approach, but to me it's really just another example of good manners. Being upfront and honest with people to me is the ultimate sign of respect. It's how I treat people, and it's how I hope people will treat me.

Are You Coachable?

No matter who you work with—black or white, men or women, gay or straight—to reach your full potential, you must remain open to good advice. I don't care how skilled you are, what sort of accolades you've received, or how big your check is. Your continued evolution depends on being able to accept criticism and advice from people who are more experienced than you.

When you make the mistake of thinking you know it all, you're going to shut yourself off from so much wisdom. I see talented people fall into this trap all the time. They experience a little success and then think their talent is enough to carry them the rest of the way to the top. If they meet someone who doesn't seem as gifted, or skilled, as they are, they'll dismiss that person's advice out of hand. But here's a little secret: there are a lot of people out there whose main talent *is* their ability to coach.

Phil Jackson wasn't a star as an NBA player, but he's probably the greatest coach in the history of the game. Providing instruction, vision, and guidance is his gift. Imagine if Michael Jordan and Scottie Pippen had ignored Phil just because he wasn't an All-

Star when he played in the league. They would have missed out on so much wisdom and might have never won all those rings.

Or take Coach K, aka Mike Krzyzewski of Duke. The man who is perhaps the greatest college basketball coach of all time. Coach K wasn't a pro player himself. He's a short white guy with a funny-looking face and an unspellable last name (you should have seen how I spelled it before this book was edited). Still, he has an undeniable gift of being able to communicate with and inspire his players. By being open to his instruction and buying into his system, a lot of guys have been able to make millions of dollars for themselves in the NBA.

There might be a Phil Jackson or a Coach K waiting to come into your life too. They probably won't be a basketball coach, but they could be a supervisor, a manager, or just a coworker. Someone who on the surface might not seem to have the talent that you do but still can clearly see what is needed to be done in order for you to take that step to the next level. If that person approaches you, will you be receptive? As long as you give yourself the credit you deserve for being stupid, you'll make the right choice. When you can freely admit "I don't know everything," then you're always going to be open to more instruction.

I've been very fortunate to learn under some great coaches over the years. Individuals who were able to point out the aspects of my game that I needed to improve. Who didn't back away from my brashness but stepped up and showed me how to turn it into a strength.

There was Ron White, the music director at Z93 Jamz in Charleston. As well as George Cook, who gave me my first full-time job in radio at Hot 98.9 in Charleston. George is the person who planted the seed in my mind that I could host a morning show.

I'm also indebted to Mike Love, who hired me at the Big DM 101.3 in Columbia, South Carolina. I actually dubbed him "Phil Blackson" because he was such a great coach and strategist.

One of my greatest coaches (and great friends) is Cadillac Jack. He's absolutely one of the smartest, most driven and deliberate people I've ever met. He and Geespin are the reason not only that there is *The Breakfast Club*, but also that it's the hit that it is today. I like to say that Geespin's gift is identifying the talent and that Cadillac's is showing the talent how to grow. There's no doubt in my mind that Cadillac's guidance is one of the reasons my career was able to go to the next, next level.

Cadillac blessed me with so many gems during our time together, but probably the greatest was teaching me the "Law of Ten." It states that when a media personality puts an opinion or an idea out into the world, three people will like it unconditionally, three people will hate it unconditionally, and four people will be on the fence about it.

Cadillac taught me that a lot of on-air personalities waste their time trying to win over the three haters. It's easy to understand why. If someone keeps tweeting, *Charlamagne, you are such a moron*, my natural inclination is try to show that person that I'm not.

Cadillac knew better. "Just ignore the haters, because nothing you say is going to change their opinion," he told me. "They're not interested in your ideas. They just get off on attacking *you*." Instead of exhausting precious energy on the three people who already hate me, Cadillac coached me to focus on the four people who are undecided. "Those are the people who are worth your effort. The other ones are already a lost cause."

Man, that advice truly saved me, especially in this time when everyone not only has an opinion but also a platform to express it. If I had kept paying attention to the haters on Twitter, Instagram, and the comments sections of YouTube, I would have gone crazy. Instead of playing verbal Whac-a-Mole with people who weren't ever interested in having a real dialogue, the "Law of Ten" showed me the value in sharpening my "I don't give a fuck" skills to a razor's edge. I think I also gravitated toward Cadillac's advice because it reminded me of something my father always told me, "You're never as good as they say you are, and you're never as bad as they say you are."

Not everyone in my position would have made themselves so open to Cadillac's coaching. He's a lot older than me. He's white. He's a Top 40 DJ who never played a lot of hip-hop. He's from Boston. The list goes on and on. But I didn't care about any of those factors. I could tell that Cadillac was trying to help me, and I wanted to soak up all the game he had to share.

From Cadillac and Geespin to my current coach Thea, so many people have helped me grow and prosper professionally. But again, only because I stay receptive to both new people and new information.

Coachable in the Bedroom

I'd be negligent if I didn't add that being open to new information is a mandatory mind-set for the bedroom as well. I learned this back in Columbia from a female friend who was also in the radio business. We don't talk that often anymore, but she knows that if she ever needed anything from me, I would be there to hold her down. That's how I am with my real friends.

One night back in the day, we left the club high and drunk out of our minds. One thing led to another and we ended up fucking.

First that night, and then more regularly. "Friends with benefits," as they say. I'm sure some of you have been in a similar situation.

"Friends with benefits" status is great for many reasons, not the least of which is that your friend will keep it real with you. Especially when it comes to your skills, or lack thereof, between the sheets.

That was the case the first time I went down on my friend. I though I was putting in real work, but she stopped me in mid-slurp and told me straight up, "Charlamagne! You do not know how to eat pussy!" A lot of men would have gotten upset in that moment. Not me.

Like I said, I've always prided myself on being *extremely* open to constructive criticism. Even when I'm standing on the verge of getting it on.

I didn't take offense, because if you're truly coachable, then you know there's a difference between someone being honest with you because they just want to break you down, and being honest with you because they want to build you up. I could tell she was only trying to help me.

My friend was so sincere in trying to help me earn my "licker license" that she gave me a book called *The Ultimate Kiss*. The first half was dedicated to teaching men how to eat box correctly, while the second half instructed women how to return the favor. I studied that book like a student cramming for a test until I was sure I had the technique down.* Then my friend was kind enough to let me practice on her until I worked out any remaining kinks and got it absolutely right. Hey, that's what real friends are for.

It's only because of her willingness to be a cunnilingus coach that today I can proudly say I am one of the best pussy eaters

---

*For those of you who want to practice right away, here's the CliffsNotes version: Work your tongue like a light switch, off, on, off, on, off, on. That's what makes a girl cum!

on the planet. Yes, I've gotten a five-star rating from every girl who has had my big-ass mouth go down on her. *Ultimate Kiss* is the reason that my wife squirts every time I put my face in her fur burger. So, moral of the story is, always be open to coaching, whatever form it may come in. You never know what skill set it will help you improve.

Stay Open to Growth in Your Relationships

Okay, speaking of going down on women other than my wife, I want to address the issue of my infidelities. And I hope you'll see that one of the most important things you can stay open to in life is the possibility of change in your relationships.

As you might have noticed, I didn't have the best role model when it came to male monogamy. My father was a serial cheater before leaving my mother for the woman who is now his wife. He was fairly unapologetic about it too. When I was about seventeen or eighteen, I decided to confront my father about how he was flaunting all his side chicks. I was sitting on my bed while he rode an exercise bike I used to keep in my room. We were just bullshitting when suddenly I blurted out, "Why are you so sloppy cheating on Mom? The whole town can see!"

I'll never forget what my father did next. He looked me dead in the eye and pointed to a picture I had on the wall of my girlfriend at the time.

"You ever cheat on that girl?"

"Nope," I said truthfully.

"Well, one day you will. And then you'll understand what I'm doing."

"I won't! I'm never going to cheat on her," I shot back.

When I said that, my father just laughed. Not a nervous or inse-cure laugh, but the kind of pure laugh that can only come from someone whose lived a lot of life.

"Trust me," he repeated when he was done. "One day you'll understand."

Today I can say, "Pops, you were right. Now I *over*stand." But it still doesn't make it right. No matter how strong the temptation, you can't allow another person to ruin your family. My pops is remarried now, and, as far as I know, he's been faithful to his new wife. But I know my father's never truly been happy since leaving my mom. Every so often he tells me, "One of the worst mistakes I've ever made is leaving your mother."

Despite my father's infidelity literally being the talk of the town, my mother refused to let her pain and humiliation show, as far as I could see. She was so good at making it appear that their divorce wasn't hurting her that for a long time I believed her.

The only time I saw—or I should say, heard—the pain come through is when she would sit in her bedroom and play Lauryn Hill's "Ex-Factor" over and over and over again. At the time I thought it was just cool that my mom liked Lauryn, but as I've gotten older, I have to admit that was just wishful thinking. Look at the lyrics of that song:

> It could all be so simple
> But you'd rather make it hard
> Loving you is like a battle
> And we both end up with scars

I heard that song so many times that I didn't even need to goo-gle the lyrics just now. They're forever seared into my brain.

I hate that record so much because of the pain I associate with it that sometimes I get mad at Lauryn for even writing it. If I'm discussing greatest rappers of all time and Lauryn comes up, I'll downplay her impact by saying something like, "Naw, she's only got one album; she can't be in this convo." That's just misdirected energy on my part. Lauryn *is* one of the all-time greats. Yet here I am getting mad at Lauryn for expressing her pain instead of being mad at the man who caused her that pain.

I don't have the heart to ask my mother if she ever got over the hurt of my father's infidelity, but I'm pretty sure the answer is no. I've never known her to date someone else, let alone get remarried. Her life seems to be going to the Kingdom Hall and doing a little substitute teaching now that she's retired. She also loves being with her grandchildren, but she deserves a fuller life than that. And I'm going to go out of my way to give it to her.

As for my father, my cold heart loves it when he tells me he messed up, and that the worst mistake he ever made in his life was leaving my mom. That brings me joy to hear because I believe the pain and hurt he brought to our family should be equally distributed to all parties involved.

Of course gloating over my father feeling terrible isn't the answer. Instead, I've tried to focus on making sure I don't put my wife through a similar sadness. Because, for many years, if I'm being honest, I was coming close. Yes, we've been together off and on since high school, but there have been stretches when we were "on" where I wasn't fully committed. Certainly not to the level she deserved. Even after we had a daughter, I was still hesitant to put a ring on it. I wanted to have my cake and eat it too, with other women. My wife was in pain, but whenever I sensed that pain, I just made myself numb to it like I had with my mother. I avoided the hurt and told myself that our relationship was fine. We had a beautiful daughter. I was making good money. We had a nice house and fancy things. Isn't that what every woman dreams of? Why would she need a ring too?

The irony is that despite dragging my feet on the way to the aisle, I'd always been very attracted to the concept of marriage. Even as a teenager, an age when most boys aren't thinking much past getting laid, I used to literally pray for a good wife. For a woman I could settle down and start a family with. Of course, when God delivered that good woman to me, I said, "Oh, sorry, I forgot to mention I want some other women too."

I managed to stay numb to what I was doing for years, but eventually more and more cracks began to show in the wall I'd built around myself. The first was when our daughter was old enough to start asking questions. "Daddy, why don't you and Mommy have the same last name?" she'd ask. I'd come up with some lame excuse, but I'd hate myself for it. Disgusted that I was doing such a poor job at role modeling what a real relationship should look like.

Another important moment came when I was hanging out with the legendary record executive Kevin Liles at a five-star resort in the Bahamas. We got on the subject of marriage and I told him about how I wasn't sure I'd ever tie the knot. "I can't tell you whether to get married or not," he said. "But I can absolutely tell you that you need a good woman to share your experiences with. You can find plenty of women to take to a place like this, but over time you're going to start feeling like a piece of crap. Jump-offs are cool, but wouldn't you rather be sharing this beauty, this experience, with someone you really care about? You need to look for that person." I knew he had just dropped a jewel on me. I also knew I didn't have to look anywhere for that woman. She was already right under my boonky nose. I made a vow to myself right there, "I'm not going to live like this no more. . . ."

But what really brought those walls down was when I broke the sacred code and sneaked a peek at Mook Mook's diary one day while she was out.

I'm glad I did, even though what I read broke my heart. What got me was a passage she wrote just after her best friend had gotten married: *Everyone around me is getting married, but I'm still not married yet. Am I doing something wrong? Is it me? Am I not good enough?*

Nothing could have been further from the truth. There was *nothing* wrong with her. My wife is intelligent, trustworthy, talented, inspiring, an incredible mother, and definitely sexy. I was the scumbag. I was the one who had to do better. Not her.

After that, I stopped pretending that everything was "all good" and got serious about doing right by this woman. I was going to put a ring on it and give her the relationship she deserved. Before we left for a vacation on the beautiful island of Anguilla, I went to her father, said I was going to propose, and asked for his blessing, which he gave to me. (He should have, considering how much of my Rémy he's drunk over the years.)

Then one night during the trip I took her out for a beautiful candlelit dinner on the beach. At some point the talk turned to marriage, like it had so many times before. It had become an exhausting conversation for Mook Mook. "Man, I'm not thinking about that shit no more," she said.

"Well, I have been," I replied. "And I decided if I did propose to you, I want to do it right. Somewhere beautiful like Anguilla. Maybe eating dinner on the beach by candlelight."

She still didn't catch what I was up to.

"And then I would stand up," I continued, actually standing up.

"Then I would get down on my knee," as I got down on my knee.

Then I pulled the ring out and she knew what was happening. Instant tears.

I asked her to marry me.

And she said yes.

And being my true soul mate, the next words out of her mouth were: "You have no idea how good I'm going to suck your dick tonight."

Getting married was easily the best thing I'd ever done. For a long time I'd been judging whether I was "successful" by how much money I was making, or how well my career was going. Once I was married, I realized expanding my radio career or locking down more TV deals wasn't true success. Only marriage gives me a feeling of contentedness. Raising a family the right way is the only thing that brings me pure peace.

The other day I was hanging out in the kitchen of our new home with my wife. It's a beautiful place at the end of a cul de sac in a fantastic neighborhood. Don't worry about how many square feet it is, I'm not the flossy type. Just know we're living well. Suddenly I blurted out, "I feel accomplished."

"Why, because of this house?" asked my wife.

"No, the house has nothing to do with it. I feel accomplished because of us. Because of the kids. Because of this family we've built together."

I wasn't lying. The house is incredible, and radio and TV deals give me a rush, but at the end of the day as long as I have my family, I'm good. You could fire me one more time, take away the fame, repossess the house, and send me back to South Carolina to go sit under a tree and I'd still be straight. Just as long as I had my wife and kids with me. I'd eventually figure out a way to get out from under that tree, but I wouldn't cry for anything I'd lost, because I would still have everything that I needed.

Recently we were back in South Carolina and I rented a beach house for all my friends and family. We ate, drank, told jokes, and reminisced. Our kids ran around the house, jumped in the pool, and had a great time together, just like we'd done at that same age. To see that magic being re-created by another generation was one of the best sights I've ever seen. It made me so happy that I'd stopped being stubborn and finally allowed myself to evolve into the man I'd always wanted to be.

Every single one of us has the ability to break out of our bad habits and realize our full potential. To go from a bum-ass boyfriend to a happy husband. To transition from struggling to get by to enjoying sustained success. The key is to never feel like you're stuck in one place. Stay open. Be coachable. Don't rely on peers who aren't progressing, and make sure you *do* listen to your elders when they give you gems.

The other day a guy who goes by @marcmarc330 tweeted me, *Your journey has been crazy to watch. You've evolved but you haven't changed. That's dope. #Salute.* I hit him back and wrote, *Best tweet I've got all week,* but it's really one of the best tweets that I've gotten, period.

Few things have made me prouder than being recognized for my evolution. No matter where I go, I'm still always going to be Lenard, Cowboy and Julia's son from Moncks Corner. But I can always work at being a better version of that South Carolina kid who set out to make it on the biggest stage possible. A better radio personality. A better businessman. A better thinker. A better friend. A better mentor. And most important, a better husband and father.

Access Your Black Privilege

It's an honor and a privilege to be black. Period. I consider black privilege to be a spiritual force, whereas white privilege is a systemic presence. That spiritual connection comes from the access black folks seem to have to the divine, a connection that allows us to survive and thrive in this country in spite of all the obstacles we have faced. I wake up every day believing "I have the privilege of being black." How else am I supposed to feel? And if you're a black person reading this and feel otherwise, then in the words of Malcolm X, "Who taught you to hate yourself?"

I used to get my hair cut by a brother named Divine, who had a barbershop in Goose Creek. Like all hood barbershops, it wasn't just a place to get a cut, it was also a place to hang out, swap stories, and trade opinions. Divine's shop is where I saw the R. Kelly sex tape for the first time (and hence learned how to eat ass properly).

Divine and I clicked and sometimes would hang out at his place, smoking weed and discussing life. It was then that I learned that Divine was a Five Percenter. I know I've mentioned them earlier in the book, but for those who aren't familiar, the Five Percenters are an offshoot of the Nation of Islam that was founded in Harlem in the 1960s. The group's name refers to their belief that society is divided into three groups. The first group being the masses—the

85 percent of the population who are blind to God and the truth. The second group is composed of politicians, CEOs, members of the media, etc.—the elite 10 percent who know the truth but exploit it for their personal gain. That leaves the remaining 5 percent ("Five Percenters") who know the truth (namely that God is a black man), but rather than abuse it, use it to try to help people. These Five Percenters were also known as the Poor Righteous Teachers (yes, old heads, the same name as the group that had a hit with "Rock Dis Funky Joint") back in the day.

The Five Percenters might have never enjoyed mainstream popularity, but the "Gods and Earths" (as male and female members of the group call themselves) have always played an important role in hip-hop. The Five Percenters have also attracted a lot of converts in jails (for many years the prison system in South Carolina even categorized them as a dangerous gang, like Bloods, Crips, or Latin Kings). When those Gods came home, they often found themselves operating in the barbershops, street corners, and clubs of the black communities. The same places where hip-hop lived.

Many of the Gods were charismatic speakers. Shut out from New York's main mosques and churches in the early days, the Gods were forced to preach on the city's street corners. And if you're going to command a crowd on a New York corner, you'd better have the gift of gab. As a result, over the years the Gods developed an incredible command of language and sense of showmanship. Qualities that made them very attractive to people like myself who grew up respecting the same attributes in rappers.

Divine definitely could spit a mean game. When we would build, which is a Five Percenter's term for discussing their beliefs and philosophies, Divine would break down how the American black man is the actual personification of God, who himself is a black man from Asia. Or he might teach me about how "God" is a Greek word derived from the ancient Aramaic words "Gumar," "Oz," and "Dubar," which meant wisdom, strength, and beauty. He also taught me about the Five Percenters' belief, which they shared with the Nation of Islam, that white people were created six thousand years ago by a black scientist named Yakub, who sent them into the world to be a race of devils.

Those concepts might sound crazy to you, but no matter how anyone else feels about them, the Five Percenters served a very important purpose to *me*: they made me believe in myself. It might have come in an unorthodox style, but their message was very simple: I wasn't the victim of the white man. Instead, I was a God. I had power. I was special. I was *destined* to be great.

I had never heard that message anywhere else in my life at that point. Certainly not at school. Definitely not at home, where I was seen as a screwup, albeit one with potential. And not at the Kingdom Hall, where the emphasis was much more about how I better not piss off God, let alone think that I was a god myself.

When people ask, "Why do you call yourself 'Tha God'?" my answer is because of what I learned from the Five Percenters. Whether I heard it through Divine, or rappers like Big Daddy Kane, Nas, and Ghostface Killah (who all followed the Five Percenters), I never forgot that the black man is God. That isn't a blasphemous statement to me. Or even a suggestion that everyone else isn't a god, too. It was simply a way of returning to the truth about our true nature. As the Honorable Minister Louis Farrakhan tells us, "We have been turned backward. Instead of calling ourselves God we say, 'Yo, what's up, Dog?'"

I might have discovered that truth in the lyrics of a song or a barbershop chair instead of a school or a church, but it didn't diminish the gift the Five Percenters gave me: *empowerment*.

The Five Percenters' philosophy might sound radical, but it

really isn't. The importance of believing in yourself is a concept at the root of almost every philosophy and culture. It's a message that's been shared in so many different ways, words, and platforms over the centuries. One of my favorite quotes on the subject is from the metaphysical author Christian D. Larson, who wrote, "Believe in yourself and all that you are and know that there is something inside you that is greater than any obstacle."

Larson was a white guy who was born in Iowa over one hundred years ago, but he was dropping the same gem that Divine gave me in Goose Creek. A message that will never lose its shine and will always be relevant to your life, no matter who you are. In fact, let me repeat it one more time for the people in the back: "Believe in yourself and all that you are and know that there is something inside you that is greater than any obstacle."

Some of you might be having a hard time accepting that about yourself. Maybe you think you're too black. Too dumb. Too poor. Too gay. Too ugly. Too shy. Too sick. Whatever the case may be. Maybe you don't feel like you have that much to believe in. Certainly not as much as the successful people you see out there living the life you'd like to lead.

The most overwhelming evidence that you're special is that you're here at all. Fellas, next time you're about to bust a nut, shoot it on your lady's stomach and then really look at that puddle of semen. Consider all those squiggling sperm on her belly. Each one of them had one mission and one mission only: find its way into an egg and create a life! At that fateful moment your daddy decided to shoot up your mama's club (that's my expression for ejaculating inside a woman), out of the millions of sperm he let loose, YOU were the only one who accomplished its mission! A single winning sperm out of the 250 million that are in each nut.

Man, the odds for you to have succeeded are worse than Powerball and Mega Millions. But you did. You were the Shaq of semen. The King James of jizz. The Steph Curry of sperm. You were incredible. A once-in-a-lifetime talent.

So you're telling me that now that you're here, you're going to let something like racism, sexism, or homophobia slow you down? Make you give up? After all you've already accomplished? You can't allow that to happen.

You might have forgotten your epic vaginal victory, but you've already overcome much greater hurdles than any white man could put in your way.

Don't get it twisted: I'm not having an "All Lives Matter" moment here. Not for a second am I suggesting that racism isn't real. It's as real as the air we breathe. And the evidence is everywhere.

There's slavery, segregation, and Jim Crow, the effects of which are still felt strongly in every corner of America. There's the fight for civil rights, restrictions of voting rights, the prison industrial complex, systematic racism, and perhaps most wicked of all, reality TV. In particular, I'm talking about *Flavor of Love* and Mona Scott-Young, who I respectfully call "Satan Scott-Young." Especially her franchise *Love & Hip Hop*, which I prefer to call "Lies & Hip Hop," because 80 percent of all cast members lie about what they got.

Collectively, all these institutions, laws, systems, and programs have thrown all their weight behind trying to limit black progress on this planet. They have slowed some of us down and in some cases even stopped our growth completely. I'll never deny, or try to downplay, just how many hurdles we've faced as a people. Despite all of that, however, in the words of Maya Angelou:

> You may kill me with your hatefulness,
> But still like air I'll rise.

Words like that are critical to building our belief in ourselves. Black folk need reminders like "And Still I Rise." Just like we need to hear that message in songs like Nas's "I Can" or Kendrick Lamar's "Alright." We can never lose sight that we are indeed gods, kings, and queens. That we are superheroes with Luke Cage–type strength capable of running through any obstacle. We've got skin hard enough to withstand anything this wicked world throws at us. That's right, our melanin is hard as steel! We are literally "too black, too strong."

Nope, I'll never tell you racism isn't real, because it is. Just as white privilege is real too. Instead, what I'm encouraging you to do is stop letting them define you. You might say, "Well, it's a little hard to ignore it when no one ever replies to my résumé because it reads Shareka at the top." Just as you might say, "It's a little hard to ignore it when I'm pulled over ten times a year simply for driving while black."

I understand that sort of oppression can be depressing. Even deadly. But if you let it completely color your vision of the world, then you're doing the white man's dirty work for him. When all we can see is the privilege of others, then the biggest oppressor of African-Americans becomes OURSELVES. It might not be a popular sentiment, but it needs to be said.

That's why every day when you get up and look in the mirror, you need to point a finger at your reflection and say, "Fuck these crackers. White man isn't the problem here. *You* are holding me back. *You* are keeping me down. *You* are suppressing me from being great. Because *you* simply don't believe in *yourself*."

Blaming yourself for not being great might seem like an exercise in self-hate, but I promise it's actually one of the most optimistic outlooks you can have. When you hold yourself accountable, what you're really doing is freeing yourself from mental bondage.

You're saying: "Try as it might, racism can't stop me. White Privilege can't stop me. If there's something out there that I haven't gotten, it's because I haven't *taken* it." Winston Churchill once said, "A pessimist sees the difficulty in every opportunity; an optimist sees the opportunity in every difficulty." When you blame yourself instead of the white man, then you're actually being optimistic.

Everyone Is Privileged

When you first saw the title of this book, you might have said, "Charlamagne trippin', ain't no such thing as 'Black Privilege.'" Well, hopefully by now I've at least convinced you that you've got God's privilege. Certainly you can admit that God made you who you are, and that it's a blessing, honor, and PRIVILEGE to be you. To be so original, so unique, that God decided to make only one you. Every human being on this planet—even twins—are one of a kind. What's destined for you is destined for you only. That's an incredible privilege.

If there's one thing I want you to take away from this book, it's that privilege is something that *everyone* can access. I call my personal version "Black Privilege" because contrary to all the bleaching and Uncle Tom rumors, I'm 100 percent a black man. I recognize the God in me. Doing so allows me to ignore the social norms that consciously and subconsciously tell me I'm inferior because of race, gender, or class. So no one can tell me that I don't have Black Privilege.

No matter what sort of struggles you've faced, you still possess a unique privilege. Do you have arms and legs? Good. Well, then you have Limb Privilege. You have an advantage over the Iraqi vet who lost his and is trying to learn how to walk on bionic legs. Or the guy who lost his arms and had to figure out how to roll a blunt with his toes. You have tremendous privilege over people in those situations. So make the most of it!

Do you feel relatively healthy today? Good. Then you have Health Privilege. You've got an advantage over the high school teacher who has cancer. Who has to receive chemotherapy after school every day and spends her nights throwing up. Only to get back up the next morning and go teach her class.

Or the fireman who got ALS and is now confined to a wheelchair, wasting away in front of his wife and kids until the disease finally does him in. You might be unemployed, you might be divorced, you might have just been fired from your dream job, you might be thirty pounds overweight and feeling crappy about yourself, but man—if you woke up today feeling healthy, you've got incredible Health Privilege over that teacher and that fireman. Please capitalize on that privilege!

I know some of you probably think I'm downplaying, or underestimating, the power of White Privilege. That's never been my intention. Remember, I was raised a poor black male in South Carolina. I lived in a trailer. I sold drugs. I was kicked out of two high schools and did time in jail twice before I was eighteen. I had a big nose and a funny name (okay, a few). My face had several shades. I know what it means to be counted out. To be overlooked. To be profiled. I've experienced all those things. And continue to experience them to this day.

But despite all those things, I simply can't grasp the concept of someone being better than me because of the color of their skin, their position or status in life. I truly believe, as the subtitle of this book states, that opportunity comes to those who create it.

I don't care what race you are, you still have to work to unlock your privilege. Contrary to popular belief, every white person in

America is not successful. White skin is not an E-ZPass to success. I saw too many white folks living in those trailer parks in Charleston to believe that to be true. White people have to go out there and get it just like the rest of us, even though in many cases it may be easier for them and harder for us. Black Privilege isn't about what someone else is doing; it's just about being aware of who and what you are and drawing strength from that.

So please don't confuse what I'm saying here with Lil Wayne, Raven-Symonè, or another celebrity whose implied racism can't exist anymore just because *they've* made it. Yes, I've made it, but I know not everyone has. Just because your tax bracket has changed for the better doesn't mean your reality has too.

But I want it to.

I want everyone reading this book to reach their dreams just like I have. And I sincerely believe that embracing your own privilege, instead of being intimidated by someone else's, is the best way to do it.

For everybody out there born in unfortunate circumstances it's not how you start the race, it's how you finish it that matters. I don't care what your economic condition is; I don't care where you were born. If you tap into the power of God in you, then you can make it out of any situation. Faith plus hard work can change any circumstance. Do you understand what I just said? Faith plus hard work can change any circumstance. Belief in God is essential, but you still have to put the work in, too. If I tell you that one day you're going to hit the lottery, you can't just sit around and wait for those numbers to come up. You have to actually get up, go out there, and play the lottery.

Your relationship with God works the same way. You can't just pray for him to bless you. No, you must pray and then go out there and put the work in. You must allow God to help you by helping yourself. People ask me all the time, how did I get in this position? How did I go from Moncks Corner to having my own radio show in sixty-plus markets and counting? How did I end up with a TV deal on MTV, or doing movies, producing TV shows, and writing books? I give them one simple answer: God.

And if they reply, "Well, how come it doesn't happen for everybody else who believes in God?" Or "I believe in God, so why aren't my blessings coming like that?" My answer is pretty simple. I say you must not believe in God like you claim you do, because if you did, you wouldn't question him *ever*. I pray for clarity; I pray that God speaks through me; I pray that he directs my steps and moves me the way he wants me to move. I pray for forgiveness every day, several times a day. And I pray that God is with me and everybody I love and care for throughout the day.

Remember . . . Remember . . .

My own experience has taught me that believing in the privilege God has blessed you with can be the difference between winning and losing. That's probably why losers look at me like I'm Rafiki from *The Lion King* when I talk about Black Privilege. They think I'm crazy. That I'm a coon. A sellout. That what I'm saying can't be done. To that I reply, "Man, shut the fuck up forever with that pessimistic bullshit!"

If you don't think the type of privilege I'm promoting is real, then consider the "Remember who you are" scene in *The Lion King*. That's the scene where Rafiki takes Simba to the watering hole and shows him his own reflection to prove to Simba his father Mufasa isn't truly dead. Simba is skeptical, but then his father does appear in the clouds and reprimands his son for losing sight of his true self. "You have forgotten who you are," intones Mufasa. "And so have forgotten me. Look inside yourself, Simba. You are more than what you have become. You must take your place in the circle of life."

When Simba protests that he doesn't know how to go back and find himself, Mufasa tells him, "Remember who you are. You are my son and the one true king. Remember who you are. Remember, Remember, Remember . . ."

Now when you saw that scene with your kids in the theaters, you loved it, right? Maybe you even cried a little bit because it touched your soul. That's the kind of belief you need to tap into.

Please, if you're one of those people out there who feels like they can't succeed, at least stop criticizing those of us who believe we can win at life. It's hard for a loser to understand this mentality, this belief in self. It's difficult for losers to access their own privilege because they don't even believe it's sitting there dormant waiting to bloom.

This philosophy of accessing your privilege—no matter what sort of privilege it is—is only for the winners, the dreamers, and the doers. Those of us who understand opportunity comes to those who take it! Who understand that privilege exists within us all because God gave it to us. Not America, not this system, the white man, or *any man*. They can put us in chains, steal our names, deny us our rights, throw us in jail, and even shoot us dead for the color of our skin, but they *still* can't keep us from what is divinely ours.

As Mufasa said at the end of that scene: "Remember who you are. You are my son and the one true king. Remember who you are. Remember, Remember, Remember . . ."

Just like Simba, we're all kings on this earth. To reap the privilege that is divinely ours, we just need to remember it.

Acknowledgments

This is the hardest part of the book to write. When it's time to acknowledge the people who have contributed to your success, you're bound to forget somebody, especially when you're writing it the night before your final deadline, as I am now. So if I somehow do forget to mention you, just know that I love you! Blame it on my mind, not my heart!

First off, to my iHeartMedia family, thank you for taking a chance on me even though I'd already been fired from radio four times. It was a gamble that I'm pretty sure has paid off. Cadillac Jack, Geespin, Dennis Clark, Doc Wynter, Thea Mitchem, Bob Pittman, Richard Bressler, John Sykes, Tom Poleman. Thank you all!!

To *The Breakfast Club:* DJ Envy, Angela Yee, Q, Sasha Keady, EmEz. Even though Sasha and Q have moved on in their careers, in the beginning it was just the six of us and we accomplished great things. We got championships together and I will forever be grateful to each and every one of ya'll.

To the whole team at Power 105.1: DJ Prostyle, DJ Self, DJ Clue, Angie Martinez, Honey German, DJ Suss-One, DJ Will, DJ Rey-Mo, DJ Norie, DJ Whutever, love!!! Let's keep making history. To our syndication company Premiere Radio Networks' Jennifer Leimgruber, Martin Melius, and Dwayne Crawford, thanks for your support as well! (See, this is the part where I get in trouble because I start saluting my radio people, forget someone, and they will be like, "Why you didn't big me up in your book!!!")

ACKNOWLEDGMENTS

Look, to all my radio folks across the country, I love ya'll. Let's keep pushing the culture of radio forward!! Please don't be mad I didn't salute you in my acknowledgments!!! Blame it on my mind, not my heart!! Salutes to Devi Dev, K Foxx, Titi Torres, Letty Martinez, Erica America, Carolina Bermudez, Cubby Bryant, Lulu and Lala, Bobby Bones, Producer Eddie, Radio Amy, Elvis Duran, Greg T, Froggy, Scary, Bethany Watson, Danielle Monaro, Garrett Vogel, Jim Kerr, Bob Bronson, Helen Little, Big Boy, Sway, DJ Hed, DJ AOh, DJ 33, DJ Blord, DJ Chuck T, DJ D NyceSC, Kendra G, Taylor Hayes, and Nessa! To Anita Scipio, a.k.a. Mama!! Love your energy!! To Paul Anderson and Workhouse Media—Thank you.

To my Viacom family: Paul Ricci, Candida Boyette-Clemons, Chris McCarthy, Darin Byrne, Ryan Ling, Annie Gillies, Brian Saracusa, Jessica Zalkind, Lauren Zins, Tiffany Williams, Dara Cook, Rachel Edwards, Shelby Krasnoff. I don't know why MTV2 gave me a deal about four years ago, but THANK YOU for seeing that in me when I didn't even see it in myself!! Esther Park, Kathi Palminteri, Eli Lehrer, Catherine McAloon, Essence Stewart—THANK YOU ALL!!! To the wardrobe mafia—Tysha Ampadu, Alyssa Keener, and Satthra San—Thank You, Thank You, Thank You!!!

To everyone I met on this TV grind and became great friends with: Pete Davidson, Desus and Mero, Jon Gabrus, Jordan Carlos, Jessimae Peluso, Damien Lemon, Carly Aquilino, Melanie Iglesias, Lisa Ramos, April Rose, Nicole Byer, Akwafina, Chico Bean, Zuri Hall, Karlous Miller, Amanda Seales, Chip and CP, Doug Banker—I love you all and each of you have inspired me in various ways. To Randi Hatchel, thank you for providing me with so much great reading material over the years and for introducing me to Dr. Natasha Sandy, the best dermatologist in the world!!

To Matthew Benjamin and the whole team at Touchstone and

ACKNOWLEDGMENTS

Simon & Schuster, thank you. This book is the first of many and thank you for believing in my vision.

To my attorney Loan Dang, THANK YOU! To Jan Miller and Nena Madonia at Dupree Miller, thank you both very much. I knew from the first time we had lunch, Jan, that we would do great things. Even if we weren't doing business together I would still be extremely happy calling you both friends!!

Chris Morrow, thank you for telling me the two things I need to be doing: a book and a podcast. Hey, Chris, you were right and I'm glad to be getting money with you on both of those things. To the Loud Speakers crew: Combat Jack, Matt Raz, Kid Fury, Crissle, and Taxstone #BeSafeTho! My *Brilliant Idiots* partners Andrew Schulz and Greg Schulz, love ya'll and let's keep winning!!

To my people at Marvel Comics: Chris Robinson, Blake Garris, and Sanford Greene!!! Sanford, thank you for the *Black Privilege* illustration for the book!! I'm framing that!!

Jesus Christ, this acknowledgment thing is difficult, because it's impossible to acknowledge everybody. I got a really big team who I confide in and plot and plan with everyday, folks like Van Lathan, Jasmine "Jas Fly" Waters, Alesha Renee, Dollie Bishop, DJ Frosty, Karen Civil—thank you!! Ashley James, Kenta Palmer, my blood brothers and sisters Teresa, Ashley, BJ, and Julian, love you all!!

To all the websites WorldstarHipHop, Bossip, TMZ, Elliott Wilson and B Dot at Rap Radar, YBF, Necole Bitchie, ThisIs50, AllHipHop, Sohh, HipHopDx, Hip-Hop Wired, XXL, The Source, VIBE, The Shade Room, Baller Alert, DJ Akademiks, and everyone I forgot to mention, thank you all!!!

To my Triple O.G., The Honorable Minister Louis Farrakhan; Bro. Don Muhammad; and the whole Nation of Islam. Thank You.

To my great friend Marvet Britto, thank you for believing in me and encouraging me since day one, and thank you for introducing me to the beautiful island of Anguilla. To all my Anguilla folks, Shaquille Carty, Hayden Hughes, Dalicia, and everyone at Tasty's restaurant, Gwen and everyone at Gwen's Reggae Grill, salute to you all!!!

To all the McKelveys on the planet, let's build on our legacy!!! My dog Lil Duval, he swear he stay out the way of these niggas better than me, but nah bruh! Peace to N.O.R.E. and the *Drink Champs* podcast and T.K. Kirkland.

And of course, to my manager and business partner, Karen Kinney, thank you!! You have upgraded my life and you are a gift from God. Let's take over the world!!! To my assistant/sister/ adopted daughter Paige O'Donnell, I love you, kid; I knew you was special when you interviewed me for your college radio station at Penn State. After you got that internship at Power 105.1, I tried to shake you numerous times but you held on and I love you for that. Thanks for riding with the old man; I got you for life. My brother from another mother and the craziest dude I know, Wax. Something is really wrong with you and I wouldn't change you for the world (well, a few things), but you are the pure definition of loyalty and we are going to keep growing. Salute to Big Diz, 6 Fo, Hypeman Coop SDM—lose some weight with your fat ass. Beehigh, Vegas Jones, Ty Ty, Chaka, everybody at Roc Nation, thank you all. Mike Kyser, Kevin Liles, J Grand, Joey I.E., salute! Thank you to Natina Nimene, who tells me she hates me all the time but it's really because she loves me! Salute to my guys Tyrese, Wale, Timbo the King, and Killa Mike. Salute to Lisa "Kennedy" Montgomery. (Sorry, Kennedy, just felt like putting your whole government out there.)

My partner Chris Etheridge, R.I.P. to Jerrell Garnett, Miss Jimmy Sue, my cousin Dana McKelvey, La La Anthony, Cari Champion,

ACKNOWLEDGMENTS

Bakari Sellers, Angela Rye, Pastor Carl Lentz, thank you for the constant texts and reminders that God Is Real!! My favorite corporate thug motivator, Gary Vaynerchuck!! To Mike Love; George Cook; Rochdale, Queens', finest, The Evans Family: Dr. Robert Evans and Robert "Bless" Evans; everybody in Kittfield, Highway 6, and Whitesville in Moncks Corner, S.C. Peace to Berkeley High School, and my cousin Mal Lawyer . . . look, these acknowledgments could go on forever and forever but if I forgot to give you your due, just know it's almost midnight and I have to be on *The Breakfast Club* at 6:00 a.m. If you know me, you know that Gratitude is always my Attitude, and I'm definitely grateful for everyone that I have met on my journey. Always remember what God has planned for you—nobody can stop you but you!!! Thank You.

—CthaGod

About the Author

Charlamagne Tha God is a TV, radio, and social media personality, best known as the cohost of Power 105.1 FM's *The Breakfast Club*. He also appears on MTV2's *Uncommon Sense with Charlamagne* and *Guy Code*, and will soon be launching a VH1 afternoon drive-time show. Born and raised in small-town South Carolina, Charlamagne got his start on Wendy Williams's radio show and has been climbing the ranks in media ever since, becoming an iconic voice for the urban youth. His fans seek out his controversial opinions and provocative interviews across all media.